Praise for
Sing This at My Funeral

"With this exquisitely written history and memoir Slucki has gifted us a haunted and haunting work. This is a vital story of family, loss, grief, and post-war devastation, of connection across time and space, of Jewish worlds and communities made and remade. It is a book unlike any other, a must-read."

—Jordana Silverstein, author of *Anxious Histories:*
Narrating the Holocaust in Jewish Communities
at the Beginning of the Twenty-First Century

"Brick by loving brick, Slucki builds a lyrical bridge of time, over which ghosts, dybbuks, and specters of memory may come to pass. *Sing This at My Funeral* is more than a son's tender tribute to a remarkable man. It is a profound meditation on what it means to father and be fathered."

—Bram Presser, author of the National Jewish Book
Award–winning *The Book of Dirt*

"*Sing This at My Funeral* is a compelling memoir, crafted with great artistry: an eloquent meditation on fathers and sons, the forces that shape them, and the impact of grief and trauma over the generations. Slucki acts as both subject and witness, intimate participant and historian, skillfully interweaving the past and the present, the personal and the political, and the old world with the new. This riveting quest for understanding is, above all, a profound act of familial love and humanity."

—Arnold Zable, novelist, writer,
and human rights advocate

"*Sing This at My Funeral* is a passionate—and visceral—meditation on trauma, memory, loss, and legacy. In urgent yet intimate prose, David Slucki provides a memoir of his beloved late father and grandfather and, using his own life as a fulcrum, explores the impact of their lives and loss on his own identity. Probing wounds still raw after years—or decades, he unflinchingly raises questions that in many cases have no answers. What, he wonders, will his own young son inherit from this family history of Holocaust, immigration, political engagement, and love?"

—Ruth Ellen Gruber, author of *Virtually Jewish: Reinventing Jewish Culture in Europe*

"David Slucki's memoir is a gutsy reckoning with ghosts. Like the best stories, *Sing This at My Funeral* features complex characters and a curious narrator who is not afraid to keep digging. Slucki's voice is compassionate, sharp, and relentless. A page-turning family narrative that is both highly personal and highly relatable."

—Sofija Stefanovic, author of *Miss Ex-Yugoslavia*

Sing This
at My
Funeral

Sing This at My Funeral

A Memoir of
Fathers and Sons

David Slucki

Wayne State University Press
Detroit

ISBN 978-0-8143-4486-6 (paperback); ISBN 978-0-8143-4487-3 (ebook); ISBN 978-0-8143-4721-8 (hardcover)

Library of Congress Control Number: 2019935135

Wayne State University Press
Leonard N. Simons Building
4809 Woodward Avenue
Detroit, Michigan 48201–1309

Visit us online at wsupress.wayne.edu

To Arthur:
you'll read this book
much sooner than I want you to,
but I'm so proud that you want to read it
and that you want to write
the next chapter together.
Lots of love, Dada.

Contents

Preface:
"An intercourse with ghosts"
ix

The Oath
1

In the Shadows
23

Frozen
48

Return
77

Immigrants
103

Coming of Age
135

The Slucki Method
159

Warsaw, My Ancestral Home
185

Fathers
207

Ghosts
227

Epilogue:
Just like Him
247

Acknowledgments
257

Preface

"An intercourse with ghosts"

This is a story about fathers and sons. It's about my father, Charles Roger Slucki, Sluggo to most who knew him. A man with deep wells of compassion and an endless reserve of energy. Charismatic, complex. It's about his father, my grandfather, or Zaida in Yiddish. Jakub (pronounced Ya-kub) Slucki was so traumatized by what he suffered that he couldn't model how to be a father, so broken that he lived himself into an early grave. The first forty-five years of his life were so marked by tragedy that he struggled to make it through the last thirty. Two world wars left an indelible mark on him as he entered the final phase of his life, three decades in which he worked, smoked, and punished his body until his heart couldn't take it any longer. Those wars left a mark on all of us.

This book is about how sons reconceive of the world when their fathers are suddenly and unexpectedly gone. Dad was thirty when Zaida died. Zaida was fifteen when his father died. When Sluggo passed away in December 2015, I was thirty-one, my brother, Jacob, thirty-five. So far, it hasn't been the Slucki men's destiny to have a father deep into adulthood. The prospect of living the rest of my life with my father as only a ghost is sobering. The thought of my son experiencing this is, frankly, terrifying. I think often about how Dad and Zaida picked up the pieces when they lost their fathers. Zaida was just a teenager, and World War I was raging around him. He lost his mother shortly after, orphaning him before he turned eighteen. I think about how my father coped with the sudden rupture in his life, the loss of his own guide and mentor, the unexpected absence. I'm still working out how I will cope with it, still new to being fatherless. Years later, the pain still raw. Maybe it will always be.

~

This book was born in Los Angeles, a strange place for the genesis of a book about an Australian Holocaust survivor from Poland, his Australian son, and his very Australian grandson. More specifically, this book was born in West LA, somewhere near the intersection of Pico and Olympic Boulevards. An ugly, nondescript junction. A couple of modernist hotels, a gas station, a strip mall, and an old kosher deli. Nothing to write home about, but the site of the event that changed my life immeasurably, that shattered the world as I knew it. That's where my dad, suddenly, without warning, dropped dead. Sixty-seven years old. A heart attack, the coroner thought. We didn't see it coming, having just spent six weeks together in New York City and Charleston, South Carolina, where I live with my wife, Helen, and our son, Arthur. Dad seemed to be in good health, so the shock was magnified, crippling.

Then there were the letters. A year after he died, only a few blocks from where he took his last step, I found the ghosts of his father, a pile of withered, crumpled letters that Zaida had written to his brother in the postwar decades. In December 2016, I visited Henry in Los Angeles. Henry is Dad's first cousin; they'd known each other since Dad first visited Los Angeles in 1959 to attend Henry's wedding. A youthful eighty-one, Henry ferried me around his labyrinthine city as he had willingly done since my first visit in 2003. I had just come from a conference in San Diego, energized to write more about Zaida, more about Dad. But there was still a lot I didn't know. I knew the skeleton of the story, but I wanted to add the flesh, the personalities, the emotion. The key to it all, I thought, was sitting somewhere in Henry's garage: a suitcase of letters Zaida had sent to Mendel, his brother and Henry's father, in the decades after the war. I had known probably for over a year that the suitcase existed, although Henry didn't know exactly where to find it, or the exact contents. It would take some detective work to figure it out.

We sat plotting how we might find out over oily, bland pastrami sandwiches at Canter's Deli, a mainstay in the Jewish deli scene in Los Angeles. The flavorless matzo-ball soup and greasy slices of pastrami did not calm my growing fear that I was on a pointless pursuit of a mythical holy grail, which may have once existed but was now just a distant memory buried deep, landfill somewhere in the vast southern Californian landscape. While I gorged on that bland rendition of Jewish comfort food, I furiously scribbled notes as Henry told me all he knew about Zaida, about Zaida's father, and about my dad and his early trips to the United States. He still wasn't sure exactly where the letters were, nor where to find the film reel from 1959 documenting their visit. But I continued to press, determined that they would be my periscope into the past, guiding me through the choppy waters of my memory.

We walked back to the car, deeply locked in the pursuit of these hazy memories, memories that were probably always hazy—the minutiae of lives lived where those small interactions and personality quirks I was trying to uncover were too unimportant to store in the limited recesses of our subconscious. It rained, a bad sign: with a shower beginning to fall, I was worried we wouldn't be able to search in the garage with the threat of moisture seeping in. I had only twenty-four hours, and the weather was being a nuisance.

After a couple of hours, the rain eased and Henry opened the two-car garage, a vast, mysterious, cavernous mess. A life collected in boxes, bags, shelves, piles. There was a dampness to it; it looked like it had sat uninterrupted for decades. There was no rhyme or reason to how the boxes were stacked, or where the unloved furniture sat. We spent a couple of hours out there wading through the musky garage. We shifted box after box of old records, books, kitchen appliances. I tried not to breathe in too deeply; I didn't want to further disturb the thick layer of dust and mold that had settled over these decades' worth of a life. Henry had a vague idea what the suitcase looked like. Brown, so big, he told me, gesturing with his hands to show a small rectangular shape.

I climbed further into the belly of the stale, dusty beast, sure that I'd step on some phantom box with nothing in it and end up

with a cabinet on top of me. As I balanced on a pile of four boxes of
books with one foot and a stack of records with the other, I noticed
a small, coffee-colored rectangle squeezed under three or four other
boxes. I furiously dragged aside those other boxes, balancing them
delicately at the side before triumphantly opening the little suitcase.
We rushed it inside, into the safety of Henry's house. I was covered
in dust and cobwebs, hands filthy, fingernails black. But I found
it, the unassuming brown box that held the words of my Zaida, a
material link I would be able to hold in my hand. I really had no
idea what would actually be in those letters, only what I hoped they
would reveal.

An hour later, after hurriedly cramming the boxes and furniture
back into the garage, we looked through the box. It was overflowing:
letters from Zaida, but also from friends and family the world over.
Birthday cards, photos, telegrams. We spent a couple more hours sep-
arating Zaida's letters, putting them in order, before I headed down
to the UPS store to get the most thickly padded envelope I could
find, the vessel to transport my treasures and protect these priceless
heirlooms. I celebrated with some proper deli food in Beverly Hills,
hoping I might rub shoulders with Mel Brooks, who I imagined was
a regular there. This was the gold mine I had been looking for, the
key to unlocking Zaida's life, his suffering, his mental demons. The
letters would tell me the story of his survival, his wandering, his resettlement; they would tell me all about the bustling cottage in inner
Melbourne in which he raised a family, and about the children he
reared, his hopes and expectations. I hoped they would be my tour
bus through Dad's unconscious, a guide to those episodes from his
childhood that would help explain the man he turned out to be.

The letters clarified a lot about Zaida's life during and after the
war, about his marriage and immigration, and about Dad's childhood.
They confirmed stories I'd heard and revealed new ones. More important, though, was the window I got into Zaida, an elusive, tragic
hero, the patriarch whose love and approval I sought posthumously,
whose own cataclysmic story had shaped our family in ways I barely
understood. The letters brought him alive, gave him a personality, a

voice. I had something tangible to help me connect with him and make sense of him and my dad.

⁓

Franz Kafka, Czech-Jewish author and inveterate letter writer, observed in one of his many dark love letters: "Writing letters is actually an intercourse with ghosts, and by no means just the ghost of the addressee but also with one's own ghost, which secretly evolves inside the letter one is writing or even in a whole series of letters." The ghosts for Zaida were vivid, the letters a means of bringing him nearer to them, of allowing him to communicate with them supernaturally. "Writing letters," Kafka wrote, "means exposing oneself to the ghosts, who are greedily waiting precisely for that. Written kisses never arrive at their destination; the ghosts drink them up along the way. It is this ample nourishment which enables them to multiply so enormously." That might have been Zaida's intention: that his kisses and love would be intercepted by the loved ones he left behind.

These letters helped keep the ghosts at the forefront of Zaida's consciousness, and would eventually bring them vividly, with full force, into my own life. The letters helped me to see the contours of the ghosts more clearly, bring them out of the murky shadows, understand their impact on Zaida and on Dad. Because, as Kafka wrote, although the letters were addressed to Mendel, they were a means for Zaida to make sense of those voices that could not be silenced. This was him reaching out to the ever-present specter of a family that existed only in the recesses of his consciousness. Mendel, who passed away in 2003, is also a ghost of these letters: the addressee, without a voice of his own, the letters he wrote consigned to the dustbin of history.

But if these letters confirm Kafka's theory—that letter writing is an intercourse between ghosts—they also show that this is as true for the reader of the letter as it is for the writer. As Zaida noted, the ghosts of his past haunted each stroke of the pen; for me, reading them decades later, my own ghosts helped me to interpret the words, the sorrow, the glimmers of hope.

~

My father believed in ghosts. He saw ghosts, he claimed, as a young man living in Papua New Guinea and again in his suburban Melbourne apartment. A headless lumberjack sitting at the end of his bed, in that instance. These stories were part of the repertoire of experiences he drew on, although they seemed to me to be his most fantastical. As with many other stories he told us as we were growing up, it wasn't clear what the lesson or message was, or how it fit with his broader understanding of the world.

Although he believed in ghosts, Dad was an avowed atheist, a socialist, skeptical about religion, faith, and the afterlife. He had little patience for religious ritual, for synagogues, or for God. That his father had lost his first family to the Nazi onslaught was enough to convince him there couldn't be a God, at least not a benevolent one, one to be revered, feared. A strong anomaly, these ghosts.

This is a book about ghosts. Not the ghosts that my dad saw in the jungles of Papua New Guinea but the ghosts that have haunted my family for three generations. The ghost of my grandfather, my Zaida, who died six years before I was born, and who haunted my dad through most of his adult life. The ghosts of Zaida's first wife and two sons who perished in the mobile gas vans at the Nazi death camp Chelmno and the millions of dead Jews that they represent. The ghosts of my grandfather's father, killed by German soldiers in Warsaw during the First World War.

The newest ghost is my father's. Since he died in 2015, his voice and presence surround me, echoing through me as I teach, write, and raise my son. His ghost stands with me in the classroom and in the streets, hovering, watching. It lingers constantly in all my thoughts, decisions, and actions. I see it everywhere. In my dreams and my nightmares. It's inescapable. It's comforting. It's terrifying. It is the ghost that compelled me to write this book, the ghost that convinced me there were such things as ghosts.

I thought my dad's ghost stories were silly, imagined, fairy tales, spun to add drama to a life well lived. I now see what he was telling me all along—we are, and have always been, surrounded by the ghosts of the past. They guide us, challenge us, frustrate us, and insert themselves into our lives when we don't expect them to, when we don't want them to, and occasionally, when we need them most.

As it turns out, I've been on a journey with ghosts my whole life. What I thought was absence I now understand to have been an unremitting presence. I couldn't escape the ghosts of Zaida or his murdered family. I was surrounded by their presence and the presence of all the relatives of my three living grandparents, all killed by the Nazis. The reminders of the family and the world that had been lost to the ravages of Nazism are overwhelming and have never been far from the surface.

～

I didn't intend to write a memoir. My life is not that interesting. My childhood was tranquil, uneventful, especially compared to the exciting, daring life my dad led or to the adventurous and traumatic episodes that punctuated my grandparents' lives. I still think that. My story isn't one of overcoming odds. I never suffered hardships or violence. I came from a loving home with parents who, though modest in means, always managed to provide for me and my brother, Jacob. They never beat us, never berated us. They were our safety net, unconditionally. Theirs was a marriage full of love, respect, and support. They were infatuated with each other to the very end; forty years maintaining the balancing act of partnership and parenting.

This book isn't about that, although it's all in the background. It's about the ghosts that lurk just beneath that idyllic surface. The hidden pain and longing for simpler times, when sons and their fathers faced the ghosts together; when sons had their fathers. It's about the lingering memories and absence of a family brutally murdered by the Nazis. It's about the attachments to a civilization that barely survived the Nazis' onslaught. Zaida belonged to the Jewish Labor Bund, a Polish-Jewish socialist movement that was almost completely wiped out during World War II, yet he remained a true believer. So did Dad; so do I. The book is about what drove that obsession with a political movement now on life support, virtually buried in the ruins of postwar Poland. Mainly, though, it's about how the difficult memories of the past shaped the relationships between fathers and their sons, how the ghosts kept multiplying, never far from the surface.

It's not linear, though, or neat, or redemptive. It can't be; memories aren't linear, and the ways those memories of the past are passed down are fragmented, complicated, incomplete. There is no linear time when it comes to remembering our pasts, only the scraps that we gather and from which we try to make sense. This book is my attempt to make sense of those fragments.

1

The Oath

"Make sure you sing this at my funeral," Dad said to me after belting it out for what would be the last time in his life, on December 26, 2015. We had just finished singing "Di shvue" [The oath], the anthem of the Jewish Labor Bund, the political movement to which our family had been attached for around a century.

We didn't know then that three days later he'd be dead and eight days after that we would indeed be singing it by his graveside, just as he had by his father's graveside thirty-eight years earlier.

At that moment in New York City, though, together with his son at an event celebrating the Bund, Sluggo had a spring in his step. Reconnecting with friends whom he hadn't seen for forty-five years, he worked the room as if it were one of his own events, planning future projects, catching up on half a lifetime apart. We had just spent six weeks together in Charleston and New York City. On this night, two days before he was due to return home to Australia, we celebrated the living legacy of the movement that had been central to our family for more than one hundred years. After the violent twentieth century, Dad still retained his dedication to a movement that his father had joined as a teenager in World War I–era Poland. He still carried with him a kind of sunny optimism, a sense that decades after marching against the Vietnam War and leading teacher strikes in the 1960s, 1970s, and 1980s, he was still a revolutionary in temperament and outlook.

∾

Sluggo and I singing "Di shvue" together in New York, three days before he died (December 26, 2015).

My connection to the Bund, a generations-old link, was forged almost eight decades before I was born. Zaida Jakub had found the Bund early, as a teenager. Like so many around him, he rebelled against the strictures of his traditional upbringing, the suffocating, backward, premodern Jewish Warsaw in which he was raised. No one really knows how he came to the movement. His older sister, Chava, born a year before him, might have gotten there first. She later became a communist and then a Zionist, finally settling in Israel in the 1950s. Maybe he followed her into the movement, seeking the promise that the new modern Jewish politics offered young workers in the Russian Empire. That knowledge has passed with him and his contemporaries. If my grandmother Eda , Bubba Eda in Yiddish, were alive we could ask her. Perhaps Zaida's brother Mendel knew. But it's a gap that will always remain. We can now only guess what it was that drew him to the movement that was only a few years older than he. It was a connection he maintained when he left Warsaw in the aftermath of World War I for the small city of Włocławek.

During his twenty years living there, raising a family, he immersed himself in the life of the movement. He sat on the local Bund committee and might have been its treasurer, with his background as a bookkeeper. His first wife, Gitl, was a founder of the Włocławek Bund youth movement, *Tsukunft* [Future]. By the time the war broke out in 1939, his two sons, Shmulek and Chaimek, were both earnest young members of the Bund's children's organization, SKIF. In the years they lived under Nazi occupation, his family was active in the Bund's underground movement. After the war, when all was lost, Zaida reconnected with the newly reconstituted Polish Bund, working as its bookkeeper, earning barely enough to survive. Later, in Australia, he served as a kind of elder statesmen for the party and its leaders, most of whom were a generation younger than he.

He never severed his connection to the Bund, an adherent for over sixty years. His absolute dedication to his cause never weakened, no matter the tribulations he faced in his life. When it might have been easier to sink into a kind of postwar nihilism, to let go of all that he had held dear, all that he associated with his prewar life, his faith never wavered, even if his strength did. This attachment permeated the next two generations. That world, its ideals, its institutions, the sense of belonging it provided, was never far from Zaida's, or Dad's, psyche. Those were truly ghosts that followed the Slucki family from Poland to Melbourne after World War II. These ghosts persisted especially because they represented unfulfilled ambitions, a world and a life that was no longer possible.

The Bund's establishment in Vilna in October 1897 was the culmination of a decade of agitation by the Jewish intelligentsia through the Russian Pale of Settlement, the area in western Russia in which Jews had been confined since early in the nineteenth century. Set against the backdrop of growing political consciousness among Jews in Czarist Russia, the Bund was a revolutionary force on the Jewish street, trying to transform Jewish life in Eastern Europe. It was a secular, Marxist party, ultimately committed to fostering Yiddish

Zaida (back row, center) on the election committee of the Włocławek Bund, (1927).

culture and replacing capitalism with a democratic socialist state. Its leaders asserted that Jews were not simply a religious group but a nation, bound by history, culture, and language. These ideas were all relatively new in Jewish life, building over the course of a century, but taking expression only in the 1890s and 1900s, as Jews in the Russian Empire finally took their major steps toward modernity. The Bund led the way. Its forerunners in the major cities of the Pale of Settlement organized education and reading circles, where they fostered literacy and numeracy among ordinary workers—tailors, blacksmiths, artisans—who typically had no more than a rudimentary education in Jewish religious texts. Not only did it seek to empower Jewish workers through education, it also, more than any other modern Jewish political party, opened pathways for the participation of Jewish women. In the Bundist movement, not only were women welcomed as members but it was possible for them to rise into positions of authority. Jewish workers in Czarist Russia suffered under the yoke of antisemitism, which made it nearly impossible for Jews to advance outside their state of poverty. Discriminated against legally and economically, the targets of pogroms—violent anti-Jewish riots—Jews flocked to the Bund and other political movements promising a solution to their problems.

Among those, my own ancestors, Zaida and his siblings. Thousands like Zaida stayed with the Bund through the Russian Revolution, after which the original was swallowed up by the Communist Party and ultimately liquidated. They participated actively in the interwar Polish Bund, the zenith of party life and influence, when its expansive counterculture reached the homes of tens of thousands of Polish Jews and when it defended Jews against antisemitism on the streets of Poland and in its public institutions. They maintained their connection through the terrible war years, in the attempts to rebuild Jewish Poland on Polish soil, and later on the soil of Australia, Mexico, and elsewhere. Their adherence was based in ideology, yet the roots ran so much deeper than mere politics.

I'm a third-generation Bundist—actually, fourth if you include my mother Mich's branch of the family tree, but that's another story. When my turn came to learn and sing "Di shvue," that oath to party and ideology, I embraced it fully. I knew early that it bound me to my Zaida, and to a Jewish past that was relevant, usable, inspiring. It was the story of a civilization that was nearly swallowed up in the fiery conflagration that engulfed wartime Europe. This fire left Zaida's precious movement, a movement that had given Zaida entry into a world that made his father's traditional world look very narrow, in tatters. A connection to the Bund is more than ideology, to me at least, and I suspect to many of those rusted-on Bundists like Zaida and Dad. To be sure, many of us who still feel that attachment align ourselves politically with the organization. We are socialist, or social-democratic, and we believe that Jewish life ought to be fostered in all places that Jews reside and that each Jewish community must adapt to its local circumstances. We see the possibilities in Yiddish as a modern, secular Jewish language, with its rich cultural legacy and its ability to connect Jews across borders. We feel a responsibility to the

Bundist heritage keenly in the wake of its decimation during World War II.

On the other hand, there are many that come out each time the Bund in Melbourne runs a commemoration, a celebration, or a lecture who have little affection for socialism and identify strongly with Israel as *the* Jewish center. The connection to the Bund is, for these people as well as those politically aligned with the movement, familial, primordial. Maybe they are Yiddishist, maybe liberal. But their connection to the movement is not political; it comes from shared experiences, from a received set of rituals and icons passed down by parents who threw off the burden of the premodern Jewish world inhabited by their parents. Being a Bundist is a statement of identity, of belonging. It suggests your belonging not only to a group today but to a past that is glorious, inspiring, lofty, tragic. It is a connection to a tradition that today we might express only through scraps that bind us: celebrating major historical moments, a smattering of Yiddish in the movement's activities, a general liberal outlook. But there is that link, a shared history, language, experience. Something in between family, community, and religion. It is a past that young, radical Jews are increasingly claiming as their own as they search for models and inspiration for a diasporic, radical Jewish vision.

To be a Bundist in the twenty-first century is a strange way to identify. Even more so to claim to be a Bundist in the American Deep South, my home now. The only place a Bund organization formally exists is Melbourne; there is a semiregular Bundist publication in Yiddish in Israel; and a handful of nostalgic Bundists meet every year in New York to commemorate the Warsaw Ghetto Uprising. There is a growing group of young scholars and activists interested in the Bund's legacy, particularly in an era when many feel estranged from the State of Israel. I'm not really sure even if I ought to claim to be a Bundist—what does that mean in the absence of an actual movement? What does it mean when the only time Helen and I speak Yiddish is so Arthur won't understand? How do I now look back at having been imbued, brainwashed, with those ideas, that legacy, that burden?

~

After the Holocaust, the Bund was forced to develop new traditions, new rituals, a new calendar, and a new language. To be sure, these existed before the Nazis marched into Poland, but the destruction of Polish Jewry demanded new ways of thinking about the past, the present, and the future. Many doubled down in their commitment to the movement, clinging to the vestiges of a lost past, trying to raise their children in the same tradition in which they were raised in interwar Poland. Yiddish was mostly the lingua franca, although that waned in the two generations after World War II, when it became more of a ceremonial language. When I was growing up, Yiddish at a Bund meeting became like Hebrew in many synagogues—many didn't understand, and those who did were just as comfortable, maybe more comfortable, in English. The sacred dates corresponded to the Warsaw Ghetto Uprising, the anniversary of the Bund's founding, and May Day. The regular rituals ranged from the sacred—singing "Di shvue" at the end of a meeting, reading out the names of comrades who had passed since the last meeting—to the banal—soda water and *leykakh* (sponge, or angel cake) to accompany each event. The Bund had its own foundational narratives: the founding meeting of thirteen Jewish socialists in an attic in Vilna in 1897 and the martyrdom of Hirsch Lekert, the young Bundist executed after a failed assassination attempt on the governor of Vilna in 1902. More than any other, the heroism of young Bundists in resistance movements in Polish and Lithuanian ghettos during World War II became the crucial stories in our consciousness.

The Bund's icons were the intellectuals who formulated and articulately put forth the party program, those who could stand before thousands, deliver a stirring speech, and rally the average Polish Jewish worker to action. They were the workers who, through acts of bravery and daring, became the martyrs of the movement. A throwback to times when Jewish workers literally fought in the streets for tolerable working conditions, for basic political rights, for survival. The incongruity between their lives and ours was stark, but our link to them was clear. We owed a debt to those heroes and martyrs, even if we knew barely anything about them. They had fought real battles; they struggled to overthrow the czar, for a socialist Poland, against violent antisemitism. They died in battle against Nazism. Deeds that we would never, could never, live up to.

~

SKIF, the *Sotzyalistisher kinder farband* (Socialist Children's Union), was established in Poland in 1926, after a couple of decades of failed attempts to organize a Bundist children's movement. The earliest attempts to organize children in Czarist Russia failed ultimately. The Bund operated illegally, and it was difficult to incorporate children into an organization that relied on secrecy and subversion. In interwar Poland, though, where the Bund not only was legal but established itself as a major force in Polish-Jewish life, the momentum for a children's movement was irresistible. SKIF was a socialist movement that welcomed children from all different backgrounds: schoolchildren from working-class families, children who themselves were forced to work, and street children. These groups didn't always easily intermingle, but the movement's inclusive nature was central to its raison d'être. The Bund leaders who oversaw it crafted a specific Bundist teaching method, drawing on the latest ideas about education and health. They debated how best to take young people and turn them into responsible adults, citizens, Jews. A socialist organization that saw itself allied to a broader network of European socialist children's movements, SKIF became among the most popular children's movements in Poland. It focused on teaching through activities that were fun and engaging: hiking, sports, camping, drama. It proved a crucial tool to initiate a new generation into the movement—young Jews who were getting a small taste of political and religious freedom in the new Polish republic.

During World War II, SKIFistn like Zaida's two sons became active in the Bundist underground movements in the ghettos of

Poland. They acted as smugglers and couriers. SKIF ran cultural and educational programs under the most trying circumstances. SKIF children heroically participated in the resistance movements throughout occupied Europe. Many of those names became etched in my brain, as the stories of SKIFistn bravely sacrificing their lives to help save their comrades were told in ritual settings each year on April 19, at SKIF camp, and at school. Stories of SKIFistn fighting in the Warsaw Ghetto were emphasized. We memorized the feats of Dovidl Hochberg, only a teenager, who wedged his body into an opening to buy time for his comrades to escape and was shot to death by Nazi machine guns. Or Tobcia Dawidowicz, who, although wounded, led her group to safety in the sewers and then stayed behind in the ghetto so as not to burden them further. Or the brilliant and fiery Jurek Blones and his siblings, Guta and Lushek, teenagers who joined the battle. This was the most tragic episode in SKIF's short history, yet it left the greatest mark on how it would be remembered.

~

SKIF in Melbourne was founded in 1950 by survivors and refugees. Tiny when it began, it operated out of a house in the inner-Melbourne neighborhood of Carlton before moving permanently to the nearby Yiddish cultural center, the Kadimah. SKIF was the initiative of a few veterans of the Polish movement, survivors, young refugees in their twenties who had been active in the efforts to resurrect SKIF in Poland and in France after the war. They had been reared in the heady environment of interwar Poland, where politics were played out in the streets, where choosing a political movement was more than aligning yourself with a political philosophy. To join SKIF was to join a family, to provide yourself with a safety net, a political and cultural home for life. Despite their wartime suffering, this formative atmosphere stuck with those young Bundists, who tried to recreate versions of it wherever they landed after the war. Whether in the parts of western Poland where Jews were resettled in substantial numbers, in Western Europe, Israel, the Americas, or provincial

Zaida speaks to members of Melbourne's SKIF organization (1954).

Australia, Bundists tried to emulate the feeling that had lit their fire as young people.

In Melbourne, SKIF was an important tool in these efforts. Being immigrants, far removed from the Bund's original context, was a blessing and a curse. A blessing, because they could start afresh, a blank slate, unencumbered by the Polish antisemitism they faced previously, by the looming threat of war, by the desperate poverty that plagued Jewish life in the old country. New circumstances, even if they were forced upon the founders of Melbourne's SKIF organization, provided new opportunities. At the same time, a curse, because Melbourne was a faraway province without the infrastructure, without the critical mass, without the Jewish political tradition that had fast emerged in Eastern Europe. From 1950, the young leaders, veterans of Polish SKIF, ran weekly meetings on Sunday and four-week camps outside the city. As refugees came in larger numbers, SKIF opened a second location in the beachside suburb of St. Kilda, a burgeoning center for Jews.

Sluggo (seated, second from right) as a *helfer* at SKIF camp, Dromana (1968).

∽

Dad was in one of the earliest groups of SKIFistn. I think he started around 1954, when he was six, a young age to go on a month-long camp. Back then, SKIF camps were four weeks long. It was probably a relief for his hard-working immigrant parents, who didn't have the space or means to look after their kids during their summer vacation weeks. It was a win-win for Zaida. Not only was there somewhere for Dad and his sister, Miriam, to go in the sweltering hot Melbourne summers, when he and Bubba were stuck in the knitting factory, but the camp they went to was their initiation into that tradition that was so central to him. SKIF wasn't only for fun; its leaders were more than babysitters. Maybe it wasn't primarily for fun, except where there was some educational justification for fun. SKIF, at least for Bundists like Zaida, was a pathway, a way to induct a new generation of young Jews into the movement, into the tradition. Sluggo would follow in the footsteps of Zaida's first two sons, cut down in their tender youth, the hope of a family and a movement now resting on his shoulders.

Dad rarely talked about his time as a SKIFist. What he really remembered fondly was his role as a *helfer* (leader) in the movement. Pretty much all of his SKIF stories were of his time as a *helfer*. The time that one camper was too scared to go to the outhouse at night, so he neatly pushed his clothes to one side of his suitcase and did his business in the other half. The hikes to the beach, when the *helfer* would leave the campers to go to the pub and watch cricket. That visitors' day when members of the Bund committee, the founders of SKIF, tried to come up early, and Sluggo locked the gates and wouldn't let them in. I barely remember a story of him as SKIFist. They were mostly stories of times he bent or broke the rules, ways in which he inspired the kids, tales of mischief and daring.

He was fifteen or sixteen when he graduated to become a *helfer*. He was hugely popular, known to be funny, easygoing, generous, and forgiving. A straight shooter, he'd tell you if you screwed up, but it was never personal. He'd cut you slack, always be on your side. His cousin, Moshe, remembers his ability to engage with the SKIFistn of all ages. During Moshe's first camp, Sluggo was his *helfer*. The first thing Sluggo did was insist they all choose a nickname for themselves. Moshe, recalling an older Aussie kid that used to hang around Dad's house in Canning Street, chose for himself the nickname Spud. That stuck, a small but meaningful way Sluggo exerted his influence on young people's lives. He had, as Moshe recalls, an amazing ability to make young people feel they were important, interesting. He was a master, even as a sixteen-year-old, at engaging them on their level. As a *helfer*, he no doubt imbibed the philosophy of his maternal grandfather, Zaida Yitzhak, who used to tell his grandchildren that you should never humiliate or embarrass other people. It was, Moshe recalls, the number one rule in the family, and something that Sluggo embodied as a *helfer*, one of the things that made him so popular. If he needed to admonish a SKIFist, he knew how to do it quietly, privately, to take the sting out of a situation. He had the instinct for the different personalities

Sluggo with his SKIFistn at *apel* (roll call), Apollo Bay (late 1960s).

he was dealing with, and could adjust according to all the different needs of the kids in camp.

For Sluggo, then, SKIF and the Bund were even more than ideology and family. They gave him the start in his life, put him on his path to being an educator, and helped him craft his teaching approaches, his approaches to people. He didn't know that he wanted to be a teacher yet, but it was the years of being a *helfer* that certainly convinced him that it was the career for which he was chosen. Moreover, like it did for so many others, he found that SKIF imbued in him the instinct for helping others. He used to often note the kinds of professions the people around him went into, service professions devoted to helping and healing: social workers, teachers, doctors, those working in public policy. Clearly, there was something about SKIF that shaped the lives of its participants and the kinds of people they became. It was not surprising that he wanted his own sons to have that same life-shaping opportunity.

There was never even a question about whether we would go to SKIF, or if we would one day become *helfer*. Like going to school, these steps were the natural progression. It didn't even occur to my parents that we might go to another youth movement, or not go to one at all. By then, SKIF and the Bund were just our extended family. At times dysfunctional, at times with people whom we didn't want to see at family functions, but family nonetheless. SKIF's secular, Yiddish-focused Jewishness was our own; its members were our cousins, our family friends, kids whose parents and grandparents had known our grandparents in the Soviet Union and Poland. What's more, Sluggo maintained a strong connection to Yiddish Melbourne, sitting on the Bund committee or working in the Yiddish theatre. If ever there was a family that embodied the connectedness of the Bund, its ability to shape the lives of its members, it was the Sluckis.

We became immersed in its values. Dad constantly told me that the most important thing he wanted to teach me was *mentshlekhkayt*, humanity, that quality by which we inherently treat others with dignity. More than any kind of Marxian socialism, it was *derkherets*, respect, that he emphasized with me and Jacob. This was what he drew from the spirit of the Bund. All the other stuff was important, too, but without that foundation of *mentshlekhkayt*, all the rest meant very little.

I first went to SKIF camp when I was eight. Camp Reefton. I don't even know where that is today or how far outside Melbourne—it felt like a world away. I was really excited to start SKIF that year. I was going to be in my friend Josh's *kraize* (circle, or age group), my parents told me, and I was sold. I ended up in the *kraize* below, but it didn't dampen my enthusiasm too much. Going through those gates at 62 Wellington Street, St. Kilda, the headquarters of the Bund, gave eight-year-old me a thrill, running around the playground, playing soccer or basketball or volleyball, singing together at *apel*, roll call. The parents hanging around chatting to each other, catching up, remembering the times when they ran around 62 Wellington Street or at the older SKIF headquarters in the northern Melbourne neighborhood of Carlton, first stop for Jewish refugees like my dad and his parents. The connection was deep, strong.

That first camp in 1992, I was terribly homesick. I cried a lot for my parents. Quite the cliché. I don't remember too much of it, mainly impressions—that seems to be how my memory works. Details are often sketchy, but I see the broad outlines. There was the river in which we swam, canoed, and kayaked. I remember Olympiade, the yearly sporting competition in which we were divided into countries and were taught about those countries, their histories, and some of the present-day geopolitical issues that they faced. Olympiade, brought to SKIF camp in the 1970s by Sluggo after his stint at SKIF's counterpart in New York, was the highlight of camp for many, when we'd mix with groups of all ages, write some of the more memorable songs, and break up the usual routine of the camp. We played more sports during Olympiade, which suited me fine. I remember at Camp Reefton the *helfer* waking us up in the middle of the night for a fake Olympiade opening, an annual prank that *helfer* played on the campers. That camp left a lasting impression. Despite my tears, I was hooked.

In some ways SKIF camp was like any summer camp. Tents or cabins, sports activities, kids getting into mischief, making lifelong friends, and taking advantage of the chance to forge our own selves away from our parents. These are the hallmarks of summer camps—a place for parents to send their children, somewhere fun, with an educational bent.

In other ways, though, SKIF was unique. There was the ideological component, the three pillars that SKIFistn learned early: *chavershaft*, comradeship, the socialist pillar of the movement; *doikayt*, literally "here-ness," the conviction that Jewish life ought to be fostered anywhere that Jews live, a counterpoint to Zionism, which imagined a Jewish center and periphery; and *yiddishkayt*, a commitment to a secular Jewishness with Yiddish at its core. We were the torchbearers of a glorious and tragic past, in which children—many of whom did not make it beyond childhood—were seen as the key to a socialist future, a more just world. Our responsibility was grave.

Our SKIF camps were modeled on the SKIF of old. When we grew up in the movement in the 1990s, we were part of this longer, well-established chain, inheriting an educational approach that had been handed down to us over several generations. Like in Poland, our SKIF camps aimed to empower children, to involve them in the decision making, to provide a platform where, for two weeks in the summer, they could live in a democratic-socialist way. SKIF ran, as far as was practical, democratically. Children would elect a *lager rat*, a camp council, which would meet regularly throughout camp to discuss issues that would arise and represent the interest of campers to the *helfer* group. We sang songs about the coming of the proletarian revolution, about a children's republic where, together, *we* would raise the SKIF flag, a red falcon on a blue background. Each meal began with a *shtiler minut*, a moment's silence, a symbolic gesture so that all campers would start the meal together. There was no money at camp, no snack shops. If you wanted to bring chocolates, candy, it went into the communal *kraize* bag, which the *helfer* would bring out every other day during *ru-tsayt*, the afternoon rest period. Luxuries like that were to be shared among the group. A small nod to the abolition of private property, at least for those two weeks. Each *kraize* had a roster for *dizur*, the after-meal cleanup. The younger kids would be responsible for clearing the tables, the older kids for washing the dishes. No one was allowed to leave until the whole job was done. From each according to this ability, to each according to his needs—an unspoken rule that we lived. *Chavershaft*, comradeship, was our mantra, repeated each day throughout the day, a greeting, a statement.

Very few SKIFistn, by the time I came along at least, spoke Yiddish. Most weren't interested in learning it—when we did have Yiddish lessons when I was much younger, campers mostly resented it. But Yiddish was a constant presence on camp, at least symbolically. The rhythm of the day was marked out in Yiddish. Each morning at *apel*, the *tog komendant*, the *helfer* in charge that day, would read out the day's proceedings in Yiddish: *oyfshtand* (wake up), *gymnastik* (exercise), *apel* (roll call), *frishtik* (breakfast), *aktivitet* (activity), *natur-gang* (hiking), *mitog* (lunch), *ru-tsayt* (rest), *klubn* (arts and crafts), *shport* (sport), *ovntbroyt* (dinner), *nakht aktivitet* (night

Me as a *helfer* at SKIF camp. Here I was leading the boys in my *kraize* in a water polo match (2005).

activity), *nakht apel* (evening roll call). Roll call each morning and evening was almost entirely in Yiddish, we sang Yiddish songs, tried to write Yiddish songs.

What most distinguished SKIF, I think, from a typical American summer camp, or at least the kind in the movies, was that those involved were not only there for fun, and not even there because they were attached to an idea. Over time they developed an attachment to the movement and its legacy. *Chavershaft* and *doikayt* weren't simply empty terms for those who went through SKIF. They were ideas that shaped the people those SKIFistn became. This was true in other Jewish youth movements in Melbourne too—the Zionist movements connected their members to movements that had their roots in interwar Poland or pre-Soviet Russia. For many of us in SKIF, our attachment was familial, historic, almost primordial.

At SKIF, our *kraizen* were named for the Bundists of yore. One of my first groups was named Michalewicz kraize, for Beynish Michalewicz, a leading voice on behalf of Bundist youth in Russia and

Poland. Some years, *kraizen* were named for fighters in the Warsaw Ghetto, some years, for Yiddish writers. One year we carried the names of the builders of the Melbourne Bund: Weiner, Ringelblum, Mrocki, Waks, Giligich. Occasionally they were named for socialists or other icons of the Left: Nelson Mandela, Martin Luther King Jr. Many of those names didn't stick. It was the recurring names of old Bund leaders and heroes that were embedded deep into my consciousness. I don't know that any of my friends carried those names with them beyond the short window of summer camp; probably they were relegated to their subconscious. But they mattered a great deal to me. Maybe I was too serious as a kid. And anyway, isn't it weird to teach eight-year-olds about people like Lekert and ghetto partisans? What did we care about or understand why Erlich and Alter— politicians, ostensibly—mattered? How did this really connect us to the heritage of Sholem Aleichem and Y. L Peretz, to Spinoza, to Maimonides, to Moses? How could you convince children in 1980s and 1990s Melbourne that they somehow bore the legacy of the past? Didn't they just want to have fun, make friends, get a taste of Jewishness, without it being shoved down their throat?

Maybe. But the indoctrination worked on me. I can still see their portraits staring down at me from up high. I don't know if someone made a conscious decision to put those portraits high up on the wall, but the way they sat was as though they were always staring down at you, their tragic eyes staring wherever you went, reminding you of the gravity of your task, amidst the flippancy of the day-to-day work of leading SKIF. I can see Henryk Erlich, the spiritual and intellectual leader of the interwar Bund, murdered by the Soviet secret police in 1941, his deep eyes encircled by black rings, white goatee framing his wiry lips, head slightly tilted as he stares down the camera. Victor Alter, killed alongside Erlich: younger, more handsome than Erlich; an angular jaw, sharp features, thick, slicked-back hair distinguishing him from Erlich, the graying, balding elder statesman. Noyekh Portnoy, veteran of the early Bund, with his stately moustache covering any sign of a mouth, eyebrows furrowed as he cast his gaze upon us. There were the ghetto fighters on one side, the builders of the Melbourne Bund on the other. The plain black photo frames, a thick matte border surrounding the faces, lending them an air of solemnity. Each with his own solemn glare, a reminder that there were those who had struggled before us, and that our comfortable, suburban, middle-class universe did not come about by accident, did not exist in a vacuum. Faces frozen in time, their deeds immortal, their names never to be forgotten. At least by me.

Arthur, my son, was partly named for Shmuel Artur Zygielbojm, the Bund's representative in the Polish government-in-exile during World War II who took his own life in protest at the world's failure to take the Jews' plight seriously. Maybe we just liked the name and it corresponded. I don't know. It makes a nice story at least. He was almost called Leyvik, after the Yiddish poet H. Leivick and Leyvik Hodes, a founder and theoretician of SKIF in Poland. His middle name is Manny, after my Bubba Mania, Mich's mother. This fit nicely because I had wanted to call him Emmanuel, after a number of the Emmanuels who inspired me as I researched the postwar Bund, those true believers whose faith never diminished. When the question of what we should name our son came up, the figures that immediately scanned through my mind were those faces on the wall at Waks House, the Melbourne Bund's headquarters. I thought of those serious men who knew the meaning of struggle, whose commitment to a cause I had always wanted to emulate somehow.

$\approx$

When it came time to sing "Di shvue" at Sluggo's funeral, it felt like the normal thing to do. I'd heard often enough the story about hundreds of old Bundists singing it at Zaida's funeral, and we sang it on a semiregular basis at meetings of the Bund. Each time, it seemed, with fewer people. It was more than nostalgia though. Someone suggested we sing our football club's team song, "Good Old Collingwood Forever," and bury him with his football scarf. Our football team was important to us, gave us our weekly outlet, bonded us together, and connected us to another imagined community. People from every part of his life associated Dad with the Collingwood Football Club;

he went to his first match in 1958 and was a rabid supporter for the next sixty years. Everyone knew that black-and-white hooped football scarf that he wore every day when the temperature dropped.

But the football club wasn't the Bund, and it wouldn't feature at the funeral. Football was our religion, serious business, but in the end, still only a game. The Bund was truly his family, his essence, and SKIF his incubator. The movement connected him to his father and the life of a man he knew relatively little about. It filled that gap for him, and for me. It helped forge that bond between me and Sluggo, between me and the ghost of Zaida. It ensured that Zaida's ghost stayed within easy reach, something we could evoke, that we could feel as we argued about politics, about the future of the movement, about the future of socialism. SKIF taught us how to be teachers, how to be empathetic, how to fight for justice, so that each time we stepped into the classroom, or when Jacob, a lawyer, stepped into the courtroom, Zaida's ghost was there cheering us on, encouraging us to continue the work he had started but was too battered to continue. We invoked his ghost every time we sang "Di shvue." Surely Dad associated it with him; I know I did. I know also now that whenever I sing, hear, or teach it I continue to be a link in that chain, whether I want to be or not. It is an honor and a burden.

When I returned to Charleston from the funeral, I had only a few days' grace before I was thrust back into the classroom. Or before I thrust myself back into the classroom. Maybe I was being a martyr ("Don't be a martyr," Dad would say). Everyone was very accommodating, even though it was the first week of the new semester. Colleagues taught my classes, communicated with students, gave me space. I didn't even know where to start—I had planned to finish the syllabus during the winter break. Then Dad died, and the reading schedule was the last thing on my mind.

That semester I was teaching a class on modern Jewish politics. Virtually within days of singing "Di shvue" at my dad's graveside, I had to stand before a group of students and explain to them what the Bund was, its significance, and how it shaped the modern Jewish world. Partly it was easy, mechanical. I'd taught the class before, and I could fall back on old PowerPoints, old lecture notes. Summoning all that was embedded deep in my memory, I'd been teaching about the Bund and Zionism since I was a *helfer* at SKIF, and had been teaching it to university students for nearly ten years. In some ways, teaching the classes was the easy part. Just do my job, get through the day.

But it was a gut-wrenching semester, a tour through my family's history at the very moment I needed some respite, or at least the choice to have some respite. Ghosts reappeared at every turn, each week a new set of old faces from my past, my psyche, hovering at my side. Not just Dad and Zaida and all those whose stories I grew up hearing but also those faces plastered around Waks House. These faces were present class after class. Week two: antisemitism in late-nineteenth-century Russia, and the rise of Jewish political movements. Week three: Zionism. Week four: socialism and the Bund. Week six: Jewish politics in interwar Poland. Week eight: the Holocaust. Week nine: the aftermath. Week ten: the establishment of Israel. Couldn't I just teach about something else? It's probably a cliché after someone dies to say that everything reminds you of them, but in this case, I was teaching things that couldn't do anything but remind me of Sluggo.

Mostly, I managed to keep it together for those twice-weekly seventy-five-minute sessions. I thought I'd turn it into a discussion seminar, let the class run itself. The materials were interesting enough, I just needed to provide the readings a week ahead of time. I soon realized how much harder this was than lecturing. I had to be fully switched on to guide a meaningful discussion. I had to pay attention when students talked, think on my feet, give them space to explore ideas, encourage them to experiment, challenge them. In that semester it was more than I could handle. I could think only of Dad. So I lectured more than I usually do. That way, I could flick the autopilot switch, stay focused on the task, minimize the improvisation. Stay well within my comfort zone. Perform for my audience. Play the role of professor, put on a show, tell some dumb jokes, keep them entertained. The show must go on, as the theatre folks say. To take the theatre analogy further, I had learned my lines, and it was now about my performance, my delivery. I had grown up in the theatre, so that part was easy.

Some days it was like an out-of-body experience, as though I were watching myself, disconnected from what was happening inside the classroom. Most days, though, I ended up a crumpled heap on the floor of my office. I cried, breathed, cried some more. I called Helen, asked her to come and sit with me. I kept the door closed, kept my grief a secret as best I could. It wasn't always easy. I couldn't just ignore it, let it go. Could I really pretend to be detached, that teaching about the Bund and the Holocaust didn't leave me a quivering mess by the end of class? Other times I just thought about Dad: Would he be proud? What would he do in this situation? What *did* he do in this situation, thirty-eight years earlier, when his father dropped dead suddenly? How did he face his students during his period of grieving? I wondered how long this would last. There seemed to be no light at the end of this increasingly narrow tunnel, only claustrophobia and angst. Each room I walked into felt a little smaller than before.

Strange to think that SKIF somehow led me to South Carolina, but in those weeks and months after Dad died, I came, increasingly, to own that past and to connect to it. I used to hide my connection, but after Dad died, it was a legacy I couldn't disavow. I taught Jewish history, Jewish politics, and the Holocaust because of that Bundist upbringing. Probably I went into a teaching career because of my experiences in SKIF, my role as a *helfer* helping to imbue young people with a sense of their connection to the past, of the way that the past informed their present. I became a teacher because of the ghosts swirling around constantly.

The voices of those ghosts—Zaida's and now Dad's—were louder than ever.

2

In the Shadows

"I commemorate the Holocaust every day," Sluggo would often say to me. Our family's most important ritual was always the Bund's Warsaw Ghetto Uprising commemoration (*geto akademye* in Yiddish), held annually on April 19. The *akademyes* were the centerpieces of Holocaust remembrance in our Bundist community, and April 19 was the single most important date on its calendar. The commemoration was our opportunity to reflect, to remember, to weep, and to mourn for family we had not met and for those whom we were denied. Probably because their movement was decimated by the Holocaust, Bundists place the Holocaust as the pivotal episode in their historical narrative. For the Bund's followers, almost exclusively Polish-Jewish refugees and their descendants, the Holocaust was the defining event in their lives and their family history, and if the Bund serves as a kind of extended family, then it follows that the Holocaust is a central part of that bigger family history. This might not be so unusual. In many Jewish communities around the world, the Holocaust features as a central point of identification, even for those who aren't directly connected. Even in places with very few survivors, the Holocaust has come to be a major preoccupation.

I participated in the *akademye* from an early age; I probably read my first poem at about six or seven, sang with the SKIF choir from about eight. For as long as I can remember, *geto akademye* always played to a script: survivors would light candles, often with their grandchildren; a survivor would make a speech followed by a speech from a SKIF representative; then an artistic program, including

Yiddish poems and Yiddish songs performed by an ad hoc SKIF choir. Many of these traditions, such as lighting six candles, or a survivor telling their story, were not specific to the Bund. These were universal rituals, recognizable the world over. Some things were very specific to us, though: the emphasis on fallen Bundists, the ongoing presence of Yiddish as ritual language, with Yiddish recitations and songs by children as young as eight. There were also things that we didn't do that many other communities did: no kaddish or *El Male Rachamim* (mourning prayers); no *Hatikvah*, the Israeli national anthem, or any national anthems. Any hint of traditional religious symbols or Zionist imagery was unwelcome in the Bundist cere- mony. Even "Di shvue" wasn't sung then. Many of these practices were established in the immediate aftermath of the Holocaust, as communities of survivors began formulating the most appropriate, most meaningful ways to grieve for their families, now reduced to ashes in the cities, fields, and forests of Eastern Europe.

For most of my childhood, and in the years before I began par- ticipating, the *akademyes* were planned and directed by Sluggo and his best friend, Nudy (side note: Dad and his friends all seemed to have nicknames; Sluggo, Nudy, Cookie, Spud, Frog, Hanch, Dumbo, MZ, Daf, Rock). Partly, Dad took responsibility for them because of his background in the theatre. He knew how to put on a show. Even more, it was his way of fulfilling his responsibilities to his father, and to the family that he never knew. It was one of the most important things he did, not only to memorialize the victims but also to teach new generations of SKIFistn. At least as I remember it, there wasn't a lot of experimenting with the format. It was all pretty set in stone, al- most running itself. Sluggo and Nudy just needed to oil the machine, get the kids singing loudly enough and reading clearly enough, and then inject a dose of drama into their recitations. Incidentally, it was here that I began to appreciate the nuances of performing in front of an audience: how to project your voice to the back of an auditorium, how to make eye contact with an audience, how to recite a poem expressively, to bring out the real meaning of the words. It wasn't only the Holocaust Sluggo was teaching here but public speaking and performance. Confidence, really. In addition to all his other work commitments and communal involvement, Sluggo organizing *geto akademye* was just a part of our house, the Holocaust always just there in the background.

~

No wonder that I was raised with a very specific idea of what it meant to commemorate the Holocaust, of how it ought to be remembered. These annual rituals were replicated at various points throughout the year. At Sholem Aleichem College, my primary school, founded by Bundists in 1975, we had an annual memorial assembly that followed a similar script. Candles, survivor speech, poems. Windows blackened, large-scale maps of Europe identifying the sites of destruction, pictures from the Warsaw Ghetto adorning the walls. A solemn atmosphere manufactured by our teachers, the sense of sanctity unmistakable. This was as close to a religious ceremony as we got at our secular Yiddish day school. I remember watching the survivors in those ceremonies, accompanied by their grandchildren, lighting six candles, one for each million. In my preteen years, I hoped that I, too, might one day accompany my grandparents on stage to light the candles, not then understanding that because they survived in the Soviet Union, they weren't considered to be Holocaust survivors in the strange universe of shtetl Melbourne.

At SKIF camp, there was ghetto day, *khurbn tog*, every summer camp. This left a strong impression on all SKIFistn. When we were younger, most of us hated that day. It was designed to have maximum impact. We knew straightaway at *oyfshtayn*, at wake up, when we were woken up not by the customary three whistles but by the *helfer* walking solemnly into our room to wake us up, voices hushed, lacking their usual energy. The rules on *khurbn tog* were different than usual. No singing at meals, no chanting, no loud or boisterous talking. At one camp, at least, there was no talking at all at meals. Activities on those days focused on the Holocaust and on reflecting on the meaning, lessons, and legacies. There was usually a quiet reading space made available, with whatever books the *helfer* had on their (or their parents') bookshelves. It was as a ten-year-old at SKIF camp that I first read Art Spiegelman's *Maus*. I think I read the whole of the first volume in a sitting. Occasionally a survivor would come tell us their story, if not at camp then at least at one of our weekly Sunday meetings in the lead-up to April 19. The night would usually culminate in an opportunity for the campers to stand up in front of the camp and offer their own reflections: a poem, a passage from something they had read that day, a telling of their own grandparents' story of survival. We'd sit in a big circle, light candles, some kids would inevitably cry: maximum impact was the aim, or emotional manipulation. Clearly it was important for kids to learn facts: places, dates, people, events. More important was that they should develop an emotional connection, a sense of their own place in the story, of what connects them to the past but also what their responsibilities are going forward.

One year—or maybe it was more than once; I don't know, but one camp stands out for this—we were awoken by the *helfer* shouting abuse at us. It was soon clear that they were the Nazis in what was going to unfold as some elaborate role-play. We had to quickly get out of bed, and immediately we were shepherded outside the dorms, where we proceeded to march through the woods, *helfer* alongside, shouting at us. Learning by doing, I suppose, by simulating a death march. I don't know how long it took, but when we finally returned, the whole camp—maybe sixty of us—was squeezed into one small dorm room. With our bodies piled on top of each other, many of us complaining, the *helfer* closed the door. Occasionally they'd open up the door and throw water on us before closing it again, a sick reenactment of the victims' journey on the cattle cars. That night, the evening activity was an adventure activity—we were Jews in the ghettos, the *helfer* were Nazis. A hybrid of capture-the-flag and British Bulldog—the highest stakes game the *helfer* could conjure. They didn't go easy on us: as we tried to break through their lines—they with torches, we trying to evade their gaze, filled with nervous tension—they tackled us roughly, shouted at us, sent us back to the start.

I doubt this was a terribly effective way to teach about the Holocaust. Maybe I'm wrong. Maybe those *helfer* were at the pedagogical vanguard of active learning: kids learn better through targeted activities than through passively listening. In this case, the message was: if you're uncomfortable on this "death march," or in this "cattle train," or evading these "Nazi guards," imagine how it was for the actual victims. Teaching with a sledgehammer, beating the message into us, quite literally. I'm not sure I have the answer for how to sensitively teach about the Holocaust to children ranging from eight to eighteen whose families' backgrounds and experiences can be surprisingly diverse, but I'm pretty certain that this approach did not lead to kids becoming more aware of their own historical obligations or understanding any better the experience of the Holocaust. We dreaded ghetto day, knowing it would be an island of solemnity in what was usually a sea of laughter. We didn't want to give up the singing at meals or the boisterous life of camp even for a day. When things got more intense, such as with those Holocaust simulations, we were more resentful than reflective, more traumatized than enlightened. Those SKIF camp experiences, though, were only part of a broader program of indoctrination that permeated the Melbourne Jewish bubble. Along with my friends, I was battered by the ghosts of the past, implored to learn about, understand, and disseminate knowledge about the Holocaust. The holiest of all tasks.

$\sim$

Through all these yearly rituals and performances, I was reminded over and over of my responsibility to carry on Zaida's legacy, to ensure that the Holocaust would never be forgotten, that his family would never be forgotten. This, even though I knew pretty much nothing about them, not even their names. His story, along with those of my grandmothers, was a virtual mystery. I knew some of the outlines, the bare bones, but barely any specifics. The commemorations—at SKIF, and Sholem Aleichem, and the Bund—were a critical tool in inculcating me with a sense of the magnitude of the Holocaust, of what had been lost, and of what was at stake. Through the process, I learned of the Bund's role in the Warsaw Ghetto Uprising and absorbed the names of young fighters—SKIFistn, children, teenagers like me—as well as of veteran heroes of the Bundist resistance. I was taught almost nothing about non-Bundist resisters until I studied them myself years later. There were some exceptions, but it would have been easy for me to come away thinking that the uprising in the Warsaw Ghetto, and Jewish resistance around Europe, was strictly a Bundist affair.

One reason, our parents told us, that we had to remember the Holocaust was so that we could counteract the dangers of Holocaust deniers like David Irving, the loudmouth, antisemitic admirer of Hitler. Irving is a pseudohistorian, more a Jew-hating conspiracy theorist than a scholar. A narcissist in a tinfoil hat. When I was growing up in the early to mid-1990s, Irving was at the height of his celebrity, or infamy. In 1996, he infamously, and unsuccessfully, sued the Holocaust historian Deborah Lipstadt for libel after Lipstadt showed that he deliberately distorted, manufactured, or ignored evidence to try to prove that the gas chambers were a fiction. This was one of a number of major court cases in the 1980s and 1990s in which the truth of the Holocaust was tested in a legal setting. This was alarming for survivors, whose own stories and experiences were being scrutinized, and for families whose own traumatic pasts were at stake. Irving had gained notoriety in Australia a few years earlier when the Australian government refused him a visa to enter the country. This quasi-academic image that he portrayed, a wolf in sheep's clothing, alarmed many in our community and convinced Melbourne's Jews that correct and appropriate remembrance would help inoculate people against the lies peddled by Irving and his ilk. They were convinced more than ever that aggressively disseminating Holocaust memory was crucial if we were to ward off complacency. In its preparation, rehearsal, and presentation, the April 19 *akademye* was one way to ensure that young SKIFistn imbibed this message.

The date, April 19, was fixed immediately after the war, as Bundists took part in a global discussion about the most appropriate date on which to honor the memory of the victims of the Holocaust and, even more so, of the heroism of the partisans. The Warsaw Ghetto Uprising, which began on the morning of April 19, 1943, was the culmination of several months of negotiation between and preparation among the various Jewish political youth movements in the Warsaw Ghetto, particularly those on the left. The right-wing Zionists formed their own fighting units, distinct from the Jewish Fighting Organization (ZOB) that young Bundists, socialist-Zionists, and communists established in late 1942. For nearly thirty days in April and May 1943, these bands of brave young women and men, many still just teenagers, fought a guerrilla war against the mightiest military in wartime Europe. With virtually no military experience or training and very few weapons, armed with only guile, quick wits, and homemade Molotov cocktails, these soldiers staged a heroic, but ultimately tragic, insurrection. Very few survived, and the uprising did not halt the Nazi extermination efforts or meaningfully impact the course of the war. Nonetheless, as a symbol, the uprising was powerful for Jews under Nazi rule around Europe, and also for those outside Europe. It was adopted almost universally as the emblem of Jewish heroism and martyrdom.

I was deeply attached to the Warsaw Ghetto Uprising narrative. We were following the broader trend among Jews around the world to elevate stories of heroism, and this was the greatest of those. In the years after the war, the uprising quickly became the iconic instance of Jewish resistance and martyrdom across the Jewish world. It was the longest-sustained armed battle by European Jews, with the Nazi machine taking nearly a month to finally snuff out the last of the ZOB fighters. Even then, the Nazis only finally managed to do so by burning the ghetto to the ground. So whether it was in Wrocław, Paris, Melbourne, or New York, Zaida and Sluggo helped craft a certain mythology about the uprising and its significance. This wasn't the only reason we felt invested, though; it was more personal than that. Zaida was born and raised at Świętojerska 18 in Warsaw, in the Jewish quarter, just at the border of where the ghetto wall would run. He had family there through to the war years. Sluggo thought there was an aunt or some other relative that lived at the address Mila 18, which became the headquarters and bunker of the ZOB leadership. Mich's parents were both from Warsaw too. Her father, Zaida Izak, was raised in an apartment building at Pawia 49, in the heart of Jewish Warsaw and what would become the ghetto. Although we know of no family directly involved in the uprising, our connection to Jewish Warsaw meant that the uprising would have special significance. Warsaw is the place where family memories are buried, where family is buried.

The date was as important as the commemoration itself. For Sluggo, it was, as he told me repeatedly, the holiest day on the calendar, "my Yom Kippur," he would say. The irony is not lost on me. That was the day on which he would take stock and reflect on the life he had led, on his responsibility to his father and family, and on whether or not he was fulfilling the legacy his father's past demanded. He did all of those things every day of the year, but this day held special significance. There was no question that on April 19 each year, we would attend the evening commemoration, have the memories passed onto us, and then later pass on the memories to the next generation. It was simple, not up for debate. Some years, April 19 fell on one of the seder nights of Passover, that night families came together to remember the Jews' unlikely exodus from Egypt thousands of years earlier. Two holy nights clashing for primacy, two narratives of Jewish enslavement and resistance. A fierce argument would ensue in our house and among the Bund community over how to deal with the schedule clash. Should we move it a day later (impossible, April 20 was Hitler's birthday), or a day earlier (what if that was the first seder)? For many, the very idea of moving the commemoration was a desecration. After all, the brave souls who fought in the Warsaw Ghetto did so on seder night. If we were going to honor their memory, surely we could make a minor sacrifice like that, after the major sacrifice that they made. Usually, a compromise was worked out where the *akademye* would take place in the late afternoon, before the seder. Those discussions were always very tense, with members split between moving the event to allow for greater inclusion and maintaining the holiness of the date. This debate typified the way that remembering the Holocaust was imagined as a sacred, almost religious obligation. The date could not be moved, to do so was nothing less than a desecration, an abomination. In our own house, the discussion got heated. Sluggo and I disagreed on this: I felt it important to be flexible to ensure greater inclusivity; he was steadfast that "19 April is a *heylige date* (a holy date)."

This generational conflict was emblematic of how we thought about commemoration. I viewed the whole thing as stale, exclusive, and needing to be rejigged to appeal to a new generation who hadn't been brainwashed like I had. I thought the focus of the *akademye* should be on our generation and future generations. We should be looking ahead to how we could best honor and identify with the victims beyond the current moment. For Dad there was a settled set of rituals we must follow, a certain kind of decorum we must observe. To be sure, he was more flexible than others, having himself experimented with the format, but he and I still debated about what memorializing the Holocaust should look like.

∼

From when I was sixteen, I codirected then directed the commemoration on and off for about ten years. In the earlier years, I assisted in the process, helping compile the program, organize the logistics, and prepare the SKIFistn to perform. Later, in my midtwenties, I was responsible for running the show, as Sluggo had been when I was growing up, carrying the torch that had been passed down from my father. He was proud. Would Zaida have been proud?

During that period, it felt like I was constantly fighting with the Bund committee. Over the script, over the format, over the theme. I imagined myself the young firebrand trying to change the whole nature of Holocaust memory. I thought the members of the Bund committee were complacent, backward-looking, not aware that the world around them was changing. I thought they felt that they had perfected memorialization, when what I saw was the same thing year after year. The same poems, songs, narratives, themes when I was eighteen as

when I was eight. I wanted to change how the Bund commemorated. Lofty ambitions, more than just a little over the top. Not like a
Slucki to be overly dramatic. Maybe I was just being difficult because
I thought I had to fulfill some cliché about generational conflict. Or
maybe I was trying to emulate the stories that Dad used to tell me
about fighting with the Bund committee. In any case, they kept asking me back, maybe because no one else would take on the workload.
The *akademyes* were a success: meaningful for participants, interesting
and thought-provoking. I was doing my job well, I thought.

In 2010, I was slated to organize the *akademye* again, having
done so the previous two years. I was busy finishing off my disser-
tation and working out what the hell I was going to do with my
life after that, so instead of running it as I had previously, taking
responsibility for planning and delivery, I agreed that I would put
together a script and program and I'd give a speech. Each year I was
involved I tried to organize with a theme that connected everything, something I had learned to do from Dad. One year it was the
experience of children, another year women and their experiences as
victims and resisters. As convener of the *akademye,* I wanted to try
new things, to innovate. It wasn't only my responsibility to disseminate Holocaust memory, but to do so in a vernacular that connected
with the next generation. I was not convinced that Yiddish poetry
was that vehicle. I insisted that we include a slide show with translations of all the Yiddish, and that we hold the event in the Holocaust museum, just next door to the traditional venue, the Kadimah.
One year I asked one of the SKIF *helfer* to choreograph a dance
to a hip-hop song, "Never Again," by the rapper Remedy, himself
a descendant of survivors. Days before the *akademye* was due to
go ahead, the Bund committee decided to overrule the dance—it
would be offensive to the survivors, they argued, to have a hip-hop
song at an *akademye*. In the end, we reframed the dance and set it
to an avant-garde solo piano rendition of "Es brent" [Our town is
burning], a staple of *geto akademyes,* by the Krakow Yiddish poet
Mordechai Gebirtig.

But the message was perfectly clear: stay within the framework laid out over decades. The Bund committee argued that it was the survivors to whom they were sensitive, but I suspect that they used the survivors as a stand-in for their own discomfort with changing things too much, with experimenting in memorial practices.

A couple of factors shaped my vision for the *akademye* that year. The first was that the previous October, Marek Edelman, the last surviving commander of the Warsaw Ghetto Uprising, died in Poland. Edelman was an icon of the Bund, a wily, old curmudgeon who had been deputy commander of the Jewish Fighting Organization, one of the few of the leadership to survive. He was outspoken, unapologetically political. He didn't care what people thought; he felt it was his responsibility to speak the truth, no matter the consequences. After what he had suffered, what he had accomplished, he had earned the right. Edelman stayed in Poland after the war and trained to be a cardiologist. He made it his life's work to save people's lives. Very fitting. He was a true Bundist—a socialist who insisted that his place was in Poland and that no antisemite would scare him away from his home. He was a leading voice against communism and a leader in the Solidarity movement in the 1980s, highly respected for his wartime and Cold War resistance to totalitarianism. He was an inspiration to me. His sober account of the uprising written in the immediate aftermath of the war was one of the first accounts I read as a child, and his interview with Polish journalist Hanna Krall, published as the book *To Outwit God*, shaped a lot of my thinking about the Holocaust and the uprising. In the interview, he eschewed the kind of mystification of the fighters and the uprising to which I had become accustomed. There were no sacred cows—he just told it how it was, without embellishment, without heroics. There were no saints, no martyrs. The people who fought did so only because they had nothing else left to do. Better, he said, to die with guns in your hands than without. His was an account of the uprising that made me question all icons, all myths, made me think about how memory is formulated, shaped, and reshaped. Reading the account felt almost like a transgression, like I was doing something dangerous, edgy. What's more, Edelman continued to struggle against injustice his whole life. To him, the essence of being a Jew meant to always be on the side of the oppressed, never on the side of the oppressor, something that resonated strongly with me. The 2010 *akademye* was the first after he died, and we were conscious that we were honoring him as we prepared.

Given the universal significance of Edelman's struggle, I proposed a script that reflected on the reality of genocide since the Holocaust. I included poetry and narratives telling of the Rwandan and Cambodian genocides and of the dispossession and slaughter of Indigenous Australians. These were stories that sounded remarkably like the ones that we heard and read year after year, poems that could have easily told of the Warsaw Ghetto, of the extermination camps, of death marches. The Bund committee was uncomfortable with this; many didn't like the implication that others had suffered just as Jews did. Some thought this wasn't the venue to acknowledge those other groups. It was terrible what had happened to Bosnians, Armenians, Indigenous Australians, they agreed, but this was *our* night to honor *our* fallen.

The other factor that shaped my involvement that year was that April 19 coincided with Yom Ha'atzmaut, Israel's day of independence, what Palestinians called the *Nakba*, the catastrophe. That night, as we would be mourning the families denied us, thousands of Melbourne's Jews would be gathered across town to celebrate the establishment of the State of Israel. We were a left-wing, non-Zionist—once upon a time described as anti-Zionist—Jewish movement. What's more, we were honoring the legacy of a Bundist icon who never shied away from speaking his mind and demanding justice, including in the context of the Israeli-Palestinian conflict. I thought it would be incongruous to pretend that it wasn't also the date of Israel's Independence Day celebration. In reality, I was probably further to the left on Israel than most others in the movement. Israel had never really featured in my upbringing. We had some family there, but I was never raised to feel any particular attachment. I'm not sure why I drifted further to the left on the issue, but certainly I was out of step with the vast majority of Melbourne's Jews, and even with many in my own little corner of that community.

The speech I gave revolved around Edelman's position that to be a Jew meant to be on the side of the oppressed, never with the oppressor. This meant, for example, showing our solidarity with Indigenous Australians still suffering from the legacy of colonization and dispossession. But it also meant, I argued, that we ought to reckon with what it meant for Jews to hold political and military power, as they did in Israel. What responsibilities did it confer on Israel, a nation-state, that the Holocaust was part of its foundational narrative, that its leaders constantly invoked the Holocaust to justify their actions? What did it mean for a Jewish state, I asked there on stage, to wield its power over another population, to occupy them at best, terrorize them at worst? I described Israel's occupation of the West Bank as unethical, illegal. It was, I argued, immoral for Jews, perhaps more than for any other group, to subjugate others, given our own recent history, given our long story of suffering and uprooting. Mainly, I tried to challenge the audience to think about the ethical implications of being Jewish in the post-Holocaust world. I had a noble, if naïve objective: I wanted people to think, and I wanted especially for the younger audience members to reflect on their own Jewishness in the wake of the Holocaust, and on the obligations that laid on them. I didn't want to give concrete answers, simply to raise questions that I thought the situation demanded.

What was the point of standing before an audience if not to challenge them, to make them think? My parents were away that year. In Europe, I think. I e-mailed Dad the speech. He wrote back, said it would be controversial, that I should take out the word "illegal" when describing Israel's occupation. "It's the Bund," I responded. "How can it possibly be controversial to describe the occupation as illegal?" I sensed he was not entirely comfortable either with me giving that speech on that day; he was supportive, but his support was more lukewarm than usual. He would later defend me to the Bund committee, on which he sat.

I was nervous. I knew I was treading a fine line but felt that I couldn't take a backward step. As I spoke, my heart beat faster and faster, tiny beads of sweat lingering just at the top of my forehead, betraying my angst. There was a distinct air of discomfort in the room. I quoted former prime minister Paul Keating and his famous "Redfern speech," in which he challenged all Australians to imagine what it must be like to be among the dispossessed, the oppressed, the stolen. It was when I raised the question of Jewish military might that things took a turn, when I began to lose parts of the audience. I couldn't see much from up there on stage, with the theatre lights shining brightly in my eyes, a kind of mist before me with a few shapeless silhouettes at the bottom of my field of vision. But I heard it. The whispering, the shuffling in the seats, the uncomfortable coughs. I heard heckling. A family member, no less, a survivor himself, shouted loudly enough for me to hear. "He's an idiot!" he called out. I was pretty sure I knew who it was, even beyond the uniform glow that I could see before me. Certainly not the best reception I've had.

I watched the rest of the *akademye* from the wings, and lingered there a little after we all belted out the "Partizaner hymn" [Partisans' Hymn], which I did with extra vigor, feeling as though I had done something small to honor Zaida and his family. I wondered what he would have thought. I had no idea. When it finished I waited a little before facing the crowd. I thought it best to let people cool down, to let me cool down. There was too much nervous energy still. My heart had barely slowed down. I knew what was coming.

The Bund committee received complaints from members and nonmembers, and I received e-mails, mainly from those in the second generation, complaining about my lack of propriety in raising "political" issues and negatively impacting the reputation of other Yiddish institutions. I was accused of "generat[ing] anger and division" rather than "helping to bring our community together to pay respect to the 6 million." One person said that my actions impacted how people viewed the Bund and all related institutions, like Sholem Aleichem College. Didn't I know that? Wasn't I aware of how I was damaging the Bund's brand? I knew that I wasn't speaking on behalf of anyone but myself, and I didn't think it was my problem if other people couldn't figure that out. A certain level of brashness, even arrogance. In any case, it was hardly straying from Bundist history and ideas to challenge Israeli militarism and its centrality to Jewish life. The Bund was historically antagonistic to Zionism and was deeply split over the question of how to deal with the State of Israel, where it fit into its program. Some community members demanded that the Bund state whether it endorsed my remarks, which they saw as likely to drive people away from the movement. Had they read it in advance? Had they "approved" it?

I was indignant. The Bund, so far as I was concerned, was a movement that not only tolerated difference of opinion but encouraged it. One of the things that drew me to the Bund was that it encouraged people to think, to challenge authority, to undermine norms. How could these people, attending a Bund commemoration, possibly demand a speaker be censored, censured, for making a claim that was totally consistent with Bundist philosophy?

I know that it was the message that offended them—had I given a speech that extolled Israel's centrality and importance in the wake of the Holocaust, praised it as a defender of world Jewry, no one would have batted an eyelid. No one would have accused me of being political. Other commemorations routinely used the occasion to defend Israel's importance to world Jewry, rounding out the evening with a rendition of Israel's national anthem. This was the real litmus test, I think: what made it political was that they didn't agree with me. We clearly had different visions of what an *akademye* was for, who it was for, what work it ought to do in disseminating knowledge, understanding, and memory of the Holocaust.

In response, the Bund held a communal discussion on the nature of the *akademye* and on how it ought to be run in the future. Taking place months after the actual event, what transpired was an overwhelming feeling that Holocaust memorialization was not to be tampered with; that *geto akademye* was a certain set of known rituals providing comfort for the audience of survivors, their children, and their grandchildren. Remembering the Holocaust was not "political" or "academic," but was "emotional," above politics or intellectual engagement, purer. I was accused of having tainted the sanctity of the date. I was told that commemorating was "simple," that the April 19 ceremony was like standing at the grave of those who do not have graves. I was told that I had been disrespectful to survivors and victims alike. I was accused of naïveté at best, malice at worst.

This was, perhaps, the starkest example for me of how the Holocaust had taken on a kind of religious function for those around me. Its centrality to Melbourne's Jews had always been something of which I was aware, having been surrounded by so many who were so profoundly physically and mentally scarred by their experiences. But the religious overtones of those who claimed that commemorating the Holocaust should follow a set ritual, that the commemoration was akin to a funeral (and all the religious implications that had), was truly confronting for me in the role that had been handed to me and every member of my generation: that of assuming memories that would, within a decade or two, be primarily carried by us.

I found this an affront: the *geto akademye* was an event that had been non-negotiable for me for nearly two and half decades. Now, I was told that I was disrespecting it, that I must follow certain conventions of remembrance, certain rituals, as though a Holocaust commemoration was as tightly regulated as a *Kol Nidre* service. Although I, a grandson of survivors, was being forever reminded about my obligation to remember and to transmit the memories and stories of my grandparents, I was not being entrusted to do so, except within the narrow parameters set by my parents' generation. How, then, to make sense of the vexed question of how to memorialize the dead and honor the still living while carrying on the legacy that we have been constantly reminded is ours? Who decides what form Holocaust memorialization should take, what the lessons of the Holocaust are, or if indeed there are lessons? How could I continue to participate in a ritual from which I had begun to feel disconnected? Could remembering the Holocaust be as simple as singing a few

Yiddish songs and reciting a few poems, shedding a few tears as we sang the "Partizaner hymn"?

~

Sluggo, *Shmulek* in Yiddish, was named either after his grandfather, who died in 1916 in Warsaw, or after his father's first son, murdered at Chelmno in 1942. It almost doesn't matter now which; that he has carried the name of his dead half-brother his whole life meant that he always lived with a sense of absence, and stemming from that, a sense of responsibility. It wasn't something he really talked about, but it must, even subconsciously, have shaped his relationship to the Holocaust, which cast a long shadow over him. Perhaps not so surprising, then, that April 19 was his *"heylige date,"* his Yom Kippur. We sanctified the Holocaust, and all the symbols associated with it became untouchable: the language of martyrdom and holiness, the songs, the poems, and the candle lighting became part of our own Holocaust religion.

I'm less zealous about it now. In 1987, Israeli philosopher Adi Ophir criticized this Holocaust memorial culture and its sanctification of the Holocaust. He sardonically highlighted four commandments that govern how we remember the Holocaust, commandments that formed a "religious consciousness" for Jewish communities: "Thou shalt have no other holocaust before the Holocaust of the Jews of Europe; Thou shalt not make unto thee any graven image or any likeness; Thou shalt not take the name of the Holocaust in vain; Remember." This sense was pervasive in my Melbourne childhood—I absorbed it as a child and a teenager; as an adult I resented it. Now, I'm more agnostic about how to remember and commemorate, about what is appropriate, inappropriate, or effective. Whatever helps people cope is fine, I suppose, so long as it doesn't harm others.

This sense of piety, though, of the Holocaust as outside history, has been a constant in my life as a Jew growing up in Melbourne, and was only reinforced as I tried to fulfill my responsibilities to remember. Although my grandparents, all four of whom lived out the war years in the Soviet Union, probably did not consider them-selves to be survivors, we nonetheless always carried an almost sa-cred burden to remember, given what they had lost. The absence that for them was always present became central to us. My connection to the Holocaust was fostered not only through them, though, but also through my parents, my youth movement, my school, and my community more broadly. In each of these settings—family, school, community—the mandate to remember the Holocaust, and to do so in a prescribed manner, was a constant.

In *shtetl* Melbourne, the Holocaust remains a crucial part of the collective foundational narrative. Melbourne, more than most other locations, was profoundly shaped by the influx of European, and par-ticularly Polish, Jews in the postwar decades. Many of these migrants had survived Nazi-occupied Europe; many had escaped to the Soviet Union in the early months of the war. As kids, we were often told that Melbourne had the highest per capita Holocaust survivor popu-lation outside Israel, although I've heard similar claims about Skokie and Montreal. The Holocaust forms part of the curriculum in Jewish schools. These schools have their own commemorative events, and their students—at least when I was growing up—formed a combined schools choir that performed at the annual community commemora-tion. Youth movements across the ideological and religious spectrum emphasize the importance of Holocaust remembrance. The Jewish Holocaust Museum, established in 1984, is a central communal institution, the leading arbiter of Holocaust memory in Australia, through which thousands of Jewish and non-Jewish schools connect to the Holocaust. The commemorative events are many—whether the large community commemoration or the smaller ceremonies that take place at the memorials of the various *landsmanshaft*, mutual aid organizations that bind immigrants from the same town or city. The Holocaust is also regularly instrumentalized by communal leaders and institutions for a variety of purposes: in defense of the State of Israel; in emphasizing the ongoing dangers of antisemitism; as a barrier against intermarriage. At the same time, those community leaders warn against the Holocaust being exploited by others, such as those who compare it to contemporary genocides, or those who draw analogies between Israel and Nazi Germany.

For a young Jew, then, growing up in a Yiddish-speaking, socialist, survivor family, this sense of the Holocaust as holy penetrated deeply into my psyche. I was intellectually, spiritually, and physically surrounded by Holocaust memories. For me, the story of my relationship with the Holocaust is not one of absence, as can often be the case for the descendants of survivors, but of an overwhelming presence. There was never any doubt about the Holocaust's meaning, nor about my role in inheriting and passing on the stories. That is not to say that the Holocaust consumed me all day, every day, but it was an important part of the landscape of my childhood. It shaped my family in ways I wouldn't understand until I was an adult, but that were profound: my grandmother's constant fear of us traveling, knowing that when she left her family in 1939 she never saw them again; the closeness of even distant cousins, a relic of the fact that my father's mother survived only because her own father insisted that the family must stay together at all costs (he literally dragged her by her pigtails so that she would escape her town of Stary Sącz with them); our seemingly genetic attachment to the telephone, a way to constantly keep tabs on one another, as they had to do in Siberia. These are all psychological scars born in wartime and passed on to future generations. Not only my immediate family but my uncles, aunts, cousins, even those who were "like family," shared these foundational narratives and the curious habits that stemmed from them.

∼

I can't now remember when I first learned that Zaida Jakub lost his wife and two sons in a death camp, or that Bubba Mania was the only one left in the Minc family of Warsaw. I don't remember when I could first sing the "Partizaner hymn," the Yiddish anthem of the Partisans in the Vilna ghetto, by heart. Nor do I remember when I became desensitized to images of the dead bodies strewn across pits and fields, or the terrified looks or vacant stares in the victims' eyes as they stared up at me from the pages of books.

I do remember the Holocaust assemblies at primary school. I remember survivors regaling us with their remarkable tales of survival, their craftiness, ingenuity, chutzpah. I remember those stories of courage and guile in the Łódź ghetto, in Auschwitz, in many other camps. I remember those memorial days at SKIF camp. I remember visiting the old Holocaust museum, just over the road from my primary school, the yellowing photos on the wall, the scale model of the Treblinka death camp, the life-sized sculpture of victims behind barbed wire. The Holocaust pervaded all aspects of Melbourne's Jewish public sphere.

But the Holocaust stories also filtered through our family. I remember Bubba Eda's daring stories of survival in the hellishly frozen expanses of Siberia, when she secretly studied Russian by candlelight, against her father's wishes, allowing her to bribe the Russian guards for vodka, elixir for her ailing father. Or when she learned to operate a film projector and found herself indoor work during the harsh Siberian winter. Or when she taught herself to drive a tractor. She was only a teenager when they crossed into the Soviet Union, but she was wily, resourceful, and plucky enough to help her family survive in a place where many couldn't. I also remember Bubba Mania's stories of escape from Warsaw: encountering Jews in eastern Poland, seeing the Bolshoi ballet in Moscow, reading Tolstoy by moonlight (*War and Peace*—she liked it better in Polish), and starving in Uzbekistan, a refuge from the Russian winter.

I remember the stories of Zaida Jakub leading a transport of Polish Jews in Yakutsk on the long journey, first by boat, then by train, back to Poland, where they all discovered they had lost everything: their homes, their communities, their families. I remember the six permanent memorial candles in the foyer of the Kadimah, Melbourne's Yiddish cultural center, which, in our family's visual record, have been immortalized as part of the background for our bar mitzvah portraits.

Even when I was too young to comprehend them, I knew about the gas chambers and the crematoria. When I was little and Dad told me that his father's family had been burned in the ovens of a death camp, it was so far beyond my imagination I could only picture his wife and sons being squeezed into our kitchen oven, where we heated our frozen pizzas and meat pies. From the time I was a child, I have occasionally had a recurring dream where a Jeep full of Nazis drive past my home on Lahona Avenue, firing their guns into our house, me standing on the old porch watching it unfold. I don't know when it began, but that dream, that nightmare, is etched somewhere in the deepest recesses of my memory, as though it's always been there. The Holocaust has always been present, prominent. From my earliest years, though, in private and public, the Holocaust was not something from which I was shielded. That I should remember it, that it was a central event in Jewish history, was never anything I dared question. Details might have been sketchy, and the stories a tapestry without cohesion, but those ghosts were always hanging around, as a child in suburban Melbourne, as an adolescent and a young adult, and as a historian of the Holocaust, whether in Australia, Germany, France, or the United States.

In April 2014, I attended the annual communal Holocaust commemoration in Charleston. By then, I had been living there for nearly a year, teaching Jewish history at the historic College of Charleston. Charleston is a city of some six thousand Jews with a rich Jewish history. It is considered the birthplace of American Reform Judaism, and as a major port, was a significant Jewish center in the early years of the nineteenth century. Since the Civil War, however, it has been peripheral to American Jewish life. In the aftermath of the Holocaust, no more than a couple of dozen survivors settled in Charleston, although they have been active in promoting Holocaust education and the founding of an award-winning Holocaust memorial in a central city square. It's never been clear to me why there is such a vibrant Holocaust memorial culture here. When I teach the Holocaust at the college, many of my South Carolinian students have studied the Holocaust at school and heard one of the local survivors speak. But in some ways Charleston was the opposite of Melbourne: survivors here were a curiosity, rare but venerated. In Melbourne, most old Jews that I knew were survivors. There was something so commonplace about it. I didn't even realize how commonplace until I lived in Charleston, where the few survivors who made it there are virtually local celebrities. And while memorials to slavery are almost completely nonexistent, there stands a Holocaust memorial in Marion Square, the heart of the city, in its busiest public space. City officials flock to Holocaust commemorations, but not necessarily to events commemorating the suffering and subjugation of African Americans over four centuries. In Charleston, no less, where around 40 percent of all slaves from Africa first arrived to the United States, chained in ships, the early modern version of the Nazis' cattle cars, it is much easier to find a memorial to the Holocaust than to Charleston's own dark past.

I went to the annual Yom HaShoah Holocaust commemoration because, as a grandson of survivors, as a historian, and as someone who has been a participant in and organizer of Holocaust remembrance rituals for most of my life, I was curious to see how a small Jewish community commemorated the Holocaust. Mostly, though, I think what pushed me along was Sluggo's voice in my head telling me that April 19 is a *heylige date*. Although the Charleston memorial correlates with Yom HaShoah, rather than April 19, my duty was clear: it was my obligation to participate in such rituals, whether in Melbourne or in Charleston.

The ceremony included familiar aspects: lighting the memorial candles, a survivor telling his story (in this case, in very gory detail, with audible groans from the audience at various points), and an artistic performance from a local Jewish choir. More noteworthy, to me at least, were those rituals that were unfamiliar. For one, the ceremony took place in the local Reform temple, a site chosen, I was told, because of its proximity to the local Holocaust memorial. I was much more accustomed to attending theatres, auditoriums, or even Holocaust museums, but this site seemed to lend the ritual more religious or spiritual significance. At least, a different kind of religious significance; the Bundist ceremony, of course, carried its own kind of spirituality with it.

This was probably at the heart of what made the event so foreign to me: that the ceremony was dependent on religious Jewish rituals and vernacular for making sense of the Holocaust. Apart from the venue, three of the city's five rabbis and a local cantor played a central role in proceedings, dividing between them the introductory and concluding remarks, recitation of *kaddish* as well as a prayer for the six million, and the recitation of the funeral prayer *El Male Rachamim*. It was the rabbis who bookended the event, not only responsible for the formal religious components but also for framing the remembrance ritual.

Instead of the kind of sanctification I was used to, in which religious significance was imposed upon cultural and secular representations (poetry, songs, narratives), here, participants and organizers redirected existing Jewish symbols and rituals toward commemorating the Holocaust. This isn't novel, certainly, but in contrast to the annual reenactment of a Bundist version of Holocaust commemorative rituals to which I was accustomed, it was as though another event were being remembered.

Another new ritual to me was that at the beginning of the ceremony, local descendants of survivors read the names of their family members who perished during the war. This was perhaps the lengthiest portion of the ceremony, and at times, the most moving. Any Charleston resident who lost family during the war (it wasn't clear to me if there was a limit to how close the family needed to be) was invited to come up on stage with their families and read out the names of those family members who perished, before lighting a candle. Simultaneously, a slide show ticked over with the names. The thought that I couldn't escape was that if a community Holocaust commemoration in Melbourne included this in its program, the service would take weeks. That this simple and poignant ceremony would not have been possible in Melbourne hammered home the extent to which Melbourne Jewry, and my own life, my own family, and my own social circles have been shaped by the presence of Holocaust survivors.

At the end of the formal proceedings, the audience of several hundred gathered out in front of the temple and marched silently the half a mile to the city's Holocaust memorial. Walking down one of the city's main arterials was an impressive spectacle, although its significance was never really outlined. What was most unusual was that the march was led by members of the local chapter of the Knights of Columbus, a worldwide Catholic fraternal order, dressed in their ceremonial regalia and carrying American flags. No explanation was given as to why this group led the silent march, and although there should be no problem in principle for a Catholic organization participating in a Holocaust commemoration, there was something about the aesthetic of the Knights of Columbus leading the march that I found disquieting.

Finally, I was unsettled when twice during the survivor's talk, the audience applauded. Once, they applauded wildly when the survivor described the United States as "the greatest country in the world," and after he had finished, he received a standing ovation. In my twenty-nine years, I had never heard applause at a Holocaust commemoration. In Melbourne, it was always the accepted convention that these events were solemn and applause was taboo. It was here I first felt the pang that the moment lacked solemnity, gravity; that those present were not treating the affair with the requisite reverence.

Being in Charleston helped me to see the way in which I had my own narrow conception of what Holocaust memorialization ought to look like. Even though I tried to resist the impulse to lay claim over what was the "best" or "most appropriate" way to commemorate, I still fell into the trap of judging or censuring those forms that were different and unfamiliar. I defaulted, against my better judgment, to insisting on particular modes of remembrance. I demanded solemnity, reverence. These American Jews didn't *really* know how to commemorate the Holocaust, I thought, what it meant to grow up in its shadows. I was wrong, of course, but it's always been a niggling feeling that I derive a certain kind of legitimacy from my family history. I bask in the vicarious glow of my grandfather's suffering. I, too, am a victim. Aren't I?

Of course I'm not a victim. But I grow increasingly aware of the effects of being raised in the midst of Holocaust memory, surrounded by survivors, by photos of victims, those Polish-Jewish accents that I thought everyone over the age of sixty developed. I'm wary of overstating these effects: is it just that I get some kind of social or political cachet from these stories? Or do they really help explain why the first things I see in playgrounds are all the places where Arthur could fall? Or why my dad and I were constantly on the phone with one another, checking in? Or why I became a historian of the Holocaust? Am I traumatized? I doubt it. But when you grow up amidst the scars of the past, you can't help but be shaped by that, not only in ways that are apparent but also in ways that are hidden deep beneath the surface. The ghosts don't call ahead; they appear when you least expect them.

3

Frozen

The story of Zaida Jakub's life was mostly an enigma. There were snippets passed down from Dad, and from his friends who grew up in the same neighborhood. But he was mostly a shadow, an indistinguishable ghost, a caricature. I had to fill in the gaps with my imagination. I could make him whatever I wanted him to be—heroic, revolutionary to the bitter end, despite everything.

And then, around a year after Dad died, I read the letters Zaida wrote to Mendel. A revelation. I started to paint a clearer picture of him, his life, his suffering, and the anguish and the ghosts that were by his side constantly, inescapable. His letters, from the first in late 1946 to the last in mid-1978, right before he died, were soaked in the pain of those years of wandering and exile, his nerves never recovering from the blows. That first letter, dated September 1, 1946, only months after he returned to Poland, their first contact in over seven years, gives the clearest picture of the moments that his suffering began, a window into his tortured soul.

There are myriad gaps. He could write only so much with a limited amount of time, paper, and ink. He had only so much strength to tell the story. But there it was in front of me. I couldn't put the letter down. Handwritten in a hurry, it seemed. It must have been; he wrote late at night when he could carve out a little time, and the points of repetition give it away. Still, the penmanship was neat, a major relief to a historian. Yiddish cursive, compact letters, every inch of the page covered in words. No margins there; he had to use all he had at his disposal. A couple of pages lined, but mostly without lines. Fragile, rectangular, yellowing windows into the past, into my past. Surprisingly intact, not many tears, the only damage being the creases from decades of being folded away in a box.

$\sim$

Bubba and Zaida's lives during the war frame everything that came after. Every part of how our family thinks, how we relate to one another and to the world around us, was shaped by this story, this tragic tale of a man torn from his beautiful family, unable to protect them, flung to the farthest corners of the world's largest country. His epic journey is surely fodder for a Hollywood blockbuster: a broken hero, a young love interest, survival against the odds, grand Siberian landscapes, trains, boats, and trails. A redemptive ending.

There's the cast of characters, all of whom could stand in as the story's protagonist: Zaida, himself, who lived a life of suffering, but was loyal to his movement, family, friends despite everything. Fiery, impulsive, thoughtful, his haunting, sunken eyes lending him an air of solemnity meshed with wisdom, his gaunt cheeks and crooked dentures evidence of all he had endured. There was Bubba Eda, his young wife, a warm, pragmatic, modern woman who did all she had to do to protect her family. She was the handy one in the family, quick-witted, a problem solver. She could drive a tractor and wield a hammer, and brought her guile with her across the globe, keeping her family afloat. There was Zaida's first wife, Gitl Wiszniewska-Slucka, and his sons Shmulek, born in 1927, and Chaimek, born in 1932. They are a mystery. Zaida talked little about them, the wounds of their death too painful to split open.

There were Zaida's siblings. His younger brother, Mendel, fiery, warm, generous, who fought the Nazis in the French army, eventually settling in Los Angeles, via Spain, Cuba, and Brooklyn. A remarkable story in itself. They didn't see each other for nearly three decades, and were fierce political adversaries, Mendel a communist and Zaida a Bundist. But they remained close nonetheless. Chava, his older sister, was an educator who would later become a Yiddish writer of some renown in Israel. Her husband, Chaim, served in the

Soviet Red Army. Zaida was together with them, along with their daughter, Haddassah (or Dassa), in the Soviet Union toward the end of the war and they spent eighteen months together in Wrocław after Chaim was released from the Red Army. Zaida wanted to be close to Chava, but in his letters he complained incessantly about her, her long silences without responding to his letters, her requests for money, her lack of reciprocation or interest in his life and family. Still, she was his sister. I imagine Chava as tough, hardened by her experience, by her disappointment at what the Soviet Union became, and by the bitter life they led after arriving in Israel. Finally, there was Zaida's youngest sister, Chasha, killed at Chelmno along with her one-year-old daughter, who was born in the Włocławek ghetto. The family story goes that her husband was a ghetto policeman, and saved his mistress when he had the opportunity to rescue Chasha. I don't think Zaida even knew his niece's name, born as she must have been in the ghetto, killed in the death camp, all while Zaida languished in a Russian village in East Asia.

Many of these characters would not make it back. Their tragic deaths, Zaida's helplessness in the face of Nazi terror and Soviet tyranny, haunted him for the rest of his life.

～

Wrocław, the 1/IX 1946

My dear Mendel, Rukhl, and Henry,

My first words to you, my loves, must be to express the great joy that overcame me, and all of us, that amidst my broken life, you found yourselves among the living. We were torn far away from everything and everyone for seven years, not deserting our hope for miracles. We did not for a single minute stop thinking of our beloved ones, about my dear Gitl, dear sons, dear Chasha, about you my dears, about our whole family and on and on.

And we longed for the joyous moment, when, among all the tragic and terrible enough news, we would also receive the extremely happy news that you were also fortunate enough to be saved from Hitler's murderous claws.

The first opportunity I had after the defeat of Hitler's murderous bandits, I began searching all corners that I could about our family and friends, but unfortunately only received sad news. And among that news, I held a letter I had written to you in Montauban (France), returned with a note that you were no longer there. And afterward my joy was so much greater when I learned you were among us in our difficult lives, resurrected from the dead. And so the first thing I want to do is wish you long, happy healthy years of life, and let's have hope and live joyful moments, and that we, the survivors of our large family will be able to be together again and live happily.

My dear brother Mendel, I want to tell everything about my life, and I will do my best to do just that, and I want to be able to tell you everything at once. But don't forget that writing to you is a brother who went through a lot; a devastated, bloodied brother who has only courage left after such a life. A member of the masses of Jewish people that met such terrible misfortune, such a great catastrophe that no other people in history has endured. And this helps sustain me, that I'm not alone in this great misery. As we say, *tsoris rabim iz khatsi nekhome*, the woes of many is half consolation. Yes, that's how it is when millions of Jews were met with this misfortune and there only remained hundreds of thousands. We must now live in spite of all our enemies. I must gather my strength and continue to live because I am also one of the few left of the Jewish people, of the Jewish masses, of the Jewish working class, and that continues to sustain me.

I believe, dear brother, that you will be interested in all aspects of my life, so I will attempt to describe it all chronologically.

In 1939, up to the war, I ran a shoemaker-cooperative. My financial situation wasn't so lofty, but we lived and raised our children, who already gave me so much *naches*. My dear Shmulek was already in sixth grade and was very well educated. He was developing well, one of the best students in his class. I had the great pride that I could even talk with him about world problems, just like with an adult. My dear Chaimikl was already in the second grade. Really a nice one, a smart and a sincere little lad, a golden beautiful boy.

When I write you these lines, the tears flow like water, although now I only cry from time to time, because otherwise I would lose all my strength, and I still want to live.

When the war began, and people started running away from Włocławek out of fear for the Hitlerian beasts, I decided with my dear Gitl and sons not to separate, and to stay where we were. Living through the siege, we were running from place to place with the children as the bombing continued. I remember one moment when I wanted to run from one house to the next, and Gitl didn't want to risk it. My dear Chaimek gave us courage when he said: "*Tate*, you take me by the hand and *mame* will take Shmulek by the hand, and one, two, and we'll be in the next house." And we succeeded and made it out altogether.

When the Germans conquered Włocławek on 15 October 1939, our troubles truly began. They began sending us for slave labor, we had to endure beatings and insults, we had a visit from the Gestapo, had to wear yellow patches in the shape of a triangle on our shoulders. I remember a moment when an order was announced that we had to sew the yellow patches onto our outer garments, I came home and complained to my dear Gitl why she hadn't yet sewed the patches. She answered that she would do it, and with tears in her eyes, began to sew with patches from the drapes, not believing that we were seeing this in the twentieth century. When I said to my dear, lively Chaimikl that he should be careful in the streets, he answered: "*tateshi*, when I see the Germans in the distance, I already take off my hat." We already couldn't go on the sidewalks, and had to walk in the middle of the road like horses. To live, I decided to go work for a German who opened a shoe factory, but I couldn't work for long, because they threatened to arrest the German, along with me. And life became harder and harder. I used to sit in the house, not able to show myself in the street, nervously smoking fifty cigarettes a day, destroying my health. For two weeks, my dear Gitl waited and waited for the gestapo to come and arrest me. I used to stay ready with warm clothing, and while the children slept we waited every night until one or two o'clock. With the children, we used to spend those difficult days reading Sholem Aleichem, even though in the quiet they would laugh aloud.

Włocławek was a small, medieval city in central Poland, given its status as a town in the thirteenth century. It was one of those Polish towns that was constantly being trampled by whatever foreign power or world war was afflicting Poland. In the Middle Ages, it was the Teutonic Knights repeatedly invading and ultimately destroying the city. Then Sweden had its turn invading Poland, and Włocławek continued to be in the path of destruction. When Poland was partitioned between Russia, Prussia, and the Austro-Hungarian Empire at the end of the eighteenth century, Włocławek found itself in Prussia, but only for a few short decades. After Napoleon's defeat, the Congress of Vienna placed it back in the short-lived Congress of Poland, before it finally was incorporated into the Russian empire in 1830. During World War I, it fell under German occupation, was part of the newly independent Poland in the interwar period, before once again being occupied by Germany during World War II and renamed Leslau.

Włocławek's most famous resident may have been the astronomer Nicolaus Copernicus, who is said to have studied in the Cathedral School in the fifteenth century. The Cathedral Basilica has a sundial on its exterior wall that Copernicus might have built, although historians

Jakub, Gitl, Shmulek, and Chaim (late 1930s).

Shmulek
and Chaim
(late 1930s).

are not certain. Another Włocławek native is Jan Nagorski, the first pilot to fly an airplane through the Arctic Circle in 1914. The most famous Jew associated with the town was the controversial and path-breaking Yiddish playwright and author Sholem Asch, who moved to Włocławek when he was eighteen and lived there for two years, shifting away from his traditional Jewish education in nearby Kutno. In Włocławek, Asch made his living writing letters for illiterate Jews, an occupation that he described later as his advanced schooling.

Włocławek is perhaps most noteworthy for housing the first ghetto in Europe in which Jews were required by the Nazis to sew Stars of David onto their clothing to identify—no, humiliate—them. Like the ones that Gitl cut from the drapes.

On the whole, though, Włocławek was an unremarkable, industrial city and shipping port on the Vistula River. It was home to a lively Jewish community, around thirteen to fourteen thousand by the time the war broke out, around one-fifth of the total population. A century earlier, Jews had only just begun settling in the city, previously an ecclesiastical settlement. By the time Zaida arrived there as a teenager, it was home to a strong Hasidic community and political parties across the spectrum.

Zaida moved there in the interwar period from his childhood home in Warsaw after the death of both of his parents. He may have been fleeing the famine that Warsaw suffered during the First World War. No one really knows for certain how or why he left Warsaw or how he ended up in a small city one hundred miles from his home, and not much about his life there has survived. He was a bookkeeper, sat on the local Bund committee, married a Bundist, and raised two sons who he had high hopes would themselves become active in the party, agents of change, serious young men who would struggle against antisemitism, fight for a socialist future in Poland. Beyond that, though, his prewar life is a blur, impressionistic. What was he like before the war? Was he full of fire and passion? Did he smile, laugh, dance? What kind of father was he to Shmulek and Chaimek?

We have a few random vignettes: his brothers-in-law, upset that he and his wife, Gitl, had broken away from the strictures of Judaism, would throw stones at them when they broke the Sabbath. He would make a point of marking Yom Kippur by eating ham, antagonizing the strong religious community in Włocławek. He fought in the Polish army during the Polish-Soviet War. But details are sparse, probably by design. For Zaida, the details of his past were a big enough burden to carry, without passing them onto his children. The memories, which must have been at the forefront of his consciousness, were too painful. How do you talk to your son and daughter about their dead half-brothers? About the life that you hoped to lead, but that was taken from you? How do you deal with a family that is your consolation prize?

~

Just as the Germans came in, we learned that Chava and Dassa were in Warsaw starving, and Chaim had already gone east. I quickly arranged for a food package to be sent to them. Our dear, noble Chasha decided that she would travel then to Warsaw. I want to share with you an interesting moment to show how dignified Chasha remained. Chasha went to the Commander's office to get a *przepustka*, a permit. At one table was sitting a local German who told her that she would not receive a *przepustka* because she was Jewish. Chasha, knowing that her sister was starving, she went out in the corridor and cried loudly. A bailiff [*vozhni*] approached her, a Pole, and told her to try go to the second table where another German sat. When she went to the German, a Polish officer declared to the German that this *fraulein* was no Jew. Our dear Chasha didn't wait long before responding proudly "yes, I am a Jew." The pride and boldness impressed the German and he gave her a *przepustka*.

Understandably, the journey was difficult, even more so with packages. The day Chasha arrived, Chava was preparing her journey to the Soviet border. Chava told Chasha that we should leave everything and go to the Soviet side. On her return, Chasha maintained that I should go ahead and they would follow later. I asked my dear Gitl to come so we should travel together, but she didn't want to, saying that she didn't want to risk it with our dear little sons.

You know that by nature, I am a highly strung person, and in this situation, not knowing myself what to do, I decided, figuring and believing in a certain kind of humanism, that they wouldn't harm women and children. And that was how I was separated forever from my dear Gitl, little sons, Chasha on the 22 November 1939, at six o'clock in the morning, when they took me to the train.

I arrived in Warsaw, where Mania, after a day took me to the train and my further journey.

At the border, my things were stolen and I remained without any means, lying by the border for ten days. Arriving in Bielsk, I didn't see Chava and Chaim, who were already on their way to Minsk, in Belarus.

The Kestins, who you remember as good, decent people, didn't leave me on my own, seeing how broken and sick I was before I came to them. I started working, not earning enough, until I received a letter from an acquaintance that I should come to him in Sambor, a village by Lemberg.

And that moment that I decided that I would leave Bielsk saved my life, because the whole Kestin family was later all murdered by the German butchers. In Sambor I worked in a timber yard. I received letters from my dear Gitl, about how she was being tortured there, and to leave now was too difficult, especially without money. It was the same for Chasha and her husband.

~

After Germany invaded Poland, Zaida joined the hundreds of thousands of Polish Jews who fled to the Soviet-occupied part of Poland and the Soviet Union. In a number of waves throughout 1940 and 1941, these Jews were among the hundreds of thousands of Polish citizens deported into the vast interior of the Soviet Union. Zaida's

Chasha
Slucka-Fersht,
Warsaw.

wave, the second major deportation, took place at the end of June 1940, and included about seventy thousand deportees, mostly Jews, who were sent to the farthest reaches of the Soviet Union's desolate, frozen expanses.

Some were political prisoners, refusing to accept Soviet citizenship, anticommunists. Others, communists or sympathizers like my maternal grandparents, avoided deportation by accepting Soviet citizenship and spent the war years looking for food, work, and warmer weather, not always in that order. Many found their way to Kazakhstan, Uzbekistan; some escaped through Iran and made their way to

Palestine, members of the Polish armed forces under the command of General Władysław Anders.

Many of these deportees had sought repatriation back to Poland, including Zaida, who was preparing to rejoin his wife and sons in the Włocławek ghetto. Instead, they found themselves in the Soviet versions of cattle cars, transported for months to their temporary residences among the bears and elk in the Siberian wilderness. Unwittingly, Stalin was the savior of these Jews, perhaps two hundred thousand, who faced certain death had they returned to Nazi-occupied Poland. It's hard to say if it was the cruel irony of history or a lucky escape encapsulated in this episode: it would be four years before most of these escapees knew their good fortune, if you can call it that.

After the war, the survivor world would not welcome these escapees into the survivor fold. Even though many, like Zaida, knew the sting of a Nazi soldier's baton, the humiliation and fear of occupation, they were not considered to have suffered in the same way as those who remained under Nazi rule.

Not to mention all that they suffered as a result of their exile. A deportee camp in Siberia was no cakewalk; months-long train and boat journeys with no food and money, working in the icy plateaus, cut off from family, alone. Illness, disease, and starvation were a fact of life. It wasn't Chelmno, but it was closer to that than to a beach vacation. In the hierarchy of suffering, they were toward the bottom. In any other era, theirs would be miraculous stories of bravery, ingenuity, and strength. But in these unusual times, they were perversely seen as the "lucky" ones.

∼

In June 1940, I received a letter from Gitl asking why I hadn't come home; many had returned and it was now calmer. Not wanting to fall again into the Germans' hands, I decided to wait a little longer. On the 30 June 1940, I was sent away from Sambor by the Soviet powers into administrative exile in the taigas. We traveled from the 30 June until

5 September without any financial means, living like convicts. A transport of 1,100 people until we arrived at the spot of the gold mines 2,000 kilometers from Yakutsk (12,000 kilometers from Włocławek), starving the whole way without our own means.

Arriving in that place, the situation changed for me. I received work as a bookkeeper in an office (already knowing some Russian) and my material situation improved. But the climate, with its freezing weather as low as 65 degrees below zero, strongly affected my health and made me very sick, but I returned to normal.

I was in contact with Chava the whole time. She couldn't help me at all though, because letters took up to three months to arrive, and a package a year. One package appeared from Włocławek, and every three months I received letters, and that kept me going. The single thing that brought me closer to my dearest were the letters that I hold as a treasure and a photograph that Chava had. And in each letter, Shmulek and Chaimek had to write separately.

I threw myself into my work, working twenty hours a day without rest, anything so that the time would go quicker. More than one night lamenting my bitter destiny, regretting that I left my dearest.

Gitl lived a difficult life in Włocławek. They were all imprisoned in the ghetto. Chasha, noble Chasha, did everything she could to help, and my comrades helped a lot. She worked as the director of the community kitchen, Shmulek started learning a trade, writing me that he wanted to help his dear mother to live through the difficult times. Chasha did not badly, her husband Yisrolik earned enough. Chasha taught Chaim (there were no schools). I believe you received letters from them and that they wrote to you all.

Financially, things had improved. At work, I was promoted to head bookkeeper, but apart from that, life was very difficult alone.

Jakub (front row, left) in Yakutsk (1943).

At the beginning of 1941, I received a letter from Gitl, unfortunately the last one, where she wrote me that she had a talk with our sons about "when our Jakub is coming home." The children thought it would be in 1941, and she didn't protest, but unfortunately that's not what happened.

At the end of 1941, I received amnesty and I planned to travel to Chava who was still in a kolkhoz in the Saratov region. I started collecting ruble after ruble, but at the beginning of 1942 I was robbed and I had no possibility to travel to her (Chaim was already then in the Red Army), and I decided to travel to the city of Yakutsk. There, I worked as a head bookkeeper, financially not bad, but once again all alone, torn from my love, not receiving any news.

Yakutsk, as Bubba Eda used to tell me, is the coldest city on earth. There's not even a train that reaches there; they could only go as far as Irkutsk, perhaps halfway. From there they had to take a boat up the

Angara River, then a 250-kilometer trail to Ust-Kut, then another boat thousands of kilometers up the Lena River. From Yakutsk, they traveled further to the deportee settlement of Minor, almost at the easternmost part of Russia. There were no trains, few roads. The only way was by boat. It was summer when they traveled, the only saving grace. I imagine that in the winter, those rivers would have been unavailable, frozen arterials isolating Aleksandr Solzhenitsyn's Gulag Archipelago to the northeast of Yakutsk.

It was a gold-mining region in the sparsely settled, vast expanses of the Siberian taiga, dotted with slave labor camps to which political prisoners and dissidents were sent by Stalin during his terrifying reign. These gulags, particularly in this northeastern part of Siberia along the Kolyma River, were notorious as places where dissidents went and from which they often didn't return. Luckily, Zaida's work as a bookkeeper helped him to avoid the most arduous outdoor work that had been responsible for the demise of countless "enemies of the state." Educated, numerate, literate—the model of a worker-intellectual—Zaida was saved from certain death by his trade.

Still, life was no picnic. During his time in Yakutsk, Zaida fell ill with scurvy, a result of malnutrition and probably overworking. As a result he lost almost all his teeth. Maybe that's why he never smiled in photos; those very rare photos that have him smiling do not reveal much of his dentures. He had false teeth made on his return to Poland, although, like everything in the postwar years, they were of poor quality. To survive, they had to be wily, quick thinking. They had to learn Russian, learn how to grease the guards and protect themselves in the frosty inferno to which they'd been flung.

News from home was sparse. Zaida received occasional letters from Gitl, Shmulek, and Chaimek, but they took months to arrive and they didn't tell him much. I found those letters when I was clearing out Dad's study a couple of years after he died. Zaida kept them, then Bubba, then Dad. They were the last remaining link Zaida had to that family, the last contact with his beloved. Written in Polish, there was nothing in there about the Nazis' treatment of the Jews, and the letters revealed a kind of ennui that characterized their lives. All they had to look forward to were Zaida's letters; the only thing that gave them hope was the possibility that they would see Zaida again. Mostly the letters were just updates about who they knew was still alive, and how they were surviving. They were full of warmth, longing, love. In 1940, his family was sent into a ghetto that was built in Rakutówek, an estate on the outskirts of town. Gitl took a job in a soup kitchen, Shmulek worked in a suitcase workshop, Chaimek took lessons with Chasha, since there were no schools to go to. Most striking in the letters were Gitl's apologies to Zaida. She felt guilty that he had been cast to the ends of the earth, worried about him and his health. She mustn't have known that he was the lucky one. He would later feel that same guilt.

In Siberia, Zaida maintained a friendship with a young woman, barely twenty, from southern Poland who had been in the settlement with him and found herself in Yakutsk after the government offered Polish citizens amnesty, a recognition they were now allies in the fight against Hitler. That young woman, Eda Fertig, helped to mitigate the sense of isolation he felt, especially after he stopped receiving quarterly letters from Gitl, Shmulek, and Chaimek. She was intelligent, compassionate, always giving. He didn't know then that only a short couple of years later, she would become his wife, as he was forced to start his life anew.

At the end of 1944, the Soviet government allowed our transport of 1,100 Polish citizens to travel to the Saratov region where I met up again with Chava and Dassa, who found themselves in a difficult situation. Together, we settled there in Saratov, where I once again worked as head book-keeper in a factory. Chaim was, at that time, at the front.

Life then was very difficult, but we managed to survive. I was a member of the Union of Polish Patriots; I was very busy in my job and with communal work, and once again weaving the thread of wanting to persevere and maintaining illusions that perhaps my love would also survive. But unfortunately, after the liberation of Włocławek, I received the tragic news from one of my comrades who remained alive that I could have no more hope, and that my dear love shared the fate of all Jews in Poland and died a martyr's death in the gas chambers, on the 27 April 1942 in Chelmno (a manor between Kolo and Kitne), where 1,130,000 Jews died.

There lie the ashes, mixed in with the soil, of my dear Gitl, of my dear Shmulek, of my golden Chaimek, of our beloved and dear Chasha with her one year old daughter, and other family, friends, and acquaintances. The news, you yourself understand, broke me completely, all my hope was shattered, all my illusions burst, and I felt totally useless, that my role in the world, now overshadowed by eternal misfortune, was now redundant. But my love, my current wife Eda, who worked with me, didn't allow me to despair and think I was useless in the world, and I must live further.

I have endured a very difficult period in my life. Sorry that I had been saved, that I was not killed alongside my beloved, that I was saved when my beloved are no longer here. But the instinct to live prevailed, when I realized I had to continue on and begin my life anew. With my heart forever bloodied, wounded, I have to start building my new life, broken, already having toiled so hard for a little *nakhes*, joy, never had an easy life, with hope that my children would grow up into earnest people. My head pounding and my eyes wet as I begin to picture how my beloved family struggled in the last moments of their lives.

After I returned to Włocławek, to the cemetery of a prosperous Jewish community, I met a few younger comrades who were liberated from the camps, including one of my old comrades, my friend Chaim Tabachnik-Gostinski (you might remember him, the military tailor). I absorbed every word he told me about my darlings, because he was with them in the ghetto until 22 April 1942. He helped them (because he was vice chair of the Jewish *kehille*). Gitl worked, doing community work in the underground committee from the Bund until the last moments. My darling Shmulek was active in the underground SKIF, Chaimikl was a golden, beautiful boy with gorgeous eyes. They didn't forget me even for one moment. I stood in the place of the ghetto, the houses burned down, potatoes growing there, no sign of them remained. The ghetto was located by the Jewish cemetery. Nothing remained of the cemetery. Standing in the spot where the ghetto stood, I recognized a Polish woman, an acquaintance of Gitl, and she recounted how she often came to see Gitl in the ghetto, how beautiful Chaimek was, how Shmulek was intelligent, how they always talked about me.

Yes, dear brother, ashes and mud are all that are left of my beautiful family life. My dear Gitl ended her blooming, beautiful, earnest life, such a tragic death at only forty-one years; my dear Shmulek, who had not yet truly learnt how to relish life, was not yet fifteen; my delicate flower Chaimek, still in his innocent years, was only ten; my dear sister Chasha, blossoming at thirty years old with her dear one year old daughter. Innocents killed by murderers, the beastly German fascists, and me, completely broken. They are forever engraved in my life. No matter what happens to me in my life, my heart will always be bloodied.

∼

I had assumed that Zaida's family were killed at Treblinka, where nine hundred thousand Jews were transported between 1942 and 1944. I knew it wasn't Auschwitz, that icon of the Holocaust and the Nazis' cold, mechanical efficiency. I figured I would have known if it was Auschwitz. So, I assumed Treblinka was the camp, the major destination for the large transportations from Warsaw, not so far from Włocławek. It seemed to me that Włocławek was more or less in the same "catchment area" as Warsaw. Chelmno, the first extermination camp with its relatively primitive killing methods, didn't really figure into my calculations of how Zaida's family was killed. (I suppose even the most sophisticated mass killing techniques are primitive.) As far as the death camps go, Chelmno remains relatively mysterious. The camp was dismantled in 1943, and then again after resuming operations in late 1944. Survivors of Chelmno can be counted on two hands, unlike those at Auschwitz, where thousands survived its labor camps to tell their terrible stories. Compared to the Operation Reinhard camps—Belzec, Sobibor, and Treblinka—documentation for Chelmno is sparse.

Chelmno, like most of the other extermination camps, was hidden away in a forest, far from prying eyes. Or at least that was the intention. The camp itself contained a manor house, where prisoners were lulled into a false sense of security, and the "forest camp," which was a clearing in the forest large enough to accommodate the mass graves of the 152,000 victims from the north and west of Poland. It was a major destination for deportees from the Łódź ghetto. It was also the first camp set up for the express purpose of mass murder by asphyxiation, the first industrial death factory, producing corpses in a production line, a testing ground for the mass killings that would take place in larger, more efficient death factories. Chelmno was the place the Nazis began to perfect their method.

Another of those funny tricks of memory and history: Zaida was certain in the years following the war that 1.35 million Jews were murdered at Chelmno. The number of victims was just over one-tenth of that, 152,000, but when Zaida learned of his family's fate, information was still being filtered. It must have been easy to imagine that so many people could be executed in this quiet little forest clearing, given that what had taken place was already so far beyond the bounds of imagination. Maybe the much larger number was comforting to him—Gitl, Shmulek, and Chaimek were part of something much, much larger. *Tsoris rabim iz khatsi nekhome*, the woes of many is half consolation.

～

Our brother-in-law, Israel Fersht (Chasha's husband) was liberated from the camps, but he stayed in Germany and remarried there, I wish him all the best. We have no contact with him and not even an address. No-one remains from Gitl's family, not even one of my brothers-in-law. Arieh Shklover died in the camps with his wife and two children, alongside my dearest ones. I remain proud that, until the last moments, my dear Gitl and Shmulek were actively connected to my ideals, my party, the Bund, which I have been bound my entire life. It is there I will find some comfort. There are no graves for them where I can go to cry.

In mid-June this year, I returned to Poland with Chava, Chaim (who was already demobilized), Hadassa, and my current wife. A month before leaving the Soviet Union, I decided that if I was returning to Poland, I couldn't live alone and must have a life-partner, otherwise I would have nothing else to live for and reestablish my life. I found a true friend; a kind-hearted, devoted wife to me. I must tell you she is much younger than me (born in 1922), and I'm 45 years old. But she is a serious, honest woman. I want to have a peaceful family life and have a future generation in my life. Maybe my heart will once again feel *nakhes* in this life.

You may not know how women were demoralized during the wartime, and I had to find someone who would be a friend throughout my life, with a humane character, and who was not demoralized, seeing how anguished my life had become. I met that woman, who makes up for all my aches, and stands in place of my dear Gitl and my dear children, so I won't be completely alone.

In the current situation, I am happy—although with a broken heart—that I have with me a dear friend. Although communally, she's not like Gitl, she is still young. A good-natured wife who feels all my sorrow, understands me, mourns with me in all my most difficult moments, who holds me up and allows me to continue living. In future letters, she will write to you herself. And so, in May 1946, I married once again. Perhaps now we will have the luck to live a peaceful, happy life.

Jakub and Eda at their wedding, Engels, USSR (May 2, 1946).

~

Until I was an adult, it didn't even occur to me that you would be married to someone for a reason more complex than love. My parents were a happy, loving couple; Helen's parents were too. Certainly, my mum's parents didn't seem to be living in married bliss, but I just figured they were old and jaded, a couple of old grouches weary with life and each other. That the Holocaust brought people together in these marriages of convenience, marriages born out of desperation to feel some connection, to regenerate in the face of near total annihilation, was not something I even considered. Bubba Eda remarried about a decade after Zaida died, when I was about five or six, I suppose, but it didn't last long. Her new husband, Mendel, with his perfectly round belly protruding permanently, was kind to me. He'd pick me up from school in his new, little silver sedan. I can still smell the musty new car smell, that universal sign of moving on up in the world, even on such a small scale. But theirs was also a marriage of convenience. A widow and a widower seeking solace from their loneliness, but the love and affection never developed.

When Zaida met her, Eda Fertig was a petite blonde woman from a small village in southern Poland, right near the Czech border. Still a teenager, she probably could have passed as Polish, with her blue eyes, straw-colored hair, and unaccented Polish. Twenty-two years his junior, she was not much older than Zaida's murdered sons. Torn away from her village as a teenager, she was forced to grow up quickly. She was astute beyond her years, educated, as she would say, "in the university of life." Zaida was utterly isolated during those years in Russia, and was broken by the news that Gitl, Shmulek, and Chaimek had been murdered. Bubba was his lifesaver, his de facto family during the war, that guardian angel who gave him something to live for, who mourned with him. She didn't try to replace Gitl. She was just herself: kind, gentle, endlessly supportive, patient, understanding of how deeply Zaida's wounds cut. They were scars she also had to live with. I don't know how affectionate they were to one another, but there was certainly a lot of mutual respect and love between them. Zaida and

Bubba were husband and wife, but they were truly a team, wearing the blows of their pasts together. A marriage of convenience, maybe, but not without a great deal of love and warmth.

Dad never took off his wedding ring. Ever. It's a strange little detail that I remember. When I was little, I'd jump into bed with my parents in the morning to hang out on the weekend, and one of the things that would occupy me would be trying to extract that ring off Dad's left hand. To no avail. It had become attached, grafted on almost, integrated into his hand like another nail, but one made of yellow gold, perfectly circular, a little worn and scratched. That ring had seen a lot, scuffed just the right amount, evidence of a life well lived, a marriage that endured all that the world had to throw at it. Perhaps the ring is the metaphor: by the end, no matter what, you couldn't take it off; it had become an extension of him, like his marriage. Mum and Dad, two immigrant kids, children of survivors, children of the Bund—so much that they shared, so many things that connected them.

Helen and I were married in March 2006, sixty years after Zaida married Bubba. We'd been dating since we were thirteen, met in the Yiddish theatre, married at twenty-one. Both of us grandchildren of the Bund—Helen's grandmother was from a Bundist family— and grandchildren of survivors. Maybe it was *bashert*, destined, that we would find each other, with this common legacy that we shared, common neuroses and quirks. We shared a complicated inheritance, knowing that it was Hitler who brought our grandparents together in their marriages of convenience, pushed our families out of Europe and to Australia, forged the growth of the strange little Holocaust survivor community in Melbourne. Like our grandparents had, and like our parents had, we spoke, even as teenagers, a similar language, we understood what it meant to be born into a community of ghosts, a family and a life that might have been.

∼

Returning to Poland, we settled in Wrocław (Breslau). I couldn't go live in Włocławek, where my dearest were killed, where every Pole I knew would constantly pity me, and where I would always feel lower than those who did not have the honor to help my family survive. I engaged in party work and work as a secretary-functionary in the Bund organization in Wrocław. My comrades didn't let me go work in a second job. I am pleased that I can continue to live and be active communally after all my experiences, and materially, I am secure and live as well as I can. We are living through very difficult times, Kielce pogrom, murderers among the Polish reactionaries, who won't willingly leave their positions. My future plans: I do not want to become a beggar-wanderer, just wandering around aimlessly.

I read the letter you wrote to Chava. In our party, there is the sentiment that active party members must not leave, they must be the last to remain. Only regular party members may leave, and you know how disciplined I am in fulfilling my duties.

Yes, Jews are fleeing, Jews emigrate without prospects, without a destination. I don't now, nor have I ever, subscribed to the Zionist prescription. Therefore, I have decided to write to Avram-Shimon that he should send me papers so I will be able to legally migrate with my wife to Paris. If I have those I believe I will receive the blessing of the Central Committee to emigrate. In Poland, only a small Jewish community will remain. If I don't receive legal permission to emigrate, I won't leave this place. I no longer have the strength to wander aimlessly. I understand it's very difficult to get to America, and that you know the situation there better. As I suggested to my comrades, perhaps if we have family in America, the Jewish Labor Committee or our Bundist representation will be able to do something. If you are comfortable, dear brother, it would of course be good if you could go see my comrades in the American Representation [of the Bund], such as my comrade Emanuel Nowogrodski, who knows me; your former teacher Gilinski; Salek Lichtenstein, who hails from Włocławek; and maybe other comrades of mine. If you can't, it will be hopeless. Maybe Avram-Shimen will be able to help bring me to Paris. I don't want to benefit from Zionist favors, be smuggled over the Polish border to Austria and then wander through the camps. Therefore, I will, in the meantime stay put. The address of the Bund representation is: 175 East Broadway, Room 401, New York 2 NY. If you're not comfortable, it will be hopeless.

You have certainly received letters from Chava, Chaim, and Dassa and her husband. I believe they are striving to travel to Palestine, but so far they haven't left yet. Even they don't know when it will be. They are active in the Left Poale Tsion. I wonder if you received the telegram I sent, I got your address from Avram-Shimen. I haven't yet received an answer. I wish our Chava, Chaim, Dassa with her husband only good things, but I can't agree that their plans are the right ones.

Chava showed me the photos you sent. It's truly joyous and a huge pleasure to see my surviving brother, sister-in-law and such a sweet young boy. I am so happy that you remained whole. Chava declared that she won't give me a single photograph, because she maintains they were sent only to her (that is a bit of egoism). I trust that you won't forget me and that you'll also send me some photographs. The question of the gift you sent to Chava and Dassa—until today they still haven't collected it from Warsaw, but I believe they will go do it soon.

I see Chava very often at inter-party meetings and in the Jewish committee. From time to time, we come to see each other. If you want to help me with something, do it only if there's a purpose.

Yes, I've completely forgotten our extended family. Of Mania-Moshe and their children, sadly no one was left. Of Tsilke-Naftali, I know for certain they're no longer here, but I don't know about their children. Of aunt Sore-Miriam, uncle Hershl, Ber with his wife and children, no one is left. Of dear Esther and uncle Dovid and their children, only one daughter remained, Gitl, who already has a fine son. Her husband died in the Soviet Union, and she has remarried. Her life is very difficult. Chava and I help her with what we can. Send her a letter. Gitl and her son came to stay with me for a few days in Wrocław. I am sending you a recent photo of my darling wife.

I write you our personal details in case you need them:

1. Jakub Slucki, born 20 July 1901, Warsaw

2. Etla Fertig-Slucka, born 26 September 1922, Tarnow to Izak Fertig and Rozalji Somerow.

Now, I have a big favor to ask, as my current father-in-law with his wife and two daughters are currently living in Wrocław and are preparing to emigrate to a Zionist kibbutz. They have family, cousins, in Brooklyn. Would you find out why they haven't written or helped at all? Until the war, they were in constant contact. Now, nothing. You don't need to tell them that they will soon emigrate. My father-in-law's name is Izak Fertig. He lives in Wrocław, 23 Luizen Street. Their cousin's address: Majer Siegfried, 94 Elton St, Brooklyn, New York. Or his brothers, whose address I can't find, are Mozes Siegfried and Josef Siegfried, Brooklyn, or their children. They hail from Radomyzl-Wielki, near Tarnow. You could also try their son-in-law Max Shtoyer, Brooklyn. Or my father-in-law's uncle, Szymon Fertig, Brooklyn. They live in Brooklyn and hail from Zabno, near Tarnow. Izak Fertig, the son of Shmuel Fertig from Radomyzl, is asking about them. You could probably ask the Radomir committee, or the Mielec committee of Polish Jews in Brooklyn or New York. You will be doing me and my wife a major favor. If you find anything out, please write me straight away.

Dear brother Mendel, sister-in-law Ruchel, and my dear little Henry, I fear that I have already written too much today. In coming letters, I will tell you more.

With warm kisses and embraces,
Your Jakub

Jakub before and after World War II.

My loving wife greets and sends you kisses, although she
does not know you yet. Greetings also from my father-in-
law, mother-in-law, and sisters-in-law.

∼

Zaida and Bubba lost a lot of extended family, and in those first
months after returning to Poland, they were faced with a seemingly
constant stream of bad news, a barrage of dead relatives, ghosts. For
the most part, those were names I'd never heard before reading this
letter. Each time they discovered someone among the living, they
must have felt a huge sense of relief, some brief respite from the
crushing news that they kept receiving. One of the main tasks in
those months, for them as for most of the returnees, was to search
for news, which was usually only bad.

The family that was left became crucially important. Maintaining a close bond to his siblings, nephews and nieces, cousins, and
in-laws took on central importance. In 1946, perhaps the most important family member was Henry, his nephew, Mendel's son. He

Jakub and Eda with Chava, Chaim, and Hadassah, Wrocław (1946).

was part of that regeneration, having escaped the great conflagration, just barely. He was the great hope in the future of his family, his people, the one in whose hands the memory of his murdered family rested. Zaida's surviving nephew, and later his children and his growing cadre of nieces and nephews, held the key to holding onto the memory of his own children, who didn't get to live fulfilled lives. He ended his first letter to Mendel with a short note specifically for Henry, eleven years old and himself a survivor and refugee, having escaped Nazi-occupied Paris, and then having narrowly evaded capture by the French collaborators in Vichy France.

~

My dear Henry,

I send you a heartfelt greeting and want you to know you had two good cousins Shmulek and Chaimek who died martyr's deaths in their young years at the hands of the fascist beasts, like so many Jewish children in Poland. Never forget to honor them in your lifetime, and at the same time to hate the murderous German beasts for their innocent deaths. I will reproduce a photo of them that I kept with me and send it to you. Make a little memorial in your house for them, there is no gravestone for them. With warm greetings, I hope that you'll grow to be an honest, serious person.

Your uncle,
Jakub Slucki

That letter is the most comprehensive retelling of Zaida's survival I've heard. Some of it I already knew, things that he had told Dad and Dad had passed on; the broad outline we knew, the impact was clear enough. But the wrenching details, the vivid reconstruction of his separation from Gitl, the reconstruction of his emotional state during the years of isolation are things I could previously only infer and assume. Zaida, who had been a foggy, elusive figure, no more than a shadow, now had more than just contours; there was complexity, a personality.

There are still plenty of questions unanswered, gaps in the narratives, questions I can no longer ask. There are things I suspect he deliberately didn't pass on, stories that didn't filter through to me that have now gone to the grave with Zaida and Sluggo. I can hardly blame him. The ghosts of his wife and sons, of his sister, his aunts, his uncles, his cousins, and his parents haunted him daily. Why bring them back to the fore? Why torture yourself and those around you with their presence? They were all tortured enough. We just have to learn to be comfortable with the silence, with those absences, with the ghosts that continue to haunt us, even when Zaida tried to shield his family from them, to keep them in his nightmares and not let them seep into the dreams of those closest to him. They are still with us, though, whether we like it or not.

4

Return

I first traveled to Poland in 2004, part of a bus tour throughout Europe. A pilgrimage of sorts. Helen and I and had been living in London through that winter, and we had saved enough money for a couple of months of travel around the continent. For ten months we earned a pittance, living frugally, eating dry pasta, sometimes with the luxury of cheese and tomato sauce, drinking one-quid pints of beer during whatever happy hour we could find, often at depressingly Australian-themed pubs. It was a rite of passage for young Australians. A year out of our remote island, to find ourselves, live carefree, see the world. No, to *experience* the world. Be travelers, not tourists.

Or something.

It was the first time I had traveled outside Australia. I had flown on a plane a couple of times to visit family in Sydney, but I had barely been outside our cozy nest in the southeast of Australia. I'd barely been out of the southeast of Melbourne. For us, vacations were to beachside towns a couple of hours outside town: Wilson's Promontory, Phillip Island, Lorne, Apollo Bay. Quaint seaside towns with fish-and-chip shops and simple, clean beaches. Real Australia, maybe. Nothing exotic, nothing fancy, just a chance for family to be together and kick back. In any case, we couldn't afford anything fancier than that. Byron Bay, Noosa, Bali, the United States—out of the question for a family of two teachers. Just campsites, country grocery stores, boogie boards, and beach cricket.

Now, as "adults," that simple life quickly dissipated. As kids, the Cold War was in the background, now the real world was front and center. Ethnic cleansing in Kosovo, 9/11, gun violence, a global refugee crisis—we were quickly torn away from our protected teenagehood. Our travels would expose us to the "real" world: New York City, London, Paris. Bustling cities still with their whiff of romance, but just the right amount of grime and danger. We saw Romania, Bulgaria, and Greece—southeastern European countries with rolling hills, endless farmland, and underdeveloped cities, the third world in our imagination, the allure of grittiness, edginess. Feral cats and dogs roaming the streets, citizens of countries that seemed decades behind our own. In Poland, the Czech Republic, and Germany we saw the prettiest and the grittiest that the world had to offer. We followed all the safety advice in the Lonely Planet guides: bag locks that covered our whole rucksack, money belts, hidden stashes of cash. We were naïve, scared, excited.

When Zaida returned to Poland in July 1946 with his new wife, after nearly seven years cut off in the farthest reaches of Siberia, it was a different country. The war had taken care of that. Not only were many cities destroyed but now the borders had again changed, the vast majority of Polish Jews had been wiped out, and entire ethnic populations had been moved out of the newly constituted nation. Some things continued just as before the war. Antisemitism was a persistent factor in Polish life, with many Poles blaming Jews for the destruction wrought on their country. Many of these Poles had claimed abandoned Jewish homes and property, and were unwilling to return them now that the war concluded.

After their months-long train journey, Bubba and Zaida faced what so many of those 250,000 returning Polish Jews did: antisemitism and pogroms, cities and homes that had been destroyed, and the realization that their families had disappeared in the great catastrophe. On their return to Poland, there was little choice about where to settle. Most of Włocławek's Jews had been killed. There were a handful of Jews left from Stary Sącz, Bubba's hometown in the south of Poland. Warsaw held no allure for Zaida, even though it had one of the larger survivor populations. In the end, the government allocated them to Wrocław, formerly Breslau in lower Silesia, one of those contested strips of the earth that never stays within the borders of one country too long. After the war, the Polish government, like many others in Eastern and Central Europe, embarked on a process of ethnic cleansing of the Germans that ended up within their borders. Before the war, Breslau was Germany's largest city east of Berlin. Its population was predominantly German, up to 90 percent, with substantial Polish, Jewish, and Ukrainian minority populations. Now that it fell within the borders of the newly reconstituted Polish republic, the government aimed to empty the region of its remaining German population. Many had already fled the advancing Red Army in the first half of 1945. This final expulsion of Germans left large swathes of western Poland underpopulated, so many of the quarter of a million Jews returning from exile were sent to settle there. Wrocław fast became the largest Jewish city in Poland, the lower Silesia region home to around half the country's Jews.

As they made their way from Saratov to Wrocław in July, Zaida and Bubba and her family passed through Kielce, a medium-sized city in southeastern Poland where Jews had comprised around one-third of the prewar population. After the war, the number of Jews in the city was about two hundred. An unremarkable city, Kielce became infamous only a week after Zaida and Bubba had been there when forty-two Jews were murdered in a bloody pogrom, sparked by rumors that Jews had abducted a Polish child. Not only did the surviving Jews leave the city for good at this time, but the pogrom also sparked a mass Jewish exodus from the country. Within a few years, most of Poland's surviving Jews had left, the majority to Palestine or the United States. The continuing prevalence of antisemitism convinced many of them that Jews had no future in Poland.

After making the harrowing decision to leave his family in November 1939, Zaida could barely recognize the country to which he returned. The family and community that he had left behind were no more. The capital city, in which he was born and raised, was nothing more than pile after pile of ash and rubble, little evidence of the thriving Jewish neighborhood in which his father had made and fixed shoes. Barely a sign of one of the liveliest Jewish cities in history. The large Jewish settlements and the small shtetls had been wiped off the map. Włocławek had only a handful of Jews left. Zaida had barely any family: his sister Chava with her husband and daughter, a couple of cousins, and his new wife and her family. He reunited with a few comrades, a few old friends. But reality struck hard on his return. He had almost no one left.

The atmosphere in Poland was bleak. When you sat on the tram, in the streets, Zaida said, no one talked. There was a pall over the country; people, Jews especially, didn't like to leave their houses out of fear. Maybe people would occasionally go to the theatre or the cinema, but for many, life was now a waiting game, waiting for the economy to grow, waiting for an end to antisemitism, waiting to leave.

And so they arrived in Wrocław, newly incorporated into the latest Polish republic after centuries under Prussian and German rule. A medieval metropolis. The sixteenth century's answer to Vienna or Berlin, Wrocław had been Breslau for centuries, a German city at the threshold between East and West, not quite as modernized as its Western counterparts, not quite as underdeveloped as its neighbors to the east. Wrocław: in so many ways emblematic of the twentieth century. A central European city, multiethnic in the first half of the twentieth century, at the very frontier of two world wars, reduced to ruins by 1945. It witnessed fin-de-siècle German militarism, Weimar liberalism, Nazism, and Soviet-style communism.

Bubba and Zaida had one foot out the door during their short stay in Wrocław. They both worked, lived in a few different apartments, never felt a sense of permanence. Although Zaida was invested in the regeneration of Polish Jewry, he was by then too hobbled, too weary to take part in earnest, to see through the difficult task. Mostly, they lived at Jęczmienna 27, apartment eight, not far from the center of town. When they moved there, the street was named Luizen, but with the Polonization of Wrocław, the street names also changed.

Jakub and Eda with Eda's parents, Yitzhak and Rukhche, and sisters, Sala and Hania, Wrocław (1947).

The building today looks like one that survived the war, surrounded by Soviet-style concrete boxes, utilitarian, the socialist modernist architecture that typifies so much of postwar Eastern Europe. But their building was a survivor of the war. Like Zaida: battered, weakened, but still standing, still holding some semblance of its prewar humanity, despite its utter dehumanization.

They struggled to make ends meet, like most people in Europe at that time. Reconstruction affected everyone across the smoldering continent. No one had an easy life. During the eighteen months they live there, Zaida worked as party secretary for the newly constituted Wrocław Bund, not the highest paying job he could have hoped for but lucrative enough to pay rent and put food on the table. After a few months, the party sent him to work a second job for the regional Jewish committee for Lower Silesia, where he sat on the social welfare committee, coordinating the distribution of clothing, food, and money to tens of thousands of needy Jewish refugees. There he developed a reputation as a straight shooter, honest, scrupulous. He wouldn't do favors for friends or family; everyone was in need, their

Jakub and Eda, Wrocław (1947).

very survival relied on the fair distribution of goods. It was an important and demanding job in that context: the tens of thousands of Jews in Wrocław at the time were largely expatriates from the Soviet Union, who returned with nothing, only the *shmattes*, the rags, on their backs. Bubba Eda worked as a bookkeeper for the local Jewish committee, something they both saw as temporary until they started their family.

For most of their time there, when they weren't working, they were focused on attaining visas to Paris and on locating family members and friends lost during the war. The wandering that had plagued them for the previous six years was set to continue, visas to the United States and Australia not yet available to them. They had a growing sense that Europe held no future for them.

Helen and I started in Athens in April 2004, meeting up with our bus group. They were mostly Australians and Kiwis. We found a connection quickly—Mark, the high school English teacher whose nephew played cricket with me. A wicked sense of humor, extremely warm and generous. If it's not a game of Jewish geography, then it's Melbourne geography. A good start, a good fellow to have on one's side through the ups and downs of traveling with a big group of people. A lifelong friend. Helen and I were among the youngest in the group, perhaps the most earnest among them, so having an "adult" friend was comforting, especially when the ghosts of the past joined us later in the tour.

In Athens, we visited the Acropolis. To that point we'd probably never seen anything as old or magnificent, a taste of what was to come. After that we looped up through Turkey to Bulgaria, Romania, Slovakia, and the Czech Republic before hitting Poland and then Berlin and Paris before taking the ferry back across the English Channel. All in three weeks. We didn't get to see too much of any place, a day here, two days there, followed by whole days on the bus staring out the window at the sometimes colorful, sometimes barren-looking countryside. We'd stop for lunch in some small town along the way, bathroom breaks at a gas station. For many on the bus, those hours in the countryside offered time to recover from a hangover. We collected a range of stories and characters along the way, perhaps the best a couple of nineteen-year-olds on their first adventure could hope for. We took a lot of photos, just before the explosion of digital cameras, ending up with a backpack full of film canisters.

We joked that we were on a death tour—World War II sites, cemeteries, memorials every place we turned. Civilizations that had come and gone, left some stone traces, some crumbling buildings. At the end of the first week on the road, we attended the annual World War I commemoration at the Gallipoli peninsula in the Dardanelles, the beach where Australian troops landed alongside New Zealand, British, and French soldiers in 1915. The offensive against the Ottomans ultimately failed, but the myth of the ANZAC was cultivated over the next century. It became a myth that reframed the military defeat and tactical blunder by the British as a story of plucky, brave, irreverent Australian soldiers seeking adventure. Boys becoming men. This was certainly the spirit that permeated our tour group and the thousands of young Australians sneaking beer, vodka, and anything else they could onto the site. For many of these young people, the Gallipoli peninsula was holy ground, this journey a pilgrimage to discover the so-called birth of their nation. A few of them had family that had fought there or on other World War I and World War II battlefields. But for most, the connection to that site was no more than their membership in the imagined community of Australians.

For us, joining the Gallipoli commemoration was simply a matter of convenience. A child of migrants, I felt no connection to the ANZAC myth that, in my lifetime, became the most important myth in Australian public life. Helen and I simply wanted to go on a tour that allowed us to see a lot of places and that went through Poland. This was the one that ticked both those boxes and fit inside our meager budget. Our pilgrimage was still to come.

Beyond Gallipoli, the next two weeks were like a tour of an absent Jewish civilization as we snaked through Eastern Europe, only faint outlines remaining from what had been a rich tapestry of cultural, political, and religious civilization. We saw that absent Jewish past peeking through everywhere we went—the Jewish quarter in Prague; the State Jewish Theatre in Bucharest; old synagogues in Budapest, Berlin, and Paris; and Holocaust memorials in almost every major city. Mostly reminders of Jewish death. Not yet so many signs of Jewish life.

We spent five days in Poland, much of it on a bus. We started in Krakow, a glorious Central European city with a stunning town square, charming narrow lanes surrounding it. It was not quite as glorious as Prague, but not far from it. We went and found the building that Bubba Eda's aunt had lived in, our first connection to the past. A concrete connection. We ate pierogi and *barszcz*, pottered around the marketplace. Helen and I smugly took offense at the *Schindler's List* tour, focusing as it did on the movie sets and sites, with a guide who seemed to have only a rudimentary knowledge of Jewish culture and history, unaware, it seemed, that the prewar Jewish culture she described to us was still practiced by millions of Jews today. Maybe we'd convinced ourselves that's how it would be. Confirmation bias at play. Would anything really satisfy us?

We arrived on the precipice of a much bigger boom in Jewish tourism and Jewish life in those places. It was only a decade after the fall of communism, and a couple of years after historian Jan Gross had blown apart the notion of Polish victimhood in his book, *Neighbors*. The book told the story of the village of Jedwabne in eastern Poland, where the Polish population murdered around 1,600 Jews, half the town's population. His work put a spotlight on Polish atrocities against Jews, over which a pall of silence had been cast for half a century. The controversy was still raging when we visited in 2004. Poland was still somewhere in between coming to terms with its own role in the destruction of Jews and its own wartime suffering at the hands of Nazi Germany, all the while trying to rebuild after decades of Soviet domination. Plus, we were there only days after Poland joined the European Union. It was a moment of transition. Maybe every moment is a moment of transition.

In any case, for these two young adventurers, it was difficult to process these places, difficult to place ourselves into the past that appeared only in scraps. An empty synagogue here, a plaque there, a walking tour, a ruined cemetery, Jewish-themed restaurants with klezmer bands. It was like a theme park in the Twilight Zone. Polish Disneyland: instead of "The Happiest Place on Earth," we were in "The Saddest Place on Earth." Bizarre for young Jews steeped in a still-flourishing Polish-Jewish environment. Still, with its beautifully preserved buildings, eccentric personalities, and emerging arts scene, Krakow was fun and weird. The adventure was about to get even more complicated.

Next stop: Auschwitz.

∽

We got off the bus in the parking lot at Auschwitz I, the camp mainly for political prisoners and laborers. It was weird to arrive in Auschwitz by bus, although pretty much everything about visiting a former death camp is weird. Passing under the emblematic iron gates, the *Arbeit Macht Frei* sign, that icon of Holocaust memory, left us feeling cold. I knew that most prisoners hadn't passed through there, but still, it was chilling, like we were walking through some mystical threshold. Our Polish tour guide explained each landmark in a straightforward manner, her deadpan expression and monotone seemingly appropriate for those circumstances. There is no room for emotion when your job is to guide visitors day after day through one of the bloodiest sites the world has known. After a short video, we were taken through the camp and its main exhibits. Eerie. Quiet. No leaves on the trees, talking only in hushed whispers, the crunch of the gravel path echoing through the eerie alleys.

For some reason, I took photos. For posterity, maybe? I thought I should take photos to show my parents in case they didn't get the opportunity to visit (which they would, only a couple of years later). I took a lot of photos—of buildings, small details, of pathways. I wanted to be able to show my family what it looked like there.

I remember there was a Star of David etched into the wall in a building, a crematorium maybe. Of course, looking back, I realized quickly that it was most likely some tourist or visitor who had etched it as a form of revenge or reclamation. At the time, though, I just assumed it was an extraordinary testament to the prisoners, figuring that some prisoner had etched it into the wall in his or her last moments. Then the exhibitions with the photos, floor to ceiling, of prisoners. Then the room full of shoes, maybe fifteen feet wide; a similar room full of suitcases; and then, finally, the room full of human hair. The remains of the victims right there in front of our eyes, separated from us only by a sloped window. They may as well have put the goddamn bodies in front of us. It was too much to bear. I broke down, for the first time that day, but not the last. I couldn't breathe. The display brought a nauseous, suffocating feeling, a sense of panic. The walls were closing in. The world was closing in. I stuck my head out a nearby window to sip a few breaths of the spring air, to regain my composure. I had to run outside, sit on the ground for the rest of that part of the tour.

We got back on the bus and headed toward Birkenau, Auschwitz II, the main event, the death factory within the Auschwitz complex. It was a sunny day, a few white clouds hovering above us. It seemed brighter at Birkenau than at Auschwitz I, maybe just because it was vast and open, unlike the mini-village at Auschwitz I. It seemed wrong, upside down. It should be gray and cloudy when you go to Auschwitz. Isn't that just how it was there? Did the sun even shine at Auschwitz? Hard to imagine that it did.

We climbed the watchtower. I took it all in, looked in every direction, studied every stone, tree, blade of grass. Hard to take it all in: the vastness of the site, the fence enclosing the ruins, the forest forming a secondary fence. The site was hidden, even if it was within walking distance of the local village, Oświęcim. We wandered down the train tracks, which we'd seen in so many photos. I tried to imagine the scene of a train arriving, prisoners disembarking, the sense of chaos and terror that marked the retellings so deeply. I couldn't summon it. I didn't even know if that was where the trains ended, if they stopped and were emptied of their "cargo" inside or outside the gates. Where did they go from there? Having heard all those stories, read the books, watched the movies, it was difficult to summon that picture. The imagery that had been so pervasive now eluded me. I quietly sang the Partisans' Hymn as I ambled along the track. I didn't know what else to do, or how to process it. It seemed appropriate. Not the last time I'd sing the "Partisans' Hymn" in Poland. Fulfilling my responsibilities to Zaida.

Our tour guide took us through the barracks, probably reconstructed. I didn't think too much about it then, whether or not all that we saw was exactly as the Red Army found it in January 1945, about what kind of effort went into preserving this enormous hellish landscape. We saw the bunks, the toilets. They looked like stables for horses. Another breakdown, that feeling of suffocation returning. Ugly, hysterical tears now. Exhausted, Helen and I both collapsed to the ground to get our breath back, regain our composure while everyone else wandered around exploring. I didn't even make it to see the ruins of the gas chambers and crematoria. I couldn't. I didn't need to, I'd seen all I needed.

Auschwitz-Birkenau was unnerving, existential. I'd studied the Holocaust, and, to be sure, had been surrounded by survivors, children of survivors, and all the stories, images, and quirks that came with that. Still, I wasn't ready for it. I hadn't been prepared for the emotional impact, for the feelings that overwhelmed me, that made me feel claustrophobic. It was a jarring experience to visit with a tour group full of non-Jewish antipodeans. I felt some sense of ownership of the story and place, yet I still could not quite make sense of it. These Aussies couldn't possibly understand what it was like for grandchildren of survivors to visit Auschwitz. Tears flowed liberally. This was my history, my heritage, my family story. For me, this was a pilgrimage. Everyone else was a tourist. How could they walk through here, taking pictures like it was the fucking Eiffel Tower?

Who was I to claim this as my own, anyway? This wasn't *my* history. My grandparents didn't survive Auschwitz; their families were killed elsewhere. They had been half a world away from what took place. This was Bubba Eda's neck of the woods, around ninety miles from Stary Sącz, the small village near the Czech-Polish border from which her father had dragged her by the pigtails in late 1939 to escape the coming onslaught. Helen's grandfather had been there, the wrinkly tattoo on his arm testament to that mysterious time in his life. But I could only partially identify it as my story, a symbol of the Slucki family tragedy, rather than the story itself, which unfolded two hundred miles north of where we stood.

An aside, another trick of memory. When I asked Helen if her grandmother, Bubba Regina, had been at Auschwitz, she didn't know. "She had a number on her arm," Helen told me. Helen's mother, Fay, who holds her mother's diary from the war years, confirmed she wasn't at Auschwitz. "Did she have a number on her arm?" I asked. She didn't know; maybe, she thought, but she couldn't visualize it any longer. I doubt she had one. Bubba Regina spent the war years in Gabesdorf, a camp in the Gross Rosen complex of camps at the Czech-Polish border. She likely wouldn't have had a number tattooed on her arm in that camp. Helen is almost certain she remembers it. I think she's conflating the two sets of wrinkly forearms that stirred her chicken soup.

~

Wandering through Birkenau, I was overcome with guilt. It was a guilt that I hadn't experienced the pangs of hunger or the blows of Nazi and Soviet truncheons, as my grandparents and their families had, guilt that I could visit this place as a tourist and not an inmate. Guilt that I was leaving there on a bus within a couple of hours. It was a guilt born from the minimization of any complaints: "You don't know about hunger," my grandmother would declare, telling me of the true hunger she experienced as a wartime refugee in Uzbekistan. The nagging sense that any grievance I have pales alongside the enormous suffering earlier generations endured never really goes away.

We boarded the bus to Warsaw, a four- or five-hour journey. There had been some tension brewing on the bus, I don't even remember about what. People returning late, drunken arguments. Something petty. I was still in a daze, maybe a state of shock. And now I was heading to the childhood home of my grandparents. My pilgrimage, my homecoming, was relentless. I can barely remember those two days in Warsaw. We got drunk at a bowling alley near the campsite, struggled to find the remnants of the Warsaw Ghetto wall, saw the Umschlagplatz and the Palace for Science and Culture, that Stalinist paean to Polish communism, a giant phallus in the middle of Warsaw. We visited the address that my Zaida—Mich's father—grew up in. We saw the Warsaw Ghetto Uprising memorial. Those days were much blurrier, though, than the days spent partying in the preceding weeks. Maybe it was the heat of the sun as we walked around, backpacks in tow, scurrying to find our landmarks, tick our boxes.

I didn't know, at that time, how unprepared I was to visit Poland, to return. It would only occur to me years later. I couldn't see anything more than an elaborate graveyard. I didn't know what it took to see the ghosts that had been mostly in the background, occasionally coming to the fore, and now chaotically stirring up inside me. Warsaw, my ancestral home, was a whirlwind. I barely got to see anything, let alone absorb and reflect, before we had to climb back aboard the bus for the eight-hour trek to Berlin. I certainly didn't understand the gravity of that homecoming.

Zaida made his own pilgrimages in his year and a half living in Wrocław. Although already traumatized by what he had endured in the Soviet Union, and by the uncertainty of what had happened to his family, he was determined to learn and understand more about how they had lived in those months and years after he had lost contact with them. Those days, maybe weeks—it's not clear from his description how long—that he spent traveling around, searching for clues about his family's last moments, provided no closure, only further heartache.

He heard stories from witnesses and survivors of the Włocławek ghetto, walked the paths that his beloved wife and children must have walked, breathed in the mild spring air, just as they must have years earlier. There was something that drew him back to Włocławek, to Chelmno, to Warsaw. He wanted to know. I don't know if it helped him deal with his trauma, probably it only exacerbated it. But, knowing that his sojourn to Poland was only temporary, he was determined to have the opportunity to honor his murdered family.

And so, on the fifth anniversary of their murder, Zaida traveled the roughly two-hundred-mile journey from Wrocław to his former home in Włocławek, "a very beautiful little town," as he described it to Mendel. But now, "a cemetery of Jewish life." It wasn't his first time back. He and Bubba had traveled there in 1946 around Rosh Hashanah, the Jewish new year, to meet with the handful of surviving Bundists and plan a memorial. During that visit, they stood where the ghetto had once stood, trying to make sense of what had taken place there. They spoke to locals who could tell him something about his family, walked by the home that they had shared, now occupied by a Polish family. "I stood with Eda by the window of where I lived and even recognized the curtains that my dear Gitl put up with her own hands," he recalled. Presumably these were the same drapes from which she cut the Star of David patches they were forced to wear.

When he went back six months later, in April 1947, he had a different aim, a singular focus. Now, he wanted to retrace the steps of his loved ones, to get some sense of the last days of their lives, what they were forced to endure. He wanted to be able to properly memorialize them, although no one knew what that meant. It was still so fresh. Włocławek this time was just the starting point of their journey. From there, he and a small group traveled in a convoy of trucks the less-than-fifty-mile journey toward the Chelmno extermination camp, in a forest near the city of Kolo. Along the way, Zaida was struck by the complete absence of Jewish life in the towns and villages they passed through, once upon a time small but bustling centers of religious and political activity.

Brześć Kujawski, Lubraniec, Izbica Kujawska, Kolo: vibrant little towns that once featured in the novels of great Yiddish writers, now virtually cleansed of Jews. No communities left, only individuals. Towns Zaida must have known well, now unrecognizable. Even though the buildings and the streets were still there, those places no longer existed, only in the memories of the few that survived. Whereas Jews once comprised around 10 percent of the Polish population, one-third of the country's urban population, now the towns and cities were mostly free of Jews. For the vast majority of those who returned, it was a short-lived resettlement. After waves of state-sanctioned antisemitism in 1956 and 1968, Jews were virtually invisible in Poland, their memories erased from country's official, mythical past. This was the final act, it must have seemed then, in the thousand-year epic of Polish Jewry. A civilization erased, its ruins buried in the ground, ashes scattered through the fields and waterways.

~

In his letter to Mendel after his visit to Chelmno, Zaida described the extermination process, likely the first time Mendel had heard it in such excruciating detail. Zaida had heard it from a witness,

Jakub literally trying to rebuild Poland with his Bundist comrades, Wrocław (1947).

Jakub on the Jewish Voievodish Committee, Wrocław (1947).

Zhuchovski, a butcher from Włocławek who had escaped by stabbing two SS soldiers with a butcher's knife and had found refuge with a family of Polish peasants nearby. It's now a familiar story, although it must have sounded implausible at the time: Victims rounded up and deported to the camp, lured into a false sense of security that they would serve as a slave labor force, before being shoved into the backs

Jakub and Eda visiting Chelmno (April 1947).

of vans disguised by shower blocks. The vans were hermetically sealed and rigged to direct gas into the rear chamber. The Nazis would then drive the short distance from the fake camp to pits dug by the latest trainload of prisoners, a journey of about eight to ten minutes. Afterward the victims' bodies were burned in large pits and then pounded into ash. Many were taken in large sacks to be poured into the Vistula River, the fabled waterway that connected Zaida's childhood home of Warsaw to his adopted home, Włocławek. Many of those remains, though, simply sat undisturbed in the forest, silent witnesses to the ongoing mass murder of the Jews of western Poland.

To get to the site of the extermination camp, Zaida and his group passed by a church next to the stream that encircled the nearest village. Across the stream, they saw the ruins of a mansion. There were still a couple of walls, with grated windows behind which rotating streams of Jewish prisoners had been held: tailors, shoemakers, manual laborers co-opted by the Nazis to work for short periods, then exterminated to make way for new prisoners. A conveyor belt of slave labor and mass murder. Just past the mansion, Zaida and his group found further traces. Thousands of rusty forks, spoons, and cups that victims had left behind, evidence of lives lost.

Past that, nothing but dense forest. As Zaida's group approached the site in the forest, a couple of kilometers past the mansion, little remained of the extermination camp. It had been systematically dismantled in the last months of the war as the Red Army approached. There were traces. There were a few bricks remaining from the crematoria. They also found large open graves that still contained piles of uncovered ashes and half-ground bones. Zaida collected a handful, as a memorial, determined to take them with him wherever he went. "Let it be," he proclaimed, "the symbol of remembrance for our beloved." He vowed to take them with him and hold them near to him for the rest of his life. Maybe, he thought, his beloved wife and sons were among those remains. One day, he might even get to give them a proper Jewish burial.

I'd heard of this kind of thing before: survivors bringing stones from their village or camp with them to the new country, a reminder of their past. During a research trip to New York one year, I found an archival box that contained only a large rock wrapped in tissue paper. No explanation, but presumably a material connection to the past, a tangible link to a place that now existed only in myth. I'd seen it in other settings: when we visited the battlefields of Gallipoli in Turkey, a friend collected a film canister full of sand from the beach to take back to her grandfather. I assumed he'd fought there, or his father had. It was a concrete link, she thought, to that past. I thought it was just sand.

Zaida would later bury these ashes and bones in the Melbourne General Cemetery. A statement of permanence, the final resting place for his family. He had carried those remains with him from Chelmno, back to Wrocław, and then onto Paris and finally, Melbourne. Burying them finally was no small act. It was a symbol that their wandering had finally come to an end, that even though he never fully felt Australian, the country was his home. He was under no illusion, though, during that time in Poland, that he had found his home, the place he would raise a new family and reestablish whatever shreds of his life he could put back together. No, that world was gone. Poland was a way station, and if he wanted to feel close to the traces of that world, they'd have to follow him in a container wherever he went.

For Zaida, that symbolic burial was all that he had left. Burial, at least when you have the choice about how and where to be buried, is a statement about belonging, about attachment. When Zaida buried those ashes from Chelmno, it wasn't only a memorial to the past but a declaration about the present. No one would be displacing him from here. He was a citizen, his children spoke Australian-accented English, played cricket, and ate the strange British-influenced Australian food. They were home now.

I think about that often now. Dad died while traveling in Los Angeles, but there was no question that his body should be taken back to Australia to be buried in his home. To be buried in the same city as his parents, grandparents, aunts and uncles, truly proof that Melbourne was now the Sluckis' home. Shmulek II, buried a little over thirty miles from Shmulek I, or, at least, from his symbolic resting place.

I never made it to Włocławek or Wrocław. Although I visited Poland twice, it didn't occur to me that I might set aside time to go to these places. After all, what was left? Nothing of our family. Maybe there were a few Jews in Wrocław, but I guessed not many people in Włocławek even spoke English, and I certainly didn't speak Polish, beyond a few swear words and a tongue twister, something about Peter not over-peppering the pork. I did spend time on Google Street View giving myself a virtual tour of the places they lived and walked. Wrocław, although it had been badly damaged by the war, still seemed to have retained some of its baroque grandeur, with its tall, ornate buildings and wide boulevards. Włocławek, the virtual version, still had an old town feel, run down, gray, frozen in time. It looked like those pictures you see of Cuba, old-timey cars, crumbling buildings, cobblestone streets. Just without the color. Just as I imagined it would be. Antisemitic graffiti visible, rival football club fans marking the side of a building in the old Jewish neighborhood, right by the old synagogue, as if to confirm the worst fears of all the descendants of survivors who instinctively hate Poland. See, antisemitism is just a part of Poland, they say. I know, though, it's more complex than that.

Something about that virtual look at Zaida's old haunts, though, made me feel closer to him, helped me to understand the letters, his life. I wondered how he might have reacted, taking that virtual tour, how much more I could have understood about his life by doing that with him and Bubba.

∼

In the end, leaving Poland was an easy decision for Bubba and Zaida. Like most of the tens of thousands of Polish Jews that returned, the prospect of rebuilding their community amidst the persistent antisemitism and the specter of communism was too much to bear. Too many bad memories, too many ghosts hovering. Home lost its sense of comfort, it became only a burden, the weight of the past hunching over Zaida's tiring shoulders. Now, home was a nightmare to which he didn't want to constantly return. He didn't want to be near Włocławek and Chelmno, didn't want them to be accessible. He knew the pull toward that past would be far too strong, the search for memories that were no longer available, except in his dreams. And even then, the happy memories provided little consolation. Nothing could.

The eighteen months Zaida spent in Wrocław were full of angst and uncertainty about whether he would be able to leave. Paris always seemed to be the next destination. He had a cousin, Avram, who lived there. Mendel and Ruchel had also lived there for more than a decade before the war. After losing his immediate family, Zaida was determined that they should go somewhere with family. He knew it would be tough, he'd heard the reports about the challenges with language, with finding work, with getting visas to whatever the next destination would be. But Poland had nothing left for him. Sweden was an attractive option: news out of Sweden was that the situation for Jewish refugees was comparatively comfortable, and there was a small Bund organization forming there. But there was no family in Sweden. Family was much more important now.

~

When we lived in London in 2003–4, we visited Paris a couple of times. It was so easy, on our doorstep. Cheap flights, the fast train across the English Channel. We could be in the center of Paris within hours. A novelty for two teens from Australia. A three-hour train from Melbourne might take us to Wangaratta, not quite Paris. We clearly had different priorities to my grandparents—they wanted to get as far away from Europe as they could, while we were trying to stay close. A weekend away to Paris—it sounds whimsical, ridiculous, indulgent, the kind of life my grandparents could only dream of.

Our first trip to Paris was in 2003, a surprise weekend away for Helen's birthday. It turned out to be a kind of pilgrimage. I saw the streets where Bubba and Zaida pushed Sluggo in his stroller, the apartment that Avram passed down to his children and then grand-children. I breathed in the thick Jewish atmosphere of the Marais, newly revived at that time. We viewed Paris as the romantic maze of cobblestone streets and nineteenth-century boulevards that we knew from the movies. We were there by choice, unlike Bubba and Zaida. We could come and go as we pleased.

We strolled through the narrow lanes, happy to get lost, holding hands, sneaking kisses, eating crepes washed down with tart apple cider. My heart was in my mouth as we took the great glass elevator up to the top of the Eiffel Tower. We wandered through the gardens of the Rodin Museum, we became experts in nineteenth-century art, smugly passing judgment on the brushstrokes and use of light as though we were *New York Times* critics. We met Daniel and Monique, Avram's son and daughter-in-law, who showed us how to navigate the Metro and how to order the right kind of baguette. We ate runny cheese with spoons, drank cheap French wine, and climbed the steep streets of Montmartre. It was utterly enchanting, a contrast to the black-and-white landscape we'd later see in Eastern

Europe. We felt justified that our grandparents had left those places, but wished they had stayed in Paris. I pictured baby Sluggo with his mother sitting in one of the beautiful little neighborhood parks. My dad's birthplace, my grandparents' way station to Australia.

~

At the beginning of 1948, Bubba and Zaida traveled from Wrocław to Paris, their final transit point before they finally managed to find a place to call home. By then, Bubba Eda was heavily pregnant with Dad, around six months. They lived at 30 Rue Beaubourg, a block from the site that would become the Centre Pompidou, Paris's brutalist contemporary art mecca, where Helen and I marveled at the art of Andy Warhol, Roy Lichtenstein, and Jackson Pollock and sniveled at the arrangements of neon lights and brick heaps labeled as installation art. When Zaida was there, though, the Marais neighborhood was still a run-down immigrant quarter, not the sleek, inner-city, hipster mecca that I encountered in 2003. They lived only blocks from Zaida's cousin Avram, in his tiny second-floor apartment on Rue Ferdinand Duvall, just off the historic Rue des Rosiers, where kosher bakeries and Israeli falafel stands now dot the cobblestone alley.

For Bubba and Zaida, Paris carried little of the romance that we sought out. Paris was simply the next station in their wandering, the latest chapter in their ongoing saga filled with misfortune. Nothing happened easily for Zaida. They didn't speak, read, or write French. Without the language, Zaida couldn't work in his profession. He also didn't have work rights. There were barriers everywhere. What's more, he was frail, battered. Strong as iron, he said, to live through all that he had. But still, a mouth full of false teeth, vision deteriorating, lungs that might give out anytime, and nerves frayed from a decade filled with catastrophe. An old father, an old man, long before he should have been.

Even so, they were among the lucky ones. They had a family, who, although poor themselves, still served as a safety net. Avram and his wife, Reyzl, provided them a place to sleep when they arrived; Avram helped Zaida learn the knitting trade when it was impossible for him to work legally, a skill that would come in handy once they made it to Melbourne. Mendel's in-laws, well established in Paris, gave them an apartment rent-free while they set themselves up. Although Zaida was reticent to rely on the help of others, the fact that there was a family to provide a soft landing put them in a better situation than many. The work was seasonal, not always steady, but working ninety hours a week in the winter, the busiest season, when people clamored for coats, allowed them to keep their heads above water when his hours were cut in the off-season.

Paris was mainly a waiting game. They never expected to settle permanently there. Initially they thought they might go to America. "I hope that Paris won't be the final destination in my wandering," he wrote to Mendel when they first arrived. "I hope we will see you again in this life. I am ready now for anything." But Australia was always their most likely destination. Zaida had friends from Włocławek who had gone ahead, and could help him obtain visas. The United States didn't have a pathway for a Polish-Jewish refugee in France, a pathway that would have been much easier at that time if he'd been in a DP camp, ironically. Once they were in Paris, they sent for Bubba's parents and sisters who had stayed behind, although by 1949 it was already getting difficult and expensive to leave Poland, as communism tightened its screws.

Even with his increasingly cynical outlook on life, his terrible suffering, Zaida couldn't help but be impressed by Paris. It was the biggest city he'd seen, lively, bustling. He'd lived mostly in smaller cities his whole life. Even the Warsaw of his childhood was, by comparison, a provincial East European town. But in Paris, he could recognize its splendor, its romance, even if he could not partake in it. He beheld with wonder its strange curiosities: couples kissing, "smacking lips" in the middle of the street. He was impressed by the Eiffel Tower, which he saw when he went to a public talk in a hall nearby. And he quickly began familiarizing himself with the Metro, the underground maze shepherding Parisians across the city. That, he thought, was "truly a wonder."

Jakub with his son, Shmulek, Genoa (February 1950).

∾

On February 4, 1950, the S.S. *Cyrenia* set sail from Genoa, Italy, with the Sluckis aboard. When they left, they had no idea what awaited them. Zaida had been in touch with his friends who had gone ahead, but they could only paint a picture. He knew what challenges lay before him. It wasn't his first time flung to a faraway place with a new language, new customs, new landscapes. He was now experienced at this. They'd need to take special supplies for the ship journey, to supplement the meager amount they'd be fed. He knew that finding somewhere to live and work would be the first challenges, but there wasn't a lot he could do from France. There was no Craigslist in 1950.

Zaida and Bubba were leaving Europe for the final time. They would never return. Before he boarded the train from Paris that would take him to the ship in Genoa, he was reflective. "Soon, I leave Europe and the continent of the world where I leave behind the best and the dearest that I possess. With a bleeding, teary heart, I will begin to build a new home, and hope for long, healthy years." (He always wished people *lange, gezunte yorn*—long, healthy years—in his letters). Leaving Europe felt final, even more so than simply leaving Poland. The proximity in Paris at least, both geographically and culturally, offered some continuity. Having departed Wrocław two years earlier, and Włocławek eight years before that, he knew that sinking feeling that came with emigration, leaving behind a life cobbled together. He was intimate by now with the uncertainty ahead, with those final good-byes, most likely the last time he'd see and embrace those with whom he'd struggled to piece back together some meaning after their world was so thoroughly shattered. Their former lives were now ground into ashes, drifting silently down the Vistula River, or blowing in the stiff Polish breeze.

Europe was now just a jumble of memories, at once warm and chilling, comforting and terrifying. Lives of promise and hope now strewn in the forests of central Poland. There would be no more pilgrimages, no more standing in the places where his sons had grown up, where he married his first love, where he found his sense of worth. Europe was the past, a past that would continue to haunt him, but somehow no longer real.

With the heaviness also came a sense of relief. Zaida didn't want Sluggo to grow up surrounded by the specter of another world war. "Unfortunately, we must continue wandering and will find new problems," he wrote to Mendel, "but at least now we won't be in the center of fresh cataclysms, looming wars gathering quickly, quicker than we can even imagine. Although it will reach all corners of the world, I believe Australia won't be the center of all those terrible things; it will continue to be Europe, and in the first instance, France."

Even more than relief, there was some hope amidst the trepidation. They didn't expect this move to be temporary. They felt that despite the challenges, Australia would offer them opportunities to work, to create a comfortable family life. A life unencumbered by war and the throes of European ideological excesses. Hope that little Shmulek wouldn't face the same fate as the first Shmulek. They could at last hope. I discovered their passenger landing cards in the National Archives of Australia, a short document that gave a small window into their arrival. When asked how long they intended to stay,

Bubba wrote on the card clearly, in her elegant, cursive handwriting: For Ever. There is a sense of relief in that flick at the bottom of the *F*, the swirly *E*, the final *r* stretching out as they hoped their lives in Australia would. Probably one of her first English words, maybe some anonymous customs official helped her fill it out.

For Ever.

They were done wandering.

5

Immigrants

When I was little, I don't remember how old, coming back from some summer holiday away, squeezed into our beat-up old Mitsubishi Sigma, Dad insisted on taking a detour through his childhood neighborhood, Carlton. He guided us through the broad thoroughfares, with their mix of grand Victorian mansions and tiny Edwardian workers' cottages; down Lygon Street, the commercial and cultural center now lined with tourists and below par Italian restaurants; the narrow laneways, with their endless cast of characters from our parents' past. We didn't often come to this side of town. There was no need to drive the forty-five minutes to a neighborhood that held only sentimental value. On that day, the fact that it was on the way home was a chance for us to play tourists in our own city. Dad reveled in it: that was where this family lived; here was the old bookstore; there's the old Yiddish library; here's the median strip where we used to play cricket. He got to tell his old stories, bring the characters of postwar Jewish Carlton to life. Actually, he lived in North Carlton, but Carlton was really a mythical space that existed beyond its actual boundaries. It was a suburb where Polish Jewish migrants rubbed shoulders with immigrants from Italy, Greece, Malta, and Yugoslavia.

And there, in the middle of it all, was 501 Canning Street, where Zaida Jakub and Bubba Eda carved out their own tiny slice of Jewish Poland. A tiny, Victorian-era cottage, barely ten feet across, one among dozens on their block, indistinguishable in the rows of workers' cottages that dot Melbourne's inner city. If you went today, it would look much the same, frozen in time. The cars, much more expensive, much

501 Canning Street, Photograph by Cara Mand.

more modern, the only thing that would signal you'd stepped out of the 1950s. But there was something special about that address, the beating heart of a community. Unassuming on the outside, run down on the inside, but always full of food, people, laughter, tears, and life. Step in from the quiet streets of North Carlton and you were transported back to a workers' club in Eastern Europe, where socialism ruled the day, the guttural, lyrical dialects of Yiddish filled the air, and there was always a bowl of soup or a slice of herring for the guests.

501 Canning Street: somewhere between a community center, a halfway house, and a party headquarters. A private home transformed each night into a public sphere, a working-class salon, where the problems of the world were negotiated over a drink, where the concept of family was fluid, inclusive. A house where passions flared, where tensions simmered, and no one was turned away. A house I only ever saw from the outside, but knew its inner workings intimately. An environment Helen and I have tried to emulate, mostly unsuccessfully. Too stressful, too noisy for us. It was a unique atmosphere, impossible to replicate. How did they do it, I wonder?

In 2017, the United Nations High Commissioner for Refugees reported that there were 65.6 million forcibly displaced people in the world, including 22.5 million refugees and 10 million stateless people. Amidst protracted and bloody wars in Syria, Afghanistan, South Sudan, and many other countries, the flow of desperate people seeking safety and shelter closely resembles my parents' and grandparents' flight from their historic homes. Squint and these millions of displaced Afghans and Syrians could be Jews fleeing the rubble of central Europe. The world's indifference to their struggles is eerily like its antipathy to Jews in the 1930s and 1940s.

In 2017, the United Nations High Commissioner for Refugees reported that there were 65.6 million forcibly displaced people in the world, including 22.5 million refugees and 10 million stateless people. Amidst protracted and bloody wars in Syria, Afghanistan, South Sudan, and many other countries, the flow of desperate people seeking safety and shelter closely resembles my parents' and grandparents' flight from their historic homes. Squint and these millions of displaced Afghans and Syrians could be Jews fleeing the rubble of central Europe. The world's indifference to their struggles is eerily like its antipathy to Jews in the 1930s and 1940s.

Helen, Arthur, and I are immigrants. The lucky kind, far removed from these masses of asylum seekers and displaced persons. Rare success stories in a globalizing world. Forced to leave only by a contracting academic job market, we are immigrants by choice. We came to the United States on temporary work visas in 2013, then graduated to green cards after a few years, a sign of permanence, insofar as anything is permanent. I don't know if we'll apply for citizenship one day, but for years we've lived here, paid taxes, worked with young people, forged friendships, participated in our local community. It took a long time for me to come to terms with that word, *immigrant*. We weren't immigrants, we said. We weren't settling permanently, and in any case, immigration to me was always something you did out of desperation, despair. We came here for work, not because we were forced out. We could go home whenever we wanted, our family was still there, our friends, our football team. Life would be just as we left it, wouldn't it?

To us, being an immigrant meant something completely different. Immigrants came to a new country and didn't speak the language, didn't have jobs or money. Life as an immigrant was difficult, an obstacle to overcome. If you were an immigrant, you couldn't just pack up and move to another new country. Immigration was a statement of permanence, a new life, a break from the old. A set of circumstances thrust upon you, not something you chose. Our grandparents were immigrants, not us. All those Syrians and Afghans are immigrants, right? What are we, who choose this path, who can decide where on earth we want to settle and raise a family? What should we call ourselves, we who are in so many ways embedded into the white, urban, American middle class, so steeped in American culture and politics?

"Emigration is no light matter," Zaida wrote to Mendel in 1955. After a decade traversing the globe, looking for somewhere to settle, he would have known. Even for those in the luckiest category, like us, there are major hurdles to overcome. Paperwork, uncertainty, endless waiting, endless scrutiny, invasive tests, interrogation. No freedom of movement for a period, everything we do possibly affecting our status. A feeling of being the outsider. And, for better or worse, we are the fortunate ones: Australian, white, college professor, living in Charleston. Still, we have many decisions to make about how we relate to this place, how we want Arthur to relate to it. What kind of accent will Arthur have? American? Southern? How will we feel about it being different from ours? What sort of feeling of Australianness do we want him to have? What about when we live in a place whose political culture is so different from ours, where Confederate flags wave proudly and people carrying weapons is a daily fact? Where the call for liberty often comes at the expense of those most vulnerable, at home or abroad? Where racial segregation is still so obvious, decades after being outlawed? Where white supremacists and Nazis marched the streets in 2017, more than seven decades after the Nazis were defeated, 150 years after the fall of the Confederacy? How do we connect to a place whose history is so remote from ours? What kind of Jewishness do we want to pass on, when the local Jewish community is so unlike ours?

The longer we lived in the United States, the more we saw the gaping cultural abyss. We accepted it but never felt at home. The legacy of slavery, the presence of guns, the pervasive Evangelical Christianity are simply parts of the daily vernacular here. "Which church do you go to?" we were often asked when we first arrived. I gave a talk on Jews in Eastern Europe to a local theatre group shortly after arriving. After naïvely, glibly, stating that I was an atheist—a label I'm now not so sure about—I was surprised at the audible gasp from the small audience of genteel southerners. There is also the unofficial segregation that continues to dot the urban landscapes, decades after desegregation. I am daily astonished at the obvious link between class and race in this city, and the way in which the racial makeup of neighborhoods seems to change block to block.

These issues all dovetailed in June 2015, while we were home visiting our family in Melbourne. That Wednesday night in Charleston, Thursday morning in Melbourne, white supremacist Dylann Roof entered the historic Emanuel AME Church in downtown Charleston, opened fire, and murdered nine parishioners. Two blocks from Arthur's school; four blocks from our offices; one mile from our house. I caught wind of it on Twitter, early on a Thursday morning in Melbourne, and was glued to my phone the rest of the day. The rest of the month really. Concerned for my friends and colleagues, my community, my neighborhood, I followed it obsessively.

And then, in October 2018, a gunman murdered eleven Jews in a synagogue in Pittsburgh while shouting that "all Jews must die." Another reminder of our vulnerability, a reminder that perhaps we ought to hide our Jewishness, not be too conspicuous. A sign that maybe we weren't as safe or as welcome as we'd thought. Between the violence in our backyard and the violence targeting the Jewish

Arthur and I at a Charleston vigil for the victims of the shooting at the Tree
of Life Synagogue in Pittsburgh. Earlier, I had been one of the speakers
at the Holocaust memorial in Marion Square. This photo was taken as the
vigil continued outside the Mother Emanuel AME Church, where a white
supremacist murdered nine parishioners three years earlier. Charleston,
South Carolina (October 28, 2018).

community to which we belong, our sense of security is balanced on
a tightrope, ready to collapse at the slightest tremor in the political
landscape. Is this really a place for us to raise our son?

Australia has deeply rooted problems with racism, misogyny, a
growing Far Right. Its political landscape is beginning to resemble
the circus of American political life. But mass shootings are not a

fact of life where we grew up. For Arthur, they will be. They are. How do we explain it to him? Whatever other challenges we face integrating into American life are immaterial in the face of material fears of violence, of not knowing how many people walking down King Street are packing heat. This is a cultural hurdle among many that is difficult to overcome. Daily we see these cultural differences. There are barriers to participation in American political life, and often it feels like we speak a different language. Almost every single day we are asked, interrogated, about where we are from, what we are doing here. Always very friendly, but a constant reminder that we are outsiders.

~

If immigration is principally about moving somewhere better, safer, more prosperous, we may have gotten it backward. On all statistical measures—life expectancy, health care, schools, safety, jobs, quality of life—Australia is ahead of the United States, Melbourne streets ahead of Charleston. Melbourne: the world's most livable city, whatever that means. Better public transport, I think. According to the *Economist*. Up there with Tokyo, Vienna, Vancouver, Toronto. Culturally vibrant, multicultural, with socialized medicine. Why did we leave? I'm not sure. Why would anyone leave when you read that? Maybe I just idealize it too much, a form of homesickness. The grass is always greener and all that. That's right, I couldn't get a job. Contracting academic job market. Some things are the same everywhere.

What am I complaining about? We live in a cosmopolitan city, earn enough money in our white-collar jobs, live in an upscale part of town. The challenges we face pale in comparison to those of my parents and grandparents. First-world problems, really. We can't even compare our experiences, although it often serves as a frame of reference.

I think often about how it was for Zaida, moving to a new country for the third (or was it fourth) time. He was very concerned that Dad and his sister, Miriam, were growing up as Australian kids at the expense of their *yiddishkayt*, their Jewishness. It pained him that although Sluggo and his friends all spoke Yiddish fluently, among themselves they spoke English, even at Yiddish Sunday school. "That's just how life goes," he lamented to Mendel in 1958, resigned to raising an Australian son, a faint hint of disappointment in his tone. Shmulek II would never become the serious bearer of Polish-Jewish civilization that Shmulek I might have turned out to be. The war years had taken care of that. More likely to be a larrikin, an easy-going, irreverent Aussie kid.

Jakub and Eda Slucki arrived in Melbourne on March 9, 1950, aboard the SS *Cyrenia*, their moonfaced, Francophone toddler in tow. The *Cyrenia* was then a forty-year-old Greek liner that had recently been converted into a passenger ship transporting displaced persons from Genoa to Melbourne, a trip it made a handful of times between 1949 and 1956, when it was retired. Like those on board, the old ship had seen a lot in its time. It had been a passenger ship, had been requisitioned as a military carrier, before being transformed into a commercial ship operating between Australia, New Zealand, and North America. In the late 1940s, its final assignment was to bring weary refugees to their new homes, far away from the smoldering ashes that they had left behind. A fitting duty for the ship that had, along with its cargo—desperate refugees dehumanized by the latest Thirty Years' War—seen the best and worst the twentieth century had to offer.

When they arrived, my family's nationality was listed as Polish, a step above the "Stateless" stamp that many carried, but not a designation that carried much comfort. As quickly as they could, on August 2, 1957, they shed that formal attachment to become Australian citizens, something into which I don't think they ever fully grew. I don't know if they attended a citizenship ceremony, or how they felt about being Australian. Certainly, they were grateful that Australia took them in when they were homeless. But there remained a gap between them and their Australian-raised children. They were stateless, in spirit at least, whether they liked it or not.

They came alone, their visas sponsored by Sender Burstin, an old friend of Zaida's from Włocławek who had arrived in Melbourne in the late 1920s. Burstin had founded the first Bund club in Melbourne in 1928 and was a stalwart of the Yiddish community. His earnest, bespectacled brow stared down on us at the Kadimah and Waks House through our childhoods.

A year after they disembarked, Bubba's parents and sisters joined them, all cramming temporarily into that cottage on Canning Street. More comfortable probably than their home in interwar Poland, and luxurious compared to what they had lived in during their Soviet exile. But still a small, nineteenth-century workers' cottage housing an extended family. They moved shortly after to a house around the corner, so that they'd be just a stone's throw from Bubba and Zaida. A few years later Bubba and Zaida welcomed a daughter, Miriam, into the world. Six years Dad's junior, Miriam was the apple of Zaida's eye. After three sons, finally a daughter to dote on. Theirs was a special bond, unencumbered by the same expectations placed on the first born into the new generation. Less pressure on the younger sibling; less pressure on the daughter. Little Shmulek was happy to have a baby sister, although he'd wanted a brother. "I am happy that you have born a sister for me," he wrote to Bubba in the hospital, not allowed yet to visit. In a separate Yiddish note, he made sure to tell them that he missed them and couldn't wait for them to come home.

Life was difficult for the immigrant Sluckis. The language was tough to pick up, the customs difficult to adapt to. They had to find homes and jobs, learn a new language, navigate the unfamiliar streets, pick up the social cues, adapt to the broader culture. I'm not sure Zaida ever learned to speak English particularly well. To be fair, he already spoke Yiddish, Polish, Russian, and basic French, and probably had a smattering of German and Hebrew also. But the language was a constant source of frustration for him. He was forty-nine when he arrived, a broken man. He had just lived for two years in a place where he didn't speak the language, now he had to pick up another one. Not so easy for a weary old Jew.

Family Portrait
(ca. 1961).

Nothing so unusual or unique there—a typical immigrant story. And Australia wasn't the worst place to be doing it. It was a young country still, with a tradition of immigration, even if the immigrants tended to be predominantly British until the 1950s. By the time Bubba and Zaida came, there was at least a Polish-Jewish community that had put down its roots in Melbourne. When they arrived, there were cultural and religious institutions, Jewish political organizations, grocery stores and bookstores catering to a Jewish population. There was Yiddish theatre, and Yiddish newspapers. The Carlton to which Bubba and Zaida brought their infant son already had the seeds planted for the lively Jewish center that shaped Dad's early years.

Jakub and Eda at the knitting machines (1967).

Zaida was an experienced bookkeeper, but without English, he couldn't get a job in his profession. Having learned the knitting trade in Paris, he had a skill he could draw on. Like all immigrants do, he had to adapt, find any opportunities he could, extract the most out of whatever skills could help him earn a buck. Soon after Bubba and Zaida arrived, I'm not sure how soon, they bought some button-making equipment and began producing buttons in a back room in their house. Within a couple of years, realizing that button-making was a lot of work for not enough return, they bought some knitting machines and rented a small warehouse in an adjacent suburb. Zaida wanted the "factory" to be close by the house—he didn't drive, and he worked long hours. He didn't want to add a commute to his already exhausting day.

It wasn't easy—he had to take out loans to buy the machines. More financial pressures. And those machines were quickly superseded by better, cheaper machines. The best machines, but most expensive, came from the United States and Britain, and cost up to

£3,000. The cheapest, most efficient machines were often German-produced. "Some Jews use German machines," he wrote to Mendel in 1958, "but not me. I wouldn't allow it in my workshop. My account [with the Germans] has not yet been settled." His six Swiss machines chugged away noisily in his little workshop for long hours. Not the best available, but affordable enough that he could pay them off within a few years. That account with the Germans took generations to settle. My parents didn't buy German products either. When I was seven years old and they renovated the house, there was some discussion about whether or not to buy German appliances. In the end, I think they decided against it, although I don't quite remember if it was the ethics of it, or the cost. I'm more selective. I wouldn't drive a Volkswagen, but when it came to buying a coffee grinder, the Krups machine had the best Amazon ratings and was cheap. Looks like I closed that account finally.

How to explain the contradictions? I have no idea, except that life is full of contradictions. Did I dodge the question well enough? It reminds me of a joke Danny, our cousin in San Diego, told me, about when he got into a friend's Volkswagen. Bemused that his Jewish friend was driving a German car, he opened the ashtray, announcing: "Look! Room for the whole family!"

In the meantime, Bubba was running all around the city, making deliveries, paying bills, an equal partner in the business, but also having primary responsibility for the children. After her four hours of sleep each night, she was up at 6:30 a.m. to feed and clothe the children. Bubba and Zaida were absent most of the week. "By today's standards," Dad's uncle Gooter told me, "you couldn't say they were exemplary parents." But they did all they could to fill their refrigerator, to have a refrigerator, to give their children the life that was denied to Zaida's first two sons, cut down before they even had a chance to make something of their lives.

Bubba and Zaida couldn't catch a break. Dad had his own health battles as a small child. When he was three, shortly after arriving in Melbourne, he suffered ongoing problems with fever and tonsillitis. They took him to a private hospital to have his tonsils removed,

Six-year-old Dad at the visit of
Queen Elizabeth II to Melbourne.
A sign of his assimilation? (1954).

costing them a hefty fifty pounds. No small sum for poor knitters.
Dad was also born with a defect in his neck, so that his head bowed
to one side. The doctors in Paris said there was little to be done to
stop his little head drooping to one side. They just had to monitor
it. By the time they arrived in Melbourne, it was obvious that the
crooked neck was affecting little Shmulek's development. It took an
invasive operation to fix it, and weeks in the hospital and recovery.
It healed, although, left with almost no neck, Dad could not do up
the top button of a shirt for the rest of his life. And another hefty
medical bill. Despite these difficulties, though, in some ways, Dad's
tonsillitis and his neck issues must have seemed like a relief, a sign of

normality, compared to what they had battled constantly the previous decade. The boring, everyday problems of raising children. Problems over which they had some control, that they could fix.

Still, although they never made a fortune, food was always plentiful. They managed a couple of trips together to Los Angeles. They regularly sponsored new immigrants, and put down deposits on houses for them, usually, I think, without asking to be repaid. Their lives were a struggle, something from which they could not shield their children, but their children never starved, were never without a roof over their head.

~

Another old Jewish joke: a man gets hit by a car. The paramedics rush to help him. "Are you comfortable?" they ask as they load him into the ambulance. "Ech . . . I make a living."

~

More difficult than those typical immigrant struggles: what to do about the ghosts. They hovered constantly, made their presence felt. Zaida, and those around him, brought so much baggage to Australia, not the kind that fit neatly into suitcases. These weren't just immigrants, like us, searching for opportunity. These were refugees, even if they weren't formally labeled as such by the Australian government. Its plea to "populate or perish" had reshaped Australian immigration policy in the postwar decades, expanding the target pool of migrants to include those from eastern and southern Europe, not only the British Isles and Scandinavia. Still, there was enough latent antisemitism informing the government's approach to its refugee intake that Jews didn't find passage so simple. As refugees, they carried the burden of the past, the stigma of their stories. No one understood their suffering. There was a gap, a chasm really, between survivors and other Australians, including Australian Jews. Even the other European refugees who had suffered war and its consequences couldn't connect to the Jewish experience.

Zaida wore the burden of his past like an iron cloak that weighed heavily on him, suffocated him, and which he could never remove. Moments of joy were few after half a century of bitter struggle and heartache. Only forty-nine when he arrived in Australia, he looked much older, hunched, a skeleton of his former self. When I look at photos of him from the postwar years, I'm struck by his sunken cheeks, the prominence of the cheekbones, the brow constantly furrowed. I can barely imagine him smiling. There's one photo of him in Paris grinning. Or is it Wrocław? Dad used to tell me that Zaida never smiled or laughed. I can understand why.

He lived a life of self-flagellation. If he didn't take a vow that he would suffer maximally for the rest of his life, he might as well have done so. His devotion to suffering, at least as the family describes it, sounds almost Christian to me. Not quite what Catholic studies scholar Robert Orsi describes as "an ethos of suffering," whereby pain serves a spiritual, transcendental purpose, and those who suffer are figures to be admired, emulated. Those who suffer, in this view of the world, have a better understanding than anyone else of the true teachings of Christ, who they believe embodied virtuous suffering.

A version of this came later among Jews, when survivors became virtual celebrities; the worse their suffering the greater moral authority they carried. But in these postwar years, that historic Catholic veneration of suffering, a way to embody and emulate Christ's suffering, was something different. Suffering was not revered but unavoidable, a sign of stigma. The guilt of survival plagued most survivors, and many struggled with the knowledge of what their loved ones had endured during those war years. This guilt was especially sharp for those who escaped Poland early in the war, like Zaida. For all his own suffering, it would never equal that of those he left behind. The scenes of their lives in the Włocławek underground, marching to the trains, crammed onto the carriages and then into the death factory at Chelmno—these are images that existed only in his imagination, but certainly replayed in his head many times a day. Many survivors tried to make the most of the second chance they had been given in life, the families that they could build anew, a posthumous "fuck you" to Hitler. Many got their revenge by living good lives, lives of abundance, reproducing many new Jewish children. Zaida never could adopt that kind of zest for life. He wanted to live, and hoped for a peaceful life with his new family, but had Gitl, Shmulek, Chaimek, and Chasha in his mind every minute of every day.

"The ghosts were with him all the time until his last breath— that's the true story," Gooter told me. He was dispirited, diminished. "About me, you already know," Zaida wrote to Mendel in 1959. "An old, tired Jew, maybe with face too serious, emaciated, on edge. What about my other traits? Industrious, not unlike a horse. Without any great pretensions about human society, but with only one desire: to have enough strength and good health to still take some pride in my precious children." In 1961: "About my nerves: at sixty years old, I can't just shrug them off; they accumulated over many years of suffering, although I do what I can to escape. Maybe I need to go to a mental hospital. But I don't trust doctors, and avoid them as much as I can. I do what I can just to continue in life, a little for me, but mainly for Eda and my beloved children." A mental hospital. His past worn like a straitjacket. Even though he was an old father, run down, his children still provided him some reason to continue to navigate through those ghosts and demons haunting the little sleep he allowed himself.

To try to quiet those torments, he worked to exhaustion. To forget, maybe, to keep his mind occupied. Maybe just so that he could make his body fall asleep and shut out those nightmares. He smoked heavily. He punished his weakened, crumbling bones, his fraying lungs. From the time he escaped Poland in 1940, he worked long days, whatever his job. Whether in Siberia, in Saratow, in Wrocław, or in Paris, work was his refuge from his memories, his pain. In Melbourne, that meant working from 6:30 a.m. until 10:00 or 11:00 p.m. A few hours' sleep, and then back to the grind. Six days a week. Sunday was for the family. Even with two children, together with his wife, he worked unreasonably long hours. For a while it might have been the standard migrant mode of survival, but eventually it was clear that he was punishing himself far beyond what resettlement demanded. He and Bubba lived the lives of refugees, with a decade of war and wandering weighing heavily upon them.

~

"The smallest house on the street, but the biggest heart," the novelist Arnold Zable calls it. He grew up down the road from Sluggo, at 387 Canning Street. He and his brother, Harry, were lifelong friends of Sluggo. Together with Sluggo, they experienced the best and worst life had to offer: the adventure, the heartbreak. They were SKIFistn together, traveled together, protested together, performed in the theatre. And it all began in that small, three-and-a-half-block stretch of North Carlton. Arnold and Harry were among the many hundreds of people that came through the doors of that tiny, iconic cottage between the 1950s and the 1970s.

501 Canning Street: bought for £1,700, with a £400 deposit (around US$800) in the early 1950s. After they arrived in Australia, Bubba and Zaida lived for about a month in housing provided by the Jewish Welfare Society, first for two weeks in Camberwell, far removed from the center of Melbourne's Jews, then for another couple of weeks in a hostel in Carlton. On April 24, 1950, they moved just up the road into Canning Street, where they lived for the next two and a half decades, the longest Zaida lived in any one place. He finally found that peaceful corner of the world.

They hadn't intended to buy it, but circumstances intervened. They were living there with the whole family and the landlord decided to put it up for auction. Knowing that they'd all end up on the street, Zaida went ahead and put down a slice of whatever they had managed to save in their short time working. A happy accident. He was satisfied with the price; with an influx of Italian migrants, housing prices were rising steeply. Within a couple of years, the house was already worth nearly one-third more than what he had paid. The three pounds a week he was repaying must have seemed like very little as the neighborhood changed so rapidly.

501 Canning Street, Photograph by Cara Mand.

What he didn't know then was that the true value of the house couldn't be measured in pounds, shillings, and pence. It was truly priceless. That modest four-room cottage would become one of the liveliest addresses in the neighborhood, the beating heart of that small Bundist enclave as far removed from the major centers of Jewish life as it could be. Maybe I romanticize it too much, maybe Dad did. It's hard to know. But after Bubba Eda died in 2008, and then again after Dad died, one thing that kept coming up was the fond memories people held of 501 Canning Street, its front doors like a comforting hug, the ragtag cast of characters always there on a Friday night, or a Sunday.

~

It was a small Victorian cottage, four rooms, typical of the neighborhood, according to Moshe. Long and narrow. An unassuming facade facing out onto the footpath, none of the ornate Victorian adornments that were so typical. Zaida removed the characteristic cast-iron lacework that adorned the porch, what would now be considered a charming feature. It was a quiet street, its grass median strip dividing the street in two, a makeshift cricket pitch in the sticky Melbourne summers. A place for the bands of immigrant kids to perform their integration into Australian life. As with all those cottages, visitors entered to a long, narrow corridor. To the left, Bubba and Zaida's bedroom, then Sluggo and Miriam's bedrooms, a bathroom. At the end of the long, dark path, the house opened up into a living area with a sofa and an armchair. Behind that, a connected kitchen, where the magic happened. Herring on rye bread, pickles, soup, meat. A house never short of food, the bitter lessons of a decade wandering, no fixed abode. Zaida always held court at the head of the table. He didn't eat a lot, and only drank occasionally, but this was where he was the authority, the boss, the place where he would share a conversation, some words of encouragement or wisdom, maybe a sneaky schnapps or vodka. Past the kitchen, there was a small courtyard where the neighborhood cats would come to be fed by Bubba, and then a small disconnected room with a button machine. Every weekend, Zaida would give his niece and nephews a couple of shillings, wages for pressing buttons. No one knows whether they were buttons that they used, or if it was just a lesson to the children that workers should always be paid fairly for their labor.

They lived there less than most people lived in their homes. Bubba and Zaida were out of the house from six thirty in the morning until late into the evening, usually ten or eleven o'clock. After school, the kids would go to their grandparents', their aunt's, the Kadimah—Melbourne's Yiddish cultural center—piano lessons, or sports practice. For all those times the house was teeming with people, more often it sat empty, unoccupied, except perhaps by the

Family celebration at Canning Street (mid-1960s).

ghosts that had followed the family from Europe. They were the one constant at 501 Canning Street.

In the living room, the sofa seemed to be more a place to keep old newspapers than a place to sit. In the armchair, there was usually one of a motley crew of single men, such as old Jerzyk, never married, no kids, a steady presence ghosting in and out of 501 Canning Street. This band of lonely hearts would filter through the Slucki household looking for some company, some conversation, a meal, a sense of belonging in a world in which single men had no natural home. Everyone was welcome, an open-door policy. Late at night and on Sundays, the house was crowded with recently arrived migrants, many of whom Zaida had sponsored. At these times, family was always there: Dad's grandparents, aunts and uncles, and cousins came to be together on a Sunday, the only day they could all be together, when no one worked. The kids would head off to Yiddish school, come back, head back out to SKIF. The adults would talk about life, the world, the past. They would eat, chat, shout. Just be together. Exactly the thing that helped them endure the bitter Siberian winters, the thing that made sure they made it out of Poland as a family unit. Being together, the only thing they had left after 1940.

And in that house, the tiny little beating heart of a family, of a community. It was a place where all were welcome, where people from all walks of life shared some soup and a *shmues*, a chat. The kids playing in the street, the adults sitting at the table chatting, Zaida moderating, Bubba always making sure everyone was well fed. The television on in the background; the *Jackie Gleason Show* or *World of Sport* playing with the kids huddled around. The Sluckis had the first TV in their circle. Zaida worried it would melt Dad's young mind, and thought he watched too much. But for two hard-working parents, it was one way to try to keep the children occupied while they were out of the house. Bubba and Zaida, the hard-working hosts, taking enormous *naches*, pride and pleasure, in the role they played in building the feeling of community, a sense of home and permanence.

∾

Carlton was the center of immigrant Jewish life in Melbourne, our answer to the Lower East Side of Manhattan, the East End of London, or the Pletzl in Paris. Polish-Jewish life hovered over its broad streets and tiny houses. The smells and sounds of the shtetl cut through its provincial stillness. The kosher butchers, Jewish bookstores, and cultural centers that dotted the landscape are now but a memory, barely even traceable today. It would take a skilled archaeologist to dig up traces of that shtetl.

It is difficult to imagine now. Today, Carlton is a mecca for students at the nearby University of Melbourne, hipsters, yuppies, nouveau riche. The house that Bubba and Zaida sold for $43,000 in 1976 would today fetch close to two million dollars. A cup of coffee from a local Italian restaurant, which might have been a few cents, would now be four or five dollars in a third- (or is it now fourth-) wave café. Local businesses have been replaced by big-box clothing chains, fast-food outlets, and fancy restaurants. Gone are the working-class pubs, the Jewish grocery stores, the mom-and-pop retailers. Lygon Street today resembles any inner urban shopping strip, maybe a little more hip, maybe a touch more ethnic. But certainly not the distinctive immigrant hub that bustled in those uncertain postwar decades. No more edginess about it. Vanilla.

Even when it was a Jewish shtetl, Carlton was not only a Jewish shtetl. It was a series of overlapping shtetls: Italian, Greek, Yugoslavian, working-class Australian. Each group had its own institutions, grocery stores, bookshops, community centers. They operated parallel to one another, but also interacted in the workplace, in the marketplace, and in the street. In addition to his Jewish peers, Dad's friends at school were often recently arrived immigrants from the Mediterranean; others had been in Australia for generations. The migrants were neighbors, all figuring out how to negotiate this new country, with its different climate, its small-town outlook. The Australians tried to navigate the transformation of inner-city Melbourne as a steady stream of immigrants reshaped the landscape around them.

Melbourne, a city that had once been the crown jewel in the British Empire, in the 1950s resembled a large country town. For Jews coming from central European metropolises like Vienna, Warsaw, and Berlin, Melbourne lacked a certain kind of liveliness. A common complaint. Zaida said it was difficult to get too involved in local political life, it lacked "pepper and salt." And for many like Zaida, the Left in Australia was parochial, naïve in the eyes of these European socialists, who had been reared in a much grander tradition. The Australian Labor Party had strong sympathy for and ties to the Soviet Union, anathema to most Bundists.

Still, Carlton was where the Jewish world and the Left intersected. The Kadimah was the center of that world. Founded in 1911 by a small band of Russian-Jewish immigrants, the Kadimah was by the 1950s a dynamic Yiddish space, the first stop for many new migrants. It was their social, cultural, and political space, where they could read a Yiddish newspaper, see a Yiddish play, or hear a lecture from an overseas visitor or a local Labor Party candidate. At the Kadimah, these refugees could feel as though they were being transported back in time and space. There, they found their community.

Dad spent evenings hanging around the Yiddish theatre in the Kadimah's hall, Sundays at SKIF.

The Kadimah was at the north end of Lygon Street; Trades Hall, the headquarters of Australia's union movement, at the bottom; the University of Melbourne, somewhere in the middle. Bookends marking off the space in which Zaida and his compatriots recreated, in their own small way, the atmosphere of the Jewish street in Poland. There weren't the street fights between Jewish parties, or the mass rallies, or the same sense that they were engaged in a life-and-death struggle. Their world was now far too small, but the streets of Carlton did, for a few decades in the middle of the twentieth century, have some of that distinctive character that made refugees like Zaida feel a little more comfortable, settle more easily.

There was never a prohibition against discussing difficult subjects— religion, politics, the past, the future—in the Slucki homes. That very British nod to politeness didn't apply at 501 Canning Street, or any of our subsequent homes. On the contrary, the dining room table has always been exactly the place to wrestle with the state of the world. The Sluckis don't shirk politics or political difference. We are much more continental than that, much fiercer. At the dinner table, we always discussed politics. No matter the company, whatever was in the news that day was fair game. We argued with each other about the state of the Australian Labor Party and the union movement, about the best policies toward refugees, about overseas wars. Sometimes it'd get heated, occasionally we'd shout. Bubba Mania, Mich's mother, herself a refugee, would rail against more welcoming refugee policies; I'd take the bait, charging her with callousness. Sluggo would defend the Australian Labor Party—historic attachments die hard—charging me with naïveté for my support for the Australian Greens, a minor but growing party of the Left. I'd counter that he was too set in his ways, too cynical. And always we reconciled.

This was expected at 501 Canning Street. Shouting was commonplace, politics always at the forefront. Never with a *broygez*, a grudge. Dad used to say he got the equivalent of a political science major sitting up late listening to Zaida and the ragtag band of Bundists that would filter through at the end of a long day. Over a vodka and a slice of herring, they would reminisce, mourn for those lost, and argue about Australian politics and the Cold War. The tenor of those discussions would invariably reach fever pitch, the stakes always high. But it was always good-natured, between friends. Always with an enormous amount of respect. No matter what they thought of the Vietnam War or the Labor Party, they were all part of the same extended family, a bond that was much stronger than ideology. It was a bond that tied them together over time and space and connected them to something much bigger than what was happening in that North Carlton cottage every Friday night.

When most people who remember Zaida talk about him, the thing that comes to mind is his shouting. Not aggressive, but full of passion, that Bundist fire never extinguished. In Bund meetings, he'd stand and hold court. If it was about Australian politics or communism in Europe, Zaida had opinions and never took a backward step. When he talked, he would start calmly. His fiery tone, though, fueled by all that he had suffered in his life, invariably escalated, and before long he was delivering a hot-blooded speech on the topic of the day. In one Bund meeting that Sluggo chaired, he and Zaida got into a shouting match. "Chaver Slucki [Comrade Slucki]," Dad shouted back to Zaida, "we'll talk about this when we get home!" Dad always knew how to take the sting out of a tense situation.

These political debates were never personal. Or maybe, they were deeply personal, a lifetime worth of attachments, orthodoxies, and struggles playing out in this tiny inner-urban living room. Whatever the case, Zaida never stayed angry, and his shouting was, for the most part, a matter of his passion escalating. The Bund had been a broad enough church throughout its history, internal debate the norm. So why not at Canning Street? Everyone agreed on the basics: *mentshlekhkayt* and *derkherets*, humanity and respect. The rest, to misquote Rabbi Hillel, was commentary.

The extended family (ca. 1954).

If there was a golden rule at Canning Street, it was to respect and welcome others, no matter their background or politics. Zaida was known for his shouting, but also for his relentless respect of others. When they first arrived, the family crammed into the house at Canning Street. Bubba, Zaida, and Sluggo, and Bubba's parents and two sisters. Six adults and a child in three bedrooms. It was tight, although they'd probably all lived in closer quarters in their lives. Complicating matters further, Bubba's parents, who probably never learned English in their two and a half decades in Australia, were religious Jews. Like Zaida, they didn't allow their suffering to weaken their beliefs. Bubba's father, Zaida Yitzhak (whom Helen thinks I most resemble), had been a hatmaker in Poland. He continued that trade in Melbourne, manufacturing yarmulkes. Dad used to wear his Zaida's oversized, ill-fitting silk yarmulkes when required. He insisted. Driven by nostalgia, sentimentality. *Derkherets*, respect.

Mendel and Ruchel visiting for Dad's bar mitzvah. Six-year-old Miriam is at the front (1961).

Living together meant compromise. Zaida Yitzhak and Bubba Rukhche required the house be kosher. Separate dishes, no mixing milk and meat. Strictly no *treyf*, no ham sandwiches. Like their childhood home in Poland, as Zaida described it to Mendel, also an avowed atheist. Zaida did all he could to accommodate. When he once might have made a point to eat ham sandwiches on Yom Kippur, now he participated in rituals with the family, saying the prayers at the Passover seder when his turn came, singing *Kol Nidre* to Miriam on Yom Kippur, something he remembered from his childhood. Out of respect for his in-laws, Zaida didn't work on Rosh Hashanah and Yom Kippur, although he and Bubba did work Saturdays; they had to.

When Dad was turning thirteen, the question of his bar mitzvah came up. Zaida wasn't against it in principle. He thought it ought to be small, doing his ceremonial duty in shul, followed by a modest kiddush afterward. Bubba had other ideas: it should be a big celebration, she thought, with hundreds of guests. How many opportunities,

I imagine she argued, had they had in their lives to celebrate a milestone? Neither the first Shmulek nor Chaimek managed to mark this rite of passage. It was not something to downplay. Zaida suggested in the lead-up that he might not go to the shul ceremony, not his style. Of course, he relented. Even if he disagreed with the need for the ritual, out of respect for his family and to support his son, he made that trip to the historic East Melbourne shul along with Mendel and Ruchel, visiting Melbourne for the occasion from Los Angeles, their first of eight trips to Australia.

Zaida was almost legendary within the family for his insistence that everyone was welcome, that their politics or religious practice ought to be honored. "That's how it is now in these times," he wrote to Mendel in 1952. "When I had once truly fought for my principles, I am now more flexible. I don't get hung up on every minor issue, let it be what it will be." After such a turbulent life, all he wanted was a peaceful family life. In the interests of *sholem bays*, peace in the home, he took his role as family patriarch seriously. When it was time for the Passover seder, he would bang his fist on the table to quiet down the room, he'd say the prayers with gusto when his turn came. He didn't shirk his responsibility, even if it was at odds with his politics.

⌀

The only thing missing from this new life was the family that dispersed in the aftermath of the war. Zaida found the settled life he hoped for once he settled in Melbourne, but he feared that he wouldn't see his surviving siblings again. All he had left in 1945 was a brother and a sister, and by the end of that decade, they would each reside on different continents. Although he spent a couple of years in Poland close to his sister Chava, he hadn't seen Mendel since 1931, when Mendel last visited Poland from Paris, where he and Ruchel had immigrated in the late 1920s.

Zaida and Mendel reconnected finally in 1959, when eleven-year-old Shmulek (not yet known by his moniker, Sluggo) and his father took their first plane ride, to Los Angeles via Sydney, Fiji, and Honolulu, a much longer route than what we take between the two continents today. Qantas had been flying between Australia and the United States for only five years at that stage, and air travel was inaccessible to most. The thrill for Dad, I imagine, and the anxiety for Zaida, must have been heightened as they sat on the luxurious, cigarette smoke–filled precursors to the jumbo jets that would come within the next few years. I don't know if Zaida ever imagined that he'd fly on an airplane, and he must have marveled at the distance he could cover in only a few days, particularly after his months-long journeys through the Soviet Union during and after the war, and then from Paris to Melbourne in 1950. He was probably one of the first people in his circles to travel by air, the giant airborne vessel ferrying him to reconnect with family he thought long since lost; a journey with his son, the first in the new generation of the family he had created. A minor miracle. Maybe a major one.

In the middle of 1959, they received news that Henry was engaged to be married, and Mendel and Ruchel wanted Zaida to be there to celebrate. It was a difficult decision to go: financially, Zaida was stable, but he still had debts to pay off. Plus, it was hard to take time off work in the middle of August. Winter in Melbourne, a busy time for a knitter. His biggest hesitation lay in the prospect of traveling on his own, with his limited grasp of English. After nearly nine years in Australia, he hadn't needed to learn to speak fluently; he could get by with a smattering. Maybe it's not so surprising. He worked sixteen hours a day running a small knitting workshop. When was he going to take an English class? His social and political circles were Yiddish-speaking refugees and survivors. He had learned to read, it was a way to keep up-to-date with the society in which he was living. But to his family he spoke Yiddish, to his friends, either Yiddish or Polish.

Because of this inability to communicate, he hesitated. How would he navigate the airport? The flight? Customs and immigration? Taxis? Maybe this was one of the hidden aftereffects of his suffering during the war, his ten years as a homeless, stateless refugee. A very different journey than that of the ship filled with refugees in 1950. Although he spoke at least three languages fluently, he was too timid to travel on his own. Perhaps he remembered all too keenly what had happened the last time he traveled alone, the last time he left his family behind.

Henry's marriage was momentous for the family, an occasion to celebrate, a moment of regeneration, the Slucki family moving beyond the pain and loss that had shaped the previous half century. The first major life cycle event, outside of births, that signaled continuity. And the opportunity to see Mendel for the first time in nearly three decades. Even more momentous: Henry himself was a child survivor. Born in Paris in the 1930s, he escaped to the South of France with his parents after the Nazi invasion and crossed the border into Spain before his parents managed to put him on a ship to New York, not to be reunited for another four years. Henry was smart; he looked like a cardboard cutout of a 1950s Hollywood leading man. He had big pearly white teeth, serious eyebrows, and a sharp side part that he still wears, now into his eighties. Training, at the time, to be a psychologist under the tutelage of the pioneering behaviorist B. F. Skinner, Henry was a role model for Dad, one of only two older cousins to look up to, a young prodigy with a bright future.

Bubba Eda was adamant that Zaida should go. Don't worry about work, she told him, this was far too important. We'll make it work. Leaving the country was not so complicated; they had received Australian citizenship in 1957. The solution to Zaida's hesitation: eleven-year-old Shmulek would come with him, act as his interpreter, his guide. It's common among immigrant families for children to interpret for their parents who haven't yet learned the language of their adopted homes. This was Sluggo's first experience escorting someone on an overseas trip, the first of many.

Not only had Zaida and Mendel been apart for nearly thirty years, they probably hadn't talked much in that time. Telephone access was expensive and difficult to access. And they were all working hard; even finding time to write a letter was often too big a task. They diverged politically—Zaida was a Bundist, staunchly anticommunist, while Mendel remained a true believer in communism—but these weren't intractable differences. Still, when they reunited in 1959, within minutes they were arguing about the merits of the Soviet Union, shouting at each other in the airport pickup area.

Their two weeks together passed quickly, the brothers spending some intense time together, Zaida meeting Mendel's family and friends, getting to know Henry and his new wife, Carole, and getting a taste of the life that Mendel had built in America. The feeling of closeness, the connection, came back quickly for Zaida and infected Sluggo also. Even with the relatives with whom Zaida didn't share a common tongue, that sense of warmth and connection was strong. It filled him with hope that despite being thrust to different ends of the earth, despite his trauma and frayed nerves, Zaida still had a family to which he was bound. Something to which he belonged. I imagine Mendel and Ruchel's house in Boyle Heights, the Jewish immigrant neighborhood of Los Angeles, to have been something like an American version of 501 Canning Street: warm, inviting, a revolving door of family and friends.

Zaida especially appreciated the way that the family bonded with Sluggo, and hoped that it was the beginning of lifelong relationships between Sluggo and his American cousins. He saw Henry and Carole as upstanding role models for Dad; warm, serious young people to emulate. He also saw growth in Sluggo, who matured and took greater responsibility at home after those two weeks away.

When they left, each time they parted after a visit, Zaida was filled with a sense of foreboding, of anxiety that it might be the last time they would be together. They managed to see each other a handful more times before Zaida died in 1978. Zaida visited Los Angeles again, with Bubba Eda this time, and Mendel and Ruchel came several times to Melbourne. There was always a bittersweet feeling: elation that they once again connected, that Zaida's wife and children grew close to his brother's family. But a lingering fear that their parting was the final one. He knew that feeling all too well, having already bid farewell to one family forever. It was one of the constant reminders of the impact of the war, of the challenge of immigrant life. Time with family was precious, fleeting. Although the world was getting smaller and smaller, oceans still divided the siblings. The double-edged of sword of Zaida's resettlement: he had a home to which he could return, with its mundane, day-to-day problems and challenges, yet there remained a distance that reminded him of how remote he was from the life he might have imagined for himself.

∼

We feel that way every time we say good-bye. Leaving Melbourne, seeing off our loved ones at the airport, it always feels weighty. We remind each other that we'll be together again soon, a matter of months often, maybe a year. Yet these days I constantly replay my last good-bye with Dad in New York. I remember it vividly, he wanted to take one last family photo of us before they hopped in a taxi to the airport. We cried. He cried. I can still see Mich's face through the window of the taxi as it pulled away. I had no idea it would be the last time. Now every good-bye seems too weighty. Ominous.

∼

In the year or so after Dad died, we regularly hosted *shabbes* dinners here in Charleston, maybe a couple of times a month. Anywhere between six and fifteen people crammed into our living room, a make-shift setup to accommodate visitors. Nothing fancy: challah, roast chicken, salads, dips. A far cry from the rich spread of artery-clogging Polish-Jewish fare that was the staple of Bubba's cuisine. Many more dietary quirks to accommodate: vegetarian, vegan, gluten-free, dairy-free, paleo. Anyone was welcome, friends and family of the regular guests, those newly arrived to Charleston, Jews and non-Jews. I would make kiddush, the ritual blessings to bring in *shabbes*, and we'd often talk about the finer points of politics, the 2016 election circus, what to do about Jewish life in Charleston, how to take some of that *neshome*, soul, that community we were creating beyond the walls of our apartment. We felt as though we were creating an edgy, even radical Jewish space, inspired by some of the neo-Orthodox and egalitarian communities forming in Brooklyn and Israel.

For me, though, these weekly dinners were a tribute to what had happened half a century earlier at 501 Canning Street. I often thought about Zaida and Bubba and their unassuming little workers' cottage, imagining the doors to both the front door and the refrigerator as some kind of swinging, perpetual motion devices, never shut for long when anyone was home.

I also thought back to the weekly dinners at Bubba's flat in Elsternwick when we were kids, early episodes of *The Simpsons* on the TV, her standard Jewish fare filling the house with the garlicky aromas of small-town southern Poland. I remember the regular flow of visitors sitting in her living room, her sisters, Sala and Hania, a regular presence, if not on the armchair, then yammering away in Polish on the old rotary telephone. One constant in my memory, and among the memories I inherited about my grandparents, was the constant presence of people, all different kinds of people. I think that's the greatest legacy of 501 Canning Street. All are welcome around the dinner table, all who are in search of community can find it in the Slucki home.

Maybe this is a necessity created by immigration. When you're in a new place with no friends, no extended family, you must create it yourself. With the stories of Canning Street floating around, it was perhaps obvious to us, even subconsciously, that the only way to create a life for ourselves was to emulate our immigrant grandparents. In a situation much more difficult than ours, they transformed a run-down, four-room cottage into a de facto immigrant drop-in center. We've tried to reproduce some of that atmosphere. Just like them, we were immigrants trying to build community where we felt we had none. We wanted so much for 55 Ashley Avenue to be full of life, the sounds of laughter, joy, and *yiddishkayt* emanating from the single window in our living room. While Bubba and Zaida sought to rebuild a slice of prewar Jewish Poland, though, we have tried to recreate some of the postwar Carlton that so many people remember so vividly.

6

Coming of Age

I went to my first political rally when I was thirteen years old, or at least, my first without my dad. I'm not sure if he took me to any when I was a kid, but it certainly seems possible. I like to think he did. That breezy autumn day—it seems like it was autumn, I remember wearing my school jumper—was my first taste of real political participation. It was a demonstration against a government plan to hike up university fees. Or something like that. Something that didn't directly affect me yet, and certainly not the reason I skipped school to go march that day in 1997. I do remember the chant that went as though on a loop as we made our way to the steps of Parliament House: "Hey hey, ho ho, uni fees have got to go!" I didn't go because of the issue at hand or the politics of higher education, or even to be part of something bigger. I was in year eight; I hadn't even thought about university. I was more concerned about how to get a girlfriend, how to get a kick at my weekend football match, and if I would get into the selective Melbourne High School the next year. I went, more than anything, to impress the year nine kids I'd recently befriended in the school musical. It seemed a cool thing to do, and certainly bought me some street cred. I went because of my dad, and his stories of marches in the 1960s, and teacher strikes in the 1970s and 1980s. I don't know, then, if I was trying to fulfill that legacy, or if it was just that I found Dad's stories exhilarating, intoxicating. I wanted that kind of excitement, the kind of danger that saw Dad nearly get kicked in the head by a police horse.

For both of us, I think, our political commitments can be traced to those early years of the twentieth century, when Zaida found his own calling. We wanted to carry on his commitments to the Bund, to a grand history of democratic socialist thought; we wanted to feel part of something that stretched back in time, particularly in the absence of a Jewishness premised on adherence to religious practices and texts. But more than that, it was the legacy of the Holocaust that pushed us toward those moral and political allegiances. Sluggo and I both framed our worldviews as responses to the suffering of Jews during World War II, recognizing as we did the suffering of others on that basis. The injustices and the brutality carried out against our own families were things we saw going on in the world around us. Even more than that, the guilt we felt at the relative ease with which we moved through life conferred on us a responsibility to speak out against injustice. Our response to our own survivor guilt, transmitted through the generations, was to grab a plaque and march in the streets, to write letters to newspapers, and to never shy away from the struggle for what is right.

I think.

The impact of the Holocaust didn't only manifest in the ways we thought about the past, or how we related to family, or in certain kinds of behaviors. For us, the lessons of the Holocaust were ever-present, readily apparent, and crucial in shaping us. As we grew into our mid- to late-teen years, seeking validation from our fathers, as we sought to assuage the nagging sense of shame that we had it easy (at least in contrast to earlier generations), we channeled much of that angst into political activism. In our teen years, the twin legacies of the Bund and the Holocaust became deeply intertwined for us, the figure of Zaida so present—literally for Dad, as a ghost for me. The time was ripe: we both saw echoes of Nazism, fascism, and oppression all around us, in Australia and abroad. We felt a responsibility to struggle against any potential repetition of the past. It was a way not only to connect to our fathers but also to try right the wrongs of the past.

∼

Probably every generation has its war, conflict, or incident that defines it. Certainly, that's true in the twentieth century: World Wars I and II, the Korean War, the Vietnam War, the Gulf War, the threat of nuclear attack, the assassination of President Kennedy, the dismissal of Gough Whitlam in Australia, Thatcherism in England. Maybe everyone lives through their own turning point, although I'm not sure that there are necessarily such things; every period is a turning point in a way. But I suspect everyone can identify some historical moment that marked their loss of innocence, that inaugurated them into the realities of the big bad world and helped set them on a certain pathway. The defining event in Sluggo's coming-of-age, both personally and politically, was the Vietnam War, which corresponded roughly with his own adolescence.

Dad reached adulthood in the late 1960s, amidst a generation rebelling against their parents' conservative, old-fashioned mores. This revolution in morality, style, sexuality, and political engagement shaped him deeply. From his parents' home and its re-creation of a Jewish socialist environment in interwar Poland to inner-city Melbourne with its assortment of immigrants and refugees from Europe, to the recently built Monash University, where the New Left dominated student life, Sluggo was surrounded by the momentum of a changing world and by a growing consciousness of the destruction of Europe's Jews. He grew up in the belly of a political movement still claiming its relevance, its leaders proclaiming loudly the need for socialist upheaval, his childhood home a center of the political life of the Melbourne Bund. Growing up listening to late-night arguments and debates in his own living room had an enormous effect on his worldview and pushed him into political engagement from a very early age. When he was later part of the New Left movement at Monash University, he found a voice and medium to animate the ideas that had been implanted in his consciousness from such an early age.

When Dad was still a teenager, he let his hair grow out. It wasn't so long yet, just long enough to tuck behind his ears; not the flowing

Long-haired Sluggo hitchhiking in Switzerland (1972).

locks that would come only a few short years later. Long hair, the icon of a generation of young men branching out, antagonizing their parents. Hair was their own Freudian rebellion, a symbol of growth, a contrast to the tightly styled, short-cropped hair of their fathers. A small way that they could show they were taking control of their own lives. Boys becoming men, but imagining themselves as very different kinds of men. Even Sluggo's modest locks were too much for Zaida. Dad's hair was the source of a great deal of tension in their house, something Zaida shouted at Dad about often. I'm not sure why Zaida was so angry about the hair, or about Dad's appearance. I know that he wanted him to be *an ernste mentsh*, an earnest person, devoted to family, community, and the Bund. And it's clear that the hair somehow symbolized a transgression against these wishes.

Hair was probably only a symbol, though, of the generational conflict and change that was taking place, both in Australia and at 501 Canning Street, North Carlton. And the generational conflict was a source of great concern for Zaida. He worried a lot about Sluggo from his teenage years on. Sluggo did well enough at school, but what would his career be? Would he be able to settle down, get married, find a Jewish girl, an *eygene*, one of our own? Nothing unusual there, same concerns as many other parents. But he did worry that Sluggo lacked direction, that he wandered, got in with bad crowds, didn't focus enough at university, didn't fulfill his potential. Zaida was serious, he didn't mince words. Sluggo and he talked about his prospects for the future, his seeming lack of prospects. Sluggo reassured him that was just how things were in his generation, nothing to worry about. His wasn't a full-blown rebellion. He didn't want to upset Zaida, or create a *broygez*, a grudge. That was never his way. He had too much respect for his father.

Still, these were heady days for my dad, full of excitement, a tinge of danger, and a healthy dose of generational rebellion. This New Left that he joined was a departure from the planetary orbit that Zaida inhabited. It saw itself as distinct from the old Left and its attachment to outdated *-isms*. It was part of a global movement overhauling the strictures of the 1950s, with the Cold War constantly in the background. It was a coalition of socialist, antiracist, feminist, anticolonial movements and organizations. Its loose collection of groups fought for the rights of peoples of color, for sexual revolution and women's rights, for the rights of LGBT people, and perhaps most importantly for Sluggo, for the end of colonial wars and occupation, such as the war in Vietnam.

Australia, led by the country's longest-serving prime minister, Robert Menzies, stumbled into Vietnam in the early 1960s. By mid-1965, concerned about the threat of the spread of communism in the region and its relations with the increasingly powerful United States, the government had formally committed to sending troops to fight the North Vietnamese National Liberation Front, the Vietcong. Its commitment lasted until the Labor government of Prime Minister Gough Whitlam, the first Labor government elected in over two decades, announced the final withdrawal of Australian troops in 1972.

Sluggo joined the growing opposition to the Vietnam War, for personal, political, and probably social reasons. As a young socialist, he was influenced by the increasingly radical Left on his campus at Monash University, perhaps the center of Australian student radicalism at that time. Along with his peers in SKIF and beyond, he supported the North Vietnamese against the American and Australian forces. Like so many in his sphere, he saw the war as an imperial war by the United States, in which Australia had no clear rationale to be involved. Although the Vietcong didn't bathe themselves in glory, Dad argued that they were fighting against an unjust invasion by imperial forces. Dad went to the Vietnam moratorium marches through the center of Melbourne, joining hundreds of thousands of young Australians in protest against Australia's involvement in what they saw as an unjust American invasion. He described the demonstrations as being full of vigor, anger, and community. Most thrilling was the sense of danger, the stories of protestors and police as adversaries. One day, at a demonstration, he was nearly trampled by a police horse, saved by a policeman who literally dragged him away from the horse's hoof by his ponytail. Lucky he had long hair.

More pertinent was what was at stake for Sluggo personally. In 1964, fearful that they lacked the manpower required to fulfill their multiple commitments in the Pacific and Southeast Asia, the Australian government introduced a lottery system and ramped up its conscription efforts. It was not only a way to ensure greater preparedness for battle in Vietnam, but that was certainly a major factor.

VIETNAM 1975-95

THE AGE SATURDAY 29 APRIL 1995

On 18 September 1970, TONY MASKELL was a 21 year old house photographer at Melbourne's Southern Cross Hotel when, on the spur of the moment, he decided to photograph this anti-Vietnam war demonstration. The photographs spent the next 25 years in a cardboard box until today, when they are published for the first time.

Newspaper report of a Vietnam moratorium march. Sluggo is the figure that pops out in the middle with long hair, a beard, and sunglasses (1970, the photo appeared in a Melbourne newspaper in 1995).

The "birthday ballot" would compel all twenty-year-old men whose birthdays were called up to report for two years' service, which would likely include an overseas posting.

Dad's birthdate was called. It must have been in March 1968, around the time Dad turned twenty, according to the Australian War Memorial's encyclopedia. When Dad received the dubious honor of winning that lottery, the whole family was devastated. Bubba Eda cried. I imagine Zaida was stoic, but probably panicked inside. He had already seen two sons killed in a war; he would not lose another. Immediately they hatched a plan. There was little chance he would be granted an exemption as a pacifist—it was a notoriously difficult sell. There was no religious exemption for him, so he had one option: to be physically unfit for service. This was not so simple: he was young, active, and despite a childhood neck issue, he was a model of good health. He played football, cricket, and volleyball, and had competed locally as a runner (unsuccessfully). In other words, he was exactly what the government was looking for in its effort to bolster its counterinsurgency forces.

In the weeks leading up to him being called up for his medical examination, his parents starved him, trying to ensure he wouldn't fulfill the height, weight, and general health requirements that the army demanded. In this period, he lost a lot of weight and was often sick with fever, tired, and weak. I imagine it must have been extremely difficult for Zaida and Bubba to watch. After years of starvation and near-death experiences themselves, to be faced with this choice, to forcibly starve their own son to save his life, to save him from what might await in the jungles of Vietnam and beyond. They didn't want him to have the nightmares that they had, to experience war and its consequences as they had.

He managed to avoid being drafted. Not everyone was so lucky. He used to tell us about his friends Henry and Leon, twin brothers, neighbors and friends throughout his childhood. They had been drafted into National Service, although managed to complete their service at home. Still, they were deeply shaped by the experience. The story of evading the draft was a centerpiece in Sluggo's storytelling repertoire, I think because it underscored his rebellious nature—he would go to any length to oppose an unjust war.

An aside: this is how I remember Dad telling the story. Jacob doesn't remember it, and no one in the family seems to remember how or why he was able to evade the draft. I do have the letter stating that Sluggo did not meet the physical requirements to go fight, but it doesn't provide any detail. Maybe I'm misremembering, a hopeful story, or folding other versions of that story into Sluggo's.

Sluggo's position, and that of the SKIF *helfer*, was at odds with the Bund's leaders, many of whom were staunchly anticommunist. Theirs was an anticommunism born from their firsthand encounters with Soviet Russia—many had been deportees sent to labor camps in Siberia during World War II. Others had experienced Soviet repression firsthand as the Soviet Union exerted its influence throughout Eastern Europe from the 1920s onward. The movement as a whole took a hard anti-Soviet line after the most beloved and charismatic leaders of the Polish Bund, Henryk Erlich and Viktor Alter, were murdered by the Soviet secret service, the NKVD, in a Russian prison in 1941. The Bund leaders in Melbourne therefore welcomed Australia's commitment to containing communism and preventing its spread in their own backyard. This contrasted with the American Bund leadership, many of whom had survived in the United States, who condemned the war as a colonial incursion by their government. This was a complicated consequence of World War II for Bundists like my Zaida: Polish Jews who were ostensibly "rescued" by Stalin, yet whose moral compass led them definitively away from communism, who abhorred totalitarianism. It was also difficult for Dad and his peers, still teenagers and young adults, trying to make sense of the responsibilities conferred on them in the Holocaust's aftermath, still learning to navigate the strange ironies of history.

Dad's opposition to the war marked a generational shift in the Bund movement, and was typical of the generational conflict at the time. The political Left to which he was attached was shifting away from the orthodoxies of his parents and their comrades. Their animus toward communism wasn't as sharp, having not seen its excesses firsthand, and they saw themselves trying to overthrow the order their parents had created, the order that had led to wars in Vietnam and Algeria, lynchings in the American South, and the ongoing exploitation of the industrial working class at home. The concerns of Dad and his friends—sexism, racism, colonialism—were very different than the Bund's traditional concerns, centered around class, even if they weren't completely disconnected.

The Vietnam War was an important coming-of-age moment for Dad, when he found his own voice, when he left the comfort of his family home and joined a movement much bigger than he could have imagined. It was an era of expectation, the possibility for change, change for the better. A time when young people filled the streets, when booze and pot flowed freely at parties, when the possibilities for sex and dating opened up for a generation of baby boomers, raised in exhausted postwar homes and communities that were still reestablishing themselves. And all these stories were energizing to us, a generation raised in the 1990s, when the Cold War collapsed and we thought we'd won. Dad was a regular visitor to SKIF camp, enlisted by the *helfer* to talk about his youthful activism. He was a captivating storyteller, and with his signature cheeky grin, he knew how to draw in his teenage audience. He could often embellish the details. "Don't ruin a good story with the truth," he'd joke to us when we occasionally called him out on some fact and memory that sounded more fantastical with each retelling. He was the perfect guest for camp, though; he'd come talk to a group of teenagers about marching against the war, about traveling between West and East Berlin, about campaigning for George McGovern while living in New York City. He'd always leave his audience wanting more. I remember as a SKIFist and as a *helfer* beaming with pride, basking in the reflected glow from how cool my dad was, and knowing I was lucky to get to see my dad midcamp, a rare treat. He could talk to anyone, including teenagers, and leave them enraptured. The perfect guest.

Sluggo's excitement filtered down to me. I wanted to be part of that change. Out with the old, in with the new. I don't know if I really understood the old or knew what the new should be, or that those things that Sluggo described actually helped overturn the old order. But hearing those stories made me want to be a socialist, an activist; to be a part of something, to feel like I could play my role in fixing the broken world.

~

If he was part of a generation rebelling against its parents, though, Sluggo's was an ambivalent rebellion. To be sure, he and his father had different takes on the world and how to fix it. Unlike Sluggo, Zaida continued to be a more orthodox Marxist, reared in a socialist movement that still saw hope in the promise of revolution, that still saw society as progressing toward something better, even when there were setbacks. He was anticommunist, like most Bundists since the 1920s and 1930s, seeing communism simply as a totalitarian

Sluggo marching with the Bund in New York City. Holding the banner with him is Melbourne's Bund icon Bono Wiener (1972).

departure from the kind of democratic society he and his generation of Jewish socialists imagined. He probably saw the New Left, like many of his comrades, as a dangerous road leading back to Stalin. Remarkably, though, despite what he had endured, Zaida somehow remained an idealist. There is no other way to explain his continued adherence to the Bund and its values. He refused to despair, refused the lure of a nihilistic ambivalence to the world around him. This is one of the more miraculous stories of Holocaust survival—that despite what they had suffered, many survivors could still retain some kind of hope in the promise that the future could be brighter, had to be brighter, and that building that future was in the hands of ordinary people. I suppose they figured it couldn't get any worse than what they'd already seen up close.

This idealism infected Sluggo. Despite his own instinct to rebel against his father, Sluggo loved and respected Zaida too much for that, and instead saw in him a role model. "He was an elder statesman" of the Bund in Melbourne, he'd tell me, mediating conflicts between various individuals and factions within the community. He was a kind of one-man Beth Din, a secular rabbi or judge ruling on the delicate matters that could tear a movement apart. If there was inner strife on the Bund committee, they'd gather at nine or ten o'clock at night at the Slucki house on Canning Street, and Zaida would arbitrate the conflict over vodka, cigarettes, and herring on rye bread. Although he was on the left of the organization, he had the ability to bring warring factions together and cut through the bullshit. When Zaida talked, or rather shouted, people listened. He brought with him a worldliness, the weight of his suffering, which brought with it a kind of gravitas. He was a generation older than many of his peers, who were born in the 1920s and 1930s. Therefore, not only had he endured the Holocaust but he brought the experience of the whole twentieth century with him: breaking out of a premodern Jewish home in Czarist-dominated Poland; suffering under German occupation during World War I and the violence and famine that accompanied it; participating in the Polish-Soviet War, as a soldier in the Polish army; and experiencing the teething problems of a new world order, the rise of totalitarianism, and the march toward global conflict in the 1920s and 1930s. He endured Europe's latest thirty years' war as an adult, which brought with it a certain soberness, world-weariness, exhaustion.

In the year after Bubba Eda died in 2008, Dad grew his hair long again, the longest it had been since he was in his midtwenties. The Slucki men are lucky like that: while many of our friends began to lose their hair in their midtwenties, we've always boasted thick, dark hair. At various times in his life, Dad had had long, curly locks, with a little bit of a wave as they draped down his neck. The pictures of him as a young hippie with a scruffy mane and long beard are etched into my memory, glimpses in old photo albums at Bubba's house, in Mich's scrapbooks. So there was something familiar when, at the tender age of sixty, Dad's locks flowed again. Not the jet black of before; now a more distinguished gray streaked through, almost silver, like a shiny new car. I was never sure why this was his response to his mother's death, and he could never really explain it. Within a year, though, his old inner hippie came to the surface, as his graying locks reached down toward his back, mostly straight, with a little curl at the bottom that bounced up as his mane rested on his shoulders, like a burden he was symbolically carrying as the realization became starker that he was an orphan, as Dad insisted he was when his mother followed his father to another world.

When does one stop being an orphan? Are you an orphan when you're sixty? Is there an age limit to orphanhood? Can adults fit into that category? Was Zaida an orphan in 1918, when, at seventeen, his mother followed his father to a tragic death? Whatever the case, Dad claimed after Bubba's death that he was now an orphan. I wasn't sure why claiming that identity seemed to carry particular weight. It seemed to make things feel more depressing; maybe this was the point, to suffer maximally in difficult times.

I'm certain that growing his hair was some response to this new situation. A throwback to an earlier time when he had both his parents? Some kind of rebellion to the situation, in a way that he had done rebellion since he was a teenager? Change for the sake of change? I really had no idea, and he had no answer, even when I tried to psychoanalyze him (clearly it's a rebellion against your father!). When I told him I thought he needed a haircut, at least to look neat for his business, he insisted he didn't need to. "You look like an aging hippy," I would tell him ungenerously, but he didn't care about those things. When he got ready in the morning, he'd come out with his hair combed back tight and a forest of curls wrapping his short neck. It became part of his charm, his persona, his quirkiness, one of those many idiosyncrasies that endeared him to people so much. He marched to the beat of his own drum. If he wanted long hair, for whatever reason he did, no one would stop him. Even Mich liked it, defending him against my ridicule and that of Jacob and Helen. He cut it after a while, but not before he'd made his point, whatever that was.

In 2016, after Dad left us, I grew my hair long, inexplicably. It took some months, and it was a conscious decision, although, like Sluggo, I couldn't explain why. Arthur grew his hair long, too, his hazel-green eyes covered by the straight brown bob, a latter-day Paul McCartney. Jacob grew his beard out, thick like Dad's. He looked like Dad, circa 1985. Or like a rabbi. It seems that for Slucki men, the way we process our grief is by letting our hair grow out. Maybe we had internalized and elaborated on the shiva customs dictating that, for the first thirty days after the burial, mourners are not allowed to shave or cut their hair. We don't do things by halves. Maybe it was the sense that a massive change in our lives required more drastic change, symbolic or real. Or maybe, for me and Jacob, it was some way to identify with Dad and the way we best remembered him: me yearning for a time in our lives when Dad and I had become close friends, Jacob for a time when bushy-bearded Sluggo was our protector. A kind of nostalgia, a way to embody what we have lost, to ensure he stays alive in us somehow. I really don't know the symbolic importance of hair in our family, and why our response to tragedy has been to let it grow. Is it too lazy a metaphor to draw on the biblical story of Samson, who derived strength from his lustrous hair? Was growing our hair some way to reclaim some of that strength that we'd lost through the loss of our father, from whom we'd derived so much inner strength and self-belief? I'm probably reading too much into it. That's what I'm trained to do. Maybe we all just grew it out of laziness.

I was fascinated by the 1960s and early 1970s, by my dad's adventure-filled coming-of-age stories. I felt I was living in the wrong era. I listened to Dad's old rock-and-roll records: Bob Dylan, Eric Burdon, Eric Clapton. I loved depictions of the 1960s in film—I imagined Forrest Gump to be an accurate representation of Sluggo's milieu, the closest I could come to imagining what it was really like. I consumed Cold War thrillers: James Bond movies; *Good Morning, Vietnam*; *JFK*. I listened to The Beatles and read Malcolm X's autobiography and Che Guevara's diaries. I had a Muhammad Ali poster and a Cuban flag hanging in my room. Sluggo's influence on me was palpable. He grew up in the excitement of a changing world, when anything seemed possible, when young people seemed empowered to overhaul the stale old politics that led only to the promise of mutually assured destruction. At least, that's how he described it, and I was hooked.

While Sluggo's defining event was the Vietnam War, the parallel for me and my generation in turn-of-the-century Australia was the Al-Qaeda attack on the World Trade Center in Lower Manhattan on September 11, 2001, and the accompanying invasion of Iraq in 2003, led by the United States. That will probably be that event I tell Arthur about when he's older—where I was, how I remember it, how it shaped me. Just as Sluggo used to tell me about how he remembered the assassination of President Kennedy in 1963, or how he swerved his car off the road after hearing on the radio that Australian prime minister Gough Whitlam had been dismissed by the governor general in 1975.

When the Twin Towers came down that morning in New York City, it was still Monday evening in Melbourne. I was in year twelve, starting to prepare for my final exams, already having decided what I wanted to study at university the following year: creative arts at the University of Melbourne. I put arts/law as my first preference, just what was expected of the Melbourne High School "elite." Really, though, after a stint playing Jesus in the school's production of *Jesus Christ Superstar*, and having aced my theatre studies performance exam, I knew that I was going to be an actor. And I knew that I wanted to go to the University of Melbourne, that glorious sandstone campus in the center of Carlton, my father's old stomping ground. Not where he studied, but where he smoked pot with his childhood friends in the Arts Building on Grattan Street and got an inside look into the emerging youth culture while he was still in high school. Something pulled me toward the historical allure of Melbourne Uni. I was certain I didn't want to go to the suburban, modernist Monash University, where Dad had thrown himself into leftist politics. Too ugly, too far away from the action, even if it was closer to home. Still, I was following in his footsteps broadly, planning for a career in the performing arts. Some rebel.

That Monday night in Melbourne, as we were driving home from the theatre at Mount Scopus Memorial College (Melbourne's biggest Jewish day school, where Sluggo was director of performing arts), the radio reports began filtering through that a plane had struck one of the towers of the World Trade Center. It looked like an accident, they reported, as we drove home through the quiet streets of Melbourne, most people not knowing yet what they were going to wake up to. It was still close to a decade before people were able to read the news in real time on their cell phones, so if they didn't have the TV or radio on, they didn't know what was going on in the world. As soon as I got home, I turned on the little TV in my room, one I had inherited from Jacob when he got something just a little more modern to play the prehistoric Nintendo. It was about twelve inches wide, probably no bigger than an iPad, with an old clothes hanger stuck in the back of it, held in position by scotch tape. I mostly watched late-night talk shows on that beat-up old box, beamed in a day late from New York City and Los Angeles. It's how I became so familiar with Jay Leno, David Letterman, Conan O'Brien, and Craig Ferguson. The picture was grainy. It usually was. I could never get the improvised antenna in quite the right position; I must have used up rolls of tape trying to get it just perfect. Still, the smoke billowing from that first tower was clear enough when I switched it on, and there was no mistaking what happened minutes after I tuned in when another plane careened into the second tower. Less than an hour later, alone in my bedroom, with the lights off, having hoped to go to sleep, I watched the towers both collapse. It was utterly unbelievable, beyond even my vivid imagination. Two of the tallest buildings in the world, etched into the iconic landscape of Lower Manhattan, iconic even ten thousand miles away, now crumbling on my miniature TV screen. By then it was clear that this was no accident, even though immediately after the second plane hit commentators were still hoping that it was.

The next morning there was no chance of class. Even though we were getting close to finishing our school careers and in the midst of the grind of exam preparation, the TVs in every classroom were switched on, the free-to-air networks competing with their across-the-board coverage of the events transpiring in New York. Commentators, news anchors, experts, and TV personalities were all trying to make sense of what we were all witnessing in real time. I don't remember talking about it with my friends, or even if we did talk about it. I do remember us all being transfixed to the TV, to the pictures in front of our eyes of burning rubble, of smoke and ash floating through the air, engulfing Manhattan. It was something we could only have imagined in an apocalyptic film, totally unreal. Dad had just been there weeks earlier with students; they went to the observation deck that was now reduced to debris, a street-level observation deck, where one could now be witness only to the carnage of the American dream.

What a bizarre thing, to watch these events unfold live, to do so from the comfort of your own cozy suburban bedroom, or in the classrooms in which you learned about Camus and French existentialism, Marxism and the Russian Revolution, Sophocles and Greek tragedy. In those rooms we'd learned about the Declaration of the Rights of Man, how to read texts like that critically, how states are formed, and how political movements operate. In real time, the raw footage felt like an attack on those very ideas. Perhaps I couldn't articulate it then, but I think I felt the sense that the civilization (whatever that meant) with which I identified and in which I felt invested was now under attack. I was under attack. By whom? I didn't know, and once we all found out, it would certainly be a test of our ideas about the world, the potential goodness of the world.

I look back on my seventeen-year-old self with a certain wistfulness, and a kind of cynicism. Did I really believe in the promise of the Enlightenment, in *Liberté, égalité, fraternité*? In the progress of history and humanity? Was I that naïve to think that such a thing still existed in the wake of the Holocaust? That this attack on 9/11 wasn't simply the logical outcome of the West's march to rule the world, casting aside the hopes and aspirations of those peoples it had dominated for hundreds of years? I had yet to read Arendt, Fanon, Beauvoir, Foucault, and the many other philosophers and thinkers who would teach me to throw those truisms aside, that they were built on the backs of slaves and on the pillaging of others. All I had then was a kind of teenage socialism, tinged with some cynical existentialist thought I had picked up from my English and French teachers, and topped with angst about the world born from the Holocaust stories with which I had grown up. Still, in hindsight, 9/11 was a critical juncture in shifting from my juvenile attachments to ideologies past, to a more critical self-evaluation I would begin only months later when I started my bachelor of arts at the University of Melbourne.

It's strange how quickly these kinds of moments become history, how rapidly something that shapes one generation is merely a relic for another: for me, seventeen years old, still living at home, going to high school, working my part-time job in a local cinema, the attack on the World Trade Center was not only shocking but formative. It was the moment for which you always remember where you were and how it affected you; a moment that forces you to reflect on who you are and where you fit in the world. I had never even been to the United States. And although it was thousands of miles away, although I was keenly aware that war and conflict were a normal part of the day-to-day experience for people in many parts of the world, something about this felt much closer to home than all those other conflicts I learned about at SKIF and in my politics class at school. I was shaken out of my naïveté, forced to reconsider my cocksure, juvenile orthodoxies and to try to work out what this meant for the world moving forward. I wasn't alone here—probably most of my peers were in the same position, getting some small taste of what subjugated peoples around the world experienced daily. Being on the cusp of adulthood, though, meant that we incorporated those events into our lives in a way that those older than I, already more set and confident in their worldview, might not, and in a way that those who were younger might have found more difficult to process.

By the time I moved to the United States in 2013 to teach classes in Jewish history, the Holocaust, and the fraught relationship between memory and history, my students were increasingly distant from the event. For them, it was already ancient history, like the Vietnam War for me, or even the Cold War, which exists only in the broad brushstrokes of my consciousness. The images of 9/11 were burned into their consciousness inevitably, the annual remembrance rituals a part of their upbringing. But the event itself was so remote that its significance barely registered as something that had shaped the world in which they'd been raised.

For me, though, the aftermath of the attacks on 9/11 pushed me into political activism in a more serious way. Although I didn't join the political parties at university, I was still involved with SKIF, and I looked down my nose at campus socialists. I was too smug and self-righteous: I was born into a socialist family, it was in my DNA, it was my birthright. Besides, I knew about suffering—I was the grandson of Holocaust survivors. What did they have to teach me, right? I wore that status like a badge of honor, derived a certain kind of cachet from it, basked in the reflected glow of my family's hardships, even having experienced nothing comparable myself.

To be seventeen again. To be so certain.

The months and years after 9/11 brought a whole range of issues to the fore in Australia: our participation in the wars in Afghanistan and then Iraq; the callous approach by the Australian government toward refugees and asylum seekers, many of whom were coming from war-torn countries like Sudan and Afghanistan; a marked and visible increase in Islamophobia; the attack by the conservative government on Australia's social democratic foundations; the reemergence in the United States and Australia of the surveillance state, justified by the so-called war on terror. It was a time of experimentation for me, politically. I joined the Fabian society; read Rousseau, Marx, Sartre, and Butler; and voted for the Australian Labor Party and then the Australian Greens as I shifted leftward. And always with the lessons of the past at the forefront of my mind, always trying to prevent another Holocaust.

Everything came to a head in 2003, when Australia joined the United States–led "coalition of the willing" in its invasion of Iraq. Elected in 1996, Prime Minister John Howard's conservative coalition government had, after over a decade of Labor rule, shifted the political landscape in Australia to the right. This was accompanied by the rise of the Queensland-based, far-right party One Nation, Australia's answer to the white supremacist movements of the United States, or the British National Party in the United Kingdom, or the *Front National* in France. This was all part of a reaction in the 1990s against the consolidation of multiculturalism, against increased recognition of Australia's historic and ongoing dispossession of its Indigenous peoples, and against a Labor government that sought to bring Australia into the globalizing economy. After more than a decade in power, which coincided with my first decade on earth, the Australian Labor Party was undergoing a period of soul-searching. My family had been loyal supporters since their arrival in 1950, and we were alarmed when our party had no answers to the conservative Liberal Party's populist, nativist rhetoric. In 2003, nearly eighteen months after having committed troops to support the US war in Afghanistan, Prime Minister Howard sought to bolster Australia's ties to the United States by providing one of the larger contributions of military personnel and resources to the "coalition of the willing." The justification ran along the same lines as that of British prime minister Tony Blair: Saddam Hussein had been secretly building an arsenal of weapons of mass destruction, which was a threat to the free world. Under Labor prime minster Kevin Rudd, Australia began to scale back its commitment in 2008.

The war was hugely unpopular, with polls showing less than one-quarter of Australians supporting Australia's involvement. Nonetheless, Prime Minister Howard pressed on with his commitment in the face of public opinion. When Australia enthusiastically declared not only its support for the US actions in Iraq but its willingness to send troops, I joined the hundreds of thousands of Australians,

young and old, in the streets of Melbourne to protest what was an
unjust and illogical war. It was a no-brainer, certainly not the first
issue for which I took to the streets. I had, by then, completed a year
of university, with middling results. I was a *helfer* at SKIF, taking a
particular interest in shaping the political program of the movement,
in making sure it was more than just a social group. We *helfer* knew
that the organization would oppose the Iraq War, even if that sentiment wasn't quite as clear in the Bund organization to which we
answered. Opposing the Iraq War was a part of my maturing political consciousness, seeing in the war only the continuation of centuries of Western colonial domination. A coalition of white countries
intervening in the Middle East with only oil on their mind. It was
clear, particularly in the echo chamber in which I moved about, that
there was no foundation for the war, no real evidence that Saddam
Hussein possessed weapons of mass destruction. And on the larger
scale, we argued, he was a small-time crook compared to some of our
so-called allies, whose human rights abuses didn't seem to bother us
quite so much.

There was perhaps an even deeper reason for my increased interest in political activism at that time. Not only was I convinced
that there was no foundation for the war, I also saw myself walking
in Sluggo's footsteps along the road that he paved for me. Having
heard the stories of the Vietnam moratorium marches and his narrow escape from being sent to combat, this was the closest I could
get—at least, the closest I wanted to get—to his close brush with
danger, to the people power that so energized him decades earlier.
Even though my own politics moved to the left of his, just as he
had distanced himself from his father, I still wanted validation from
him, wanted him to be proud that I was his mini-me, that I was
continuing the tradition laid down by his father and carried on by
him, even if we were not always on the same page, sometimes not
even in the same book.

The major rally against the Iraq War on February 15, 2003, was
electrifying, the biggest demonstration in Australia's history. Bigger
than the Vietnam marches. It was probably sunny and warm, late in

the summer. I don't think we got rained on. I took the day off work, or I had the day off. I can't remember. (Damn it, when Sluggo told me those stories he knew the details so well. Did he really remember it all?) Let's say I took the day off—it makes me sound more audacious. People of all stripes and backgrounds marching through the streets of central Melbourne, waving banners, chanting, all in protest against a senseless war. We joined others on the left—university students, workers, young professionals, families, veterans of the New Left, veterans of the old Left. Iraq was our Vietnam, our May 1968. People power: the feeling that the government could not ignore the masses of people flooding the streets of Melbourne and then all the major cities of Australia. What's more, we joined millions around the world also marching. We felt like we could change the world, that through strength in numbers we could send a message loud enough to the world powers that this wasn't a war worth fighting.

At least, that's what I think we would have felt. To be honest, though, I can barely remember it, not specifically, at least. I went to many demonstrations from my teenage years through to my mid- to late-twenties—as a SKIFist and a *helfer* at SKIF, and with my colleagues and friends at university. Thinking back now, they all blend into one another. Signs, chants, diverse groups of (mainly) young people. Lots of dreadlocks, Thai fisherman pants. Some variation of the same route through the center of Melbourne, usually congregating at the imposing State Library of Victoria, with its manicured lawns and stately columns, punctuated by flashes of postmodern art and architecture. The themes changed—antiwar, pro-refugee, women's rights, LGBTQ rights, climate change—but the people stayed pretty much the same. And we always went home satisfied that we'd played our part, me feeling as though I was playing out the next chapter of the great epic of Slucki participation in the great political movements of the twentieth century. From Warsaw, to Włocławek, to Wrocław, to Melbourne (damn, couldn't quite get the alliteration in). The latest iteration of, to quote the Doobie Brothers, "Taking It to the Streets." I was fulfilling my duties, walking in the shoes of previous generations of Sluckis.

A small irony: one consequence of Australia's participation in the "coalition of the willing" was that the Bush administration created a specialist visa class for Australians seeking work in the United States. The conditions of the visa were more favorable than those of the regular work visas for temporary workers. President Bush's thank-you gift to Prime Minister Howard. That was the visa we received when we moved to Charleston. Everyone has their price, I suppose.

A lot of this changed as I continued my studies. Once I read more philosophy, sociology, and especially history, I started to think differently about the relationship between past and present. Rather than seeing events like 9/11 or the Iraq War as turning points in history or disruptions, I began to realize that they were part of a larger historic continuum. They had context; I just had to figure out what that was. My lecturers, professors, and tutors guided me through that process, teaching me to recognize the historical processes and forces that shape our world. In a way, this process of discovery as a student, as a graduate student, and later still as a professor, moved me in a different direction than Sluggo, who was a dyed-in-the-wool Bundist until the very end. I'm still attached to that movement and its values, but I'm not sure how I feel any longer about -isms. I'm not sure if I'm an idealist like Sluggo was, although I'd like to be, to have his faith in other people, on a micro and macro scale. I try to draw inspiration from him, try to emulate him, just as he did his father, but it's still a work-in-progress, a piecemeal process of cobbling together those values he taught me and trying to make them square with the world around me, the world about which I study and teach every day. I'm much more agnostic than I used to be; I've let go to a great extent of those political attachments that I held probably more for nostalgic than ideological reasons.

Just as Iraq was my Vietnam, Vietnam was probably Sluggo's own nod to his father's prewar socialism, his opportunity to fulfill his obligations. However, I think we marched against those wars for even more pressing reasons. We were constantly aware of the ghosts haunting us, those family members whom we knew only from hints of stories, a few tattered photos. We were belatedly fighting for them, to make up for what was lost. In our own way, we sought to recover their humanity. We didn't march because our dead relatives were Bundists; we marched because they fell victim to the murderous excesses of the violent twentieth century. When we saw the wars in Vietnam and in Iraq, the senseless suffering they brought, we saw reflections of World War II; we heard the echoes of our ancestors.

Our coming-of-age stories have parallels—they came at times of major political upheaval, against the backdrop of overseas wars that would profoundly shape the country and the worlds in which we lived. And we were both trying to navigate how to incorporate our pasts into that political awakening, how to balance the guilt we both felt at having not actually suffered the hardships of our ancestors, and the kind of obligations we had as a result. I suppose, like this whole exercise of trying to make sense of the family legacy, it's all still ongoing. Probably it'll never settle, and Arthur will wonder how his own coming of age will parallel my own, and his Zaida's.

7

The Slucki Method

"There are no small parts, only small actors," Sluggo would tell me as I prepared for a part in the chorus of a school production, or as a villager in the Melbourne Yiddish Theatre company. I must have heard him say it hundreds of times. It was advice borrowed from Konstantin Stanislavski, the Russian actor and director who pioneered "method acting," in which actors aim to completely inhabit the character they are preparing to portray. Sluggo repeated this mantra to thousands of actors and students that he mentored in 360 plays over three and a half decades as a director and drama teacher.

When he won the Victorian Teacher of the Year award in 1995, one local newspaper led its report with the headline "The Slucki Method." The article didn't explain exactly what the term meant, but if I had to define it, I would say it was closely related to the method developed by Stanislavski. First and foremost, the Slucki Method gave every student in his charge, every member of a company, every staff member who worked with him autonomy, dignity, and self-confidence. Everyone that came into his sphere felt they were an important part of the process; if they were the lead in the musical, if they played triangle in the orchestra, or if their job was to sweep the stage, Sluggo made everyone feel that the show could not go on without them. The Slucki Method was premised on including everyone who wanted to be involved, not excluding anyone. It was about empowering people to get the job done; it was about breaking rules that needed to be broken; it was about the process and what every person learned along the way. It had no tolerance for bullshit and ego trips. He eschewed hierarchies, seeing everyone as fundamentally equal, imbued with the potential to achieve greatness. His classroom and his rehearsal spaces were democratic, inclusive, for the masses, not only the elite.

Sluggo was clear about from where his passion for drama education stemmed; it was not the product of a long family history of theatre, or even education, although his father was highly educated and his aunt Chava was a teacher and had received a master's in pedagogy and history at the University of Warsaw. Rather, Sluggo's passion for the theatre, for the classroom, and for the space in between was driven by those ghosts haunting him; they were inseparable. This seemingly unlikely space—a high school drama class—was where he could pay his debts to the past. There, he could inspire young people, not much older than Shmulek and Chaimek, to live fulfilled lives, to give back to the world, and to lift up those around them. For him, the connection between his family's past and his passion for drama education were unambiguous. He often made it clear that it was his parents' survival that drove him personally and professionally. He would regularly bring Holocaust survivors to come speak to his students, especially in his twenty years in a public school. Their experiences helped him drum home his message to students that they ought to live every day as though it were their last. As a teacher, he could not only be a *mentsh*, someone who lives his or her life with integrity and a deep concern for the needs of others, but he could teach others how to live that life. What better way to make sure that his father's suffering had not been in vain, that others would get to live the lives that Shmulek and Chaimek missed out on.

Dad liked all kinds of theatre: from the medieval Italian *commedia del'arte* style with its chaos and laughter, to Shakespeare (who doesn't like Shakespeare), to the plays of the modernist cannon: Ibsen, Chekhov, Beckett, Miller. He loved musicals and experimental works. It was in the Yiddish theatre, though, that he got his first taste, his first rush. In the modest, semi-professional Yiddish theatre companies in

Melbourne, he became intoxicated with theatre's allure, its ability to transform people, to transfix them. That tradition penetrated deep into his very being, and would shape his life as a director and teacher. Without Yiddish theatre, he would not have pursued his career in drama education, would not have changed the lives of so many young people, setting them on the path to their own careers in the arts, their own path toward self-fulfillment, whatever their profession.

In a way, he stumbled into the theatre. It was a combination of factors that propelled him onto the stage from a young age: the circumstances of his family's resettlement, their lingering trauma, and their enduring commitments to Yiddish language and culture. As the child of working-class immigrants, whose long hours in the knitting factory left little time to spend with their children after school, Sluggo found that the Yiddish theatre became a kind of babysitter for him and for a small of group of others like him. It was their refuge, somewhere to go, something to do when they got out of school. As children, he and his friends, a group of around eight or ten, were recruited to play bit parts in whatever production the Dovid Herman theatre circle was rehearsing at the Kadimah. The director would put moustaches and beards on these kids and put them in the background of a market, a wedding, or a street scene. For these children of Holocaust survivors, the theatre company at the Kadimah was not only their afterschool care but also their education in the arts, in self-exploration, in community building. The theatre was a safe space for these children, teenagers, and young adults to learn life lessons. Theatre helped them grow up quickly, and imbued them with an egalitarian sensibility.

~

In his history of the Dovid Herman Theatre Troupe, Arnold Zable wrote that Yiddish theatre in Melbourne dated back to the beginning of the century, when Samuel Weisberg, an itinerant actor from Eastern Europe, arrived to Melbourne in 1908, expecting to perform to the thousands of Yiddish-speaking families he had been assured were there. His disappointment that there were only a few hundred

Sluggo (lying down) in a Melbourne Yiddish Youth Theatre production of
Tsvey vokhn baym kineret (Two Weeks in the Kineret), directed by Tzvi
Shtolper, a visiting Israeli director (ca. 1973).

Yiddish speakers soon abated when he began a run of one-man
shows that packed houses and thrilled audiences. There wasn't much
of a market for Yiddish theatre at the time, although there was a
steady stream of activities. By the 1930s, with the trickle of migrants
having grown to a small stream, there were two competing Yiddish
theatre companies in Melbourne.

At that time, Yiddish theatre was still a relatively young tradition. Developing slowly alongside the Haskalah, the modernizing
Jewish Enlightenment movement in Central Europe, the art form
began to take hold in the last decades of the nineteenth century,
much later than other major European cultures. Tapping into the
Yiddish folk tradition and the burgeoning interest in Yiddish liter-
ary forms, Yiddish poet and playwright Avrom Goldfaden invented
a modern Yiddish theatre canon that propelled Jewish theatre into
a new century. In the next decades, Yiddish playwriting blossomed
in Eastern Europe and the Americas, and audiences flocked to see
Jewish life represented on stage. Yiddish theatre would take its place
alongside the European theatrical traditions and would come to influence ideas about acting, staging, and producing that filtered down
to Sluggo only a couple of generations later.

The Yiddish theatre in Melbourne owed its success to a part of this tradition that developed in Poland in the decades after World War I had left Europe a smoldering mess. Many of the actors and directors that would shape Australia's Yiddish theatre had been performers in the Vilna Troupe, a touring company established in 1917. Because of their itinerant nature, notes Yiddish theatre historian Debra Caplan, the Vilna Troupe operated as a kind of global brand, sending actors, directors, and casts all around the world to perform, often simultaneously sending multiple companies to different locations. Its performers spread its vision of a modernist Yiddish theatre to all corners of Eastern Europe, and ultimately, the globe. It was a two-way street, writes Caplan. The Vilna Troupe pioneered a kind of transnational theatre practice, but it also picked up along the way all the latest philosophies about drama and performance. Its actors and directors often had studied in the best academies in Europe, and many had appeared onstage for major non-Jewish art theatres in Poland and Russia.

As historian Nahma Sandrow writes in her history of the Yiddish theatre, *Vagabond Stars* (whose spine I can still see vividly on Dad's bookshelf), the Vilna Troupe particularly emphasized ensemble work, eschewing the star system that was becoming prevalent in European theatre. Despite its glut of talent, the company (like Sluggo) was heavily influenced by Stanislavski, whose method emphasized the cohesion of a company. In 1920 it premiered *Der Dybbuk* [The Dybbuk], which tells the story of a dead man's spirit inhabiting the body of his betrothed. The play drew from an early modern folk tradition rooted in Jewish mysticism in which lost souls of the dead inhabit and haunt the bodies of the living.

Sluggo liked *Der Dybbuk* a lot. He probably saw it when the Dovid Herman Troupe produced it in 1957, and he later staged it himself a couple of times. I think he identified with it. He believed in ghosts, so why not dybbuks? The dybbuks of his family past inhabited him. The lost souls of Shmulek and Chaimek, of Chasha and her nameless baby, of so many others whose names and identities were erased.

The Vilna Troupe became known as a proponent of the dark, expressionist style so popular at the time, which would also typify the Yiddish theatre in Melbourne. Although it had formally disbanded by 1935, the Vilna Troupe's influence was global, not just for Jews, but beyond, and its performers who went on to survive the war left their mark by injecting life into Yiddish theatre wherever they landed. This was part of the legacy that Sluggo saw he had to carry on. It was one of the most important innovations of the Yiddish civilization cut down by the Nazis. The theatre was a stand-in for a culture on life support after the majority of European Jews were murdered, their language and literature a secondary casualty.

His link to this glorious tradition was not simply abstract, though, or intellectual; it was material, tangible. In 1940, two of the Vilna Troupe performers settled in Melbourne, initiating a golden era of Yiddish theatre in Australia in the 1950s and leaving a permanent mark on the young Sluggo. The Dovid Herman Theatre, named for the Vilna Troupe's artistic director, came to life when two stars of the Troupe, both on world tours, found themselves stranded in Melbourne after Germany invaded Poland and the gates of Europe were shut. Yankev Waislitz and Rokhl Holzer, accidental refugees, were both Vilna Troupe graduates, having both toured Europe with the company. These two icons would work to carry on its legacy of producing serious, modernist theatre.

They were hugely influential on Sluggo. Waislitz, whom Dad described as the "Laurence Olivier of the Yiddish stage," was a graduate of the Warsaw Yiddish drama academy, Hazomir, and performed in the Vilna Troupe's original production of *Der Dybbuk*. He was a Yiddish teacher by day, principal of one of Melbourne's two Yiddish Sunday schools. He was cranky, according to Sluggo, but to watch him on stage was magic. An education in the dramatic arts just to see him perform. As well as the Vilna Troupe, Holzer had starred in the Warsaw Yiddish Art Theatre and the Polish National Theatre. She was renowned as a versatile and graceful performer, commanding the stage with her very presence. Sluggo remembered her vividly—she moved about the stage like a ballerina, wonderful to watch. No wonder he was hooked; some of the world's most talented performers were almost literally at his doorstep, entrancing him with their guile and raw talent.

~

In 1963, fifteen-year-old Sluggo performed in the production of *Di Kishefmakherin* [The Sorceress], written in 1877 by Avrom Goldfaden. It was one of the earliest plays in the Yiddish canon, an operetta about an evil sorceress trying to tear her family apart and ultimately failing. Sluggo was again drawn to stories of the supernatural rooted in the Jewish folk tradition. He had a small role alongside Abraham Braizblatt, a veteran of the Warsaw Yiddish stage, who directed the production and played the title role. Zaida wrote to Mendel that although it was a small part, "he was hailed as a very serious young man." This was his first serious taste of being onstage, with lines. It was a minor role, but it gave him a chance to work alongside accomplished performers, trained in the best academies in Eastern Europe, bringing with them all the skill, nuance, and charisma they had accumulated over decades of performing across the globe. Zaida, I think, was probably just happy that Dad was keeping occupied, and that he was getting involved in the community. These opportunities as a young man left a lasting impression on Sluggo. They opened his eyes to the opportunity acting gave a person to totally transform themself into another time and place, to assume another identity, to experience the world through another's eyes.

A decade later, alongside a group of young actors with whom he regularly worked, he once again performed in a Dovid Herman revival of *Di Kishefmakherin*, this time staged by touring director Dina Halpern. Halpern, who also played the title role, not only featured in the Polish and American Yiddish theatre but was also cast in the film adaptation of *The Dybbuk*, perhaps the most important Yiddish film of the twentieth century. Sluggo didn't think much of Halpern the director. He later recounted she'd stand in the wings, screaming at the young actors. The first five rows could hear her screaming, he'd say, and the actors would ignore her and create what they thought worked. Watching Halpern the actor, though, Sluggo was entranced. That's where he learned about method acting and how actors can transform themselves and inhabit their characters fully. He witnessed Stanislavski's method, seeing it up close, before he would study the method itself. He would later teach it to generations of young actors, showing that it was possible to emotionally tap into the character you were going to perform, to become a character. I'm not sure he was always convinced. He used to recount the famous story about Laurence Olivier and Dustin Hoffmann, about their work together on the film *Marathon Man*. When Hoffman showed up on set looking bedraggled, having not slept for days to prepare for a scene in which his character is tired, Olivier is said to have quipped, "It's called acting, my dear boy." The story is probably apocryphal; that might be true of many of Sluggo's stories. But they always served a purpose.

Nonetheless, what he would later learn in lecture halls and textbooks, Sluggo had seen up close during those long evenings watching Halpern transform into a witch. As they sat together chatting, and having their makeup done, she would slowly emerge as the witch. He was in awe at her transformation. Despite her temper as a director, as an actor her preparation, her commitment to the role, the way she could totally inhabit that character, left a lasting impression. It showed him what was possible onstage, the art of being reborn night after night as someone new.

In Melbourne's Yiddish theatre scene, then, Sluggo grew up surrounded by, learning from, inhaling the experience of veterans of the European Yiddish stage. These actors and directors had influenced the likes of Sarah Bernhardt, Stella Adler, and Eugene Ionesco, giants of the twentieth-century stage who had clamored to see touring Vilna Troupe productions. As well as the actors and directors who settled in Melbourne, the local Yiddish theatre welcomed a regular roster of touring directors and artists. These are names that have all but vanished from the historical record, but who were celebrities in the Yiddish-speaking world: Ida Kaminska, Roza Turkow, Zygmunt Turkow, Zvi Shtolper, Shimen Dzigan. From them, Sluggo received an early education in theatre history and practice: expressionism, method acting, theatre of the absurd, Brecht.

And it wasn't only performing he came to understand. He learned the craft of the theatre from these artists. They did it all: acting, directing, writing. But more than just those things. The Yiddish theatre companies he grew up in were full of people who, in addition to playing the starring roles and relishing the glory that comes with the spotlight, were also the ones sweeping the stage, building the sets, and marketing the plays. His training was comprehensive: how to stage a play, apply theatre makeup, plan a lighting design, prepare to get into character.

Although there have always been trained professional actors on its stage, this all taught Sluggo that the Yiddish theatre was, in Melbourne at least, a community endeavor. It relied on the talent, and even more so on the sacrifices and hard work, of a lot of people to be successful. He knew that sets were only going to get built if people pitched in; costumes would only get sewn by those willing to put in long hours, volunteering because they knew it mattered. Sluggo knew that preserving and fostering Yiddish culture couldn't happen from the top down, but, at its heart, must be championed at a grassroots level. Theatre was the natural vehicle for this. Producing community theatre required commitment from its participants, and the late nights and long days in rehearsals fostered a sense of camaraderie among those involved. It also demanded everyone pitch in—no one was too good, too important, or too precious to help clear the stage or paint the set. Not only did theatre require large numbers of people to produce but it could attract large audiences. Its only hope of survival in a place like Melbourne was to bring as many people into the theatrical process as possible, onstage and off.

∾

Sluggo's political values blended easily with what he was learning in the theatre. Many of the actors, writers, and directors held deep political commitments—to the Bund, to communism, or to Zionism. His adherence to the Bund, with its emphasis on equality, cultural elevation, and democratization, could not but shape the approach he developed to theatre. And it was in the context of the Bundist youth movements, both in Melbourne and in New York, that he realized why theatre could be such a powerful tool. At SKIF summer camps, theatre was a regular part of how they communicated to the SKIFistn: writing skits and rehearsing and performing short Yiddish plays.

His big transformation—that moment he realized that he wanted to make his living developing this method—came in 1972 when he traveled the globe. This was not his first foray abroad, but perhaps the most transformative. He lived overseas for over a year. He grew up a lot during that trip. He fell in love, had his heart broken, made lifelong friends. After that, he traveled with his best friend, Nudy, to Europe. They stayed in Paris with Zaida's cousin Avram. In Berlin, they passed through Checkpoint Charlie, from east to west, with a trunk full of Yiddish socialist literature, a move that was somewhere between brave and stupid. He visited Israel, where he met his aunt Chava, uncle Chaim, and cousin Hadassah for the first time. Hadassah was herself an accomplished actor in Israel, her husband, Binem Hiller, an important Yiddish poet.

The spark was lit while working with the young campers at Camp Hemshekh, the Bundist summer camp in upstate New York, where he worked as a counselor and where children of Bundists and Holocaust survivors gained so much confidence and joy under Sluggo's guidance. At Camp Hemshekh, he saw how positive an impact Yiddish theatre had on campers, on their sense of connection to their past. He saw the confidence it gave them to better interact with the world around them. It wasn't just a matter of doing something fun with the campers, but something meaningful, life-changing. There was magic in theatre. Theatre gave young people a sense of what was possible, that thing that powered Sluggo throughout his life. It was after returning from seeing the world that he finally found his calling and settled down. He dropped out of law school and enrolled in a

Sluggo at Camp Hemshekh (1972).

drama education course. He was going to be a drama teacher, marrying what he had discovered were his two biggest passions: inspiring young people and the performing arts. He did some work as a professional actor, but never really had ambitions to work full-time in the industry. He had greater aspirations, world-changing expectations.

After four years at drama school, armed with a renewed sense of purpose and determination, Sluggo began a celebrated thirty-year career as a high school drama teacher, continually developing the Slucki Method. He received many accolades in his two decades heading up the performing arts program at Highett High School, later incorporated as a junior campus of the neighboring Sandringham Secondary College. There, he built a program that was the envy of all other drama teachers, staging several major productions each year, often with over two hundred students in the cast and dozens more working behind the scenes. Sluggo found teaching thrilling. The sense of having made a meaningful contribution to the development of young people energized him daily. He loved the long hours in the theatre, where he could weave his magic with his students. His disciples, really. He was engaging, encouraging, idiosyncratic (his uniform for almost every day of his teaching career was shorts, a pencil in white socks, and a half-empty bottle of Diet Coke). He was prolific, often working eighty-hour weeks, inheriting

Sluggo the teacher (1980s).

his father's own boundless work ethic, dragging me and Jacob along with him to school, to rehearsals, to productions. Teenagers came from around the state to learn under Sluggo's tutelage, many leaving elite private schools to see for themselves who this energetic, diminutive, bearded dynamo was that took shy, enthusiastic young people and turned them into professional actors, directors, and theatre technicians. At the program's peak, Sluggo oversaw eleven upper-level theatre and drama classes, eight media studies classes, and four dance classes.

He was laid back with students, generous and convivial, always accommodating, endlessly supportive. His school productions were high quality, ambitious. Semi-professional, he'd say. He taught the fundamentals of theatre history and practice, but also drew on his life experiences to illustrate that learning happened beyond the books and the classrooms. He never excluded anyone, and he knew just how to get the best out of young people, whether through encouragement, a gentle push, or, when he thought it necessary, raising his voice at a company. "It's always controlled," he'd tell me after. A way to shake them out of their complacency. But always with love and dedication to his craft. People would come from neighboring suburbs to see the shows, filling the improvised five-hundred-seat theatres each night. Talent agents were regular audience members, knowing Sluggo's reputation for turning out disciplined, committed actors.

From 1977 until he left Sandringham in 1997, Sluggo ran weekly drama workshops at a nearby special school, pairing his own students with students with disabilities, using drama and creativity to help build their confidence and understanding of the world around them. This was a program that had a tangible effect on the lives of those in need and was meaningful for his own students. It was part of his inclusive approach to theatre education, which said everyone could be involved, everyone could grow through the theatre, no matter their ability or background. That idea he developed in those years on the Yiddish stage, that theatre was transformative, life-changing, healing, and could fix the world, underpinned his teaching.

In general, he tried to foster a sense of adventure, of possibility in his students, mixed with a healthy dose of daring and cheekiness. He was averse to bureaucracy and authority, and challenged his students to always be skeptical of adults telling them what to do. "It's better to ask for forgiveness than to ask permission" was his motto, passed on to thousands of students. He was a rule-breaker, audacious, not afraid to step on people's toes if he needed to in order to get things done, to change things for the better, to help students in difficult situations. In his first year of teaching, he twice confronted the abusive father of a student, and provided her comfort among his own family, where she could feel safe and part of a family. She was not the last student whose life he changed with his warmth, love, and daring. He was caring, intelligent, compassionate, energetic. He gave all of himself to his students.

Under his guidance, students felt that they mattered, that they had a voice. Students who were outcasts, quirky, different, or the victims of bullying and harassment felt empowered in his classrooms. They went from being shy kids in the background to leads in the school musical, performing in front of five hundred people a night. Kids from rough homes felt safe in his presence, more confident that they could tackle the world. He was much more than a drama teacher to many; he was a father figure, guiding them through their adolescence. Many told me over the years, "I'd be in prison without your dad," or even "I'd probably be dead without your dad."

In 1995, he was recognized as Victorian Teacher of the Year for his innovation and his tireless commitment to his students and to building his program. After winning the award, Sluggo was featured in the *Herald-Sun*, one of Australia's most widely circulated newspapers, and in a range of local print media. He was congratulated by senior government officials, including the minister for education. It was his just reward for a career spent nurturing young people, recognition not only for his dedication but also for his innovation and his healthy dose of chutzpah. Not bad for a public school teacher in a lower-middle-class beachside suburb. Not bad for the immigrant son of Holocaust survivors. Not bad for someone inhabited by the dybbuks of a lost world.

～

A major innovation of the Slucki Method was its emphasis on taking students out of the classroom. Not just to see a play or to sit on the lawn for class. Sluggo showed them Victoria, Australia, and the world. He accompanied students to the centers of the performing arts world: London, New York, Los Angeles. In a typical tour, the students might perform their own production; they would see up to ten Broadway shows in eight days; they would participate in workshops with professional actors, dancers, and industry professionals; they met stars such as Matthew Broderick and Henry Winkler; they toured major Hollywood studios and production companies. Sluggo went numerous times to Japan, where his friend, Shiro Kobayashi, a professor in drama at the University of Tokyo, treated him and his students like royalty. It was Professor Kobayashi who referred to Sluggo's approach as the "Highett Method." Each year he took dozens of students to the Adelaide Fringe Festival, a major international arts festival, where they would stage shows, but also would do theatre in other creative ways. He would send students out to do "guerilla theatre": one year he instructed a group to go into a shop and get into a loud, public argument over a sweater. Other times he had large groups lie down in the middle of the major shopping strip on their backs, emulating dead bugs. He would take students out of their comfort zone, encourage them to be audacious, bold, and experimental in how they looked at theatre and the world around them. He also took a production each year to country towns in northeastern Victoria, where they would tour local primary schools, performing shows like *Alice in Wonderland* or *The Lion, the Witch, and the Wardrobe*. Jacob and I each had the opportunity to join him on these trips when we were in grade five, as we helped *schlep* sets around, seeing Sluggo entrance his disciples up close.

On top of his regular teaching load, and producing several large school productions a year, Sluggo did an enormous amount of work for these tours, often during the dead of night, while we all slept. I remember drowsily coming into his study at two or three in the morning where he was on the phone to London or New York, booking hotels and workshops. Even after the advent of e-mail, he found it easier to talk directly to those across the increasingly shrinking globe. In many ways, this work was extracurricular, outside the normal demands of a teacher, and took him away from his family more than we would have liked. Yet he saw it as central to his offerings as a teacher. No doubt, this stemmed from his recognition that a youth spent exploring the world shaped him profoundly. Even more crucial in explaining how central this became to his teaching philosophy, I think, is the fact of his own immigration, his own multilayered attachments. "Conceived in Poland, born in Paris," he often quipped, describing the transnational circumstances of his own genesis. Deep in his soul, he knew that students' success depended on their willingness to be out in the world, to go beyond their own narrow bubble and open themselves up to new experiences. He was forced to do so from his very conception; it was a staple of his parents' lives. It was that restless wandering that fed his curiosity, his soul. He was like a perpetual motion machine, always on the go, ready for the next adventure. He knew that those five days in Adelaide, those three weeks in London and Los Angeles, those ten days in Tokyo were worth years of training. They were a time for students to save money and budget, to negotiate the demands of a different culture and environment, to see the many forms a career in the arts might take.

More remarkable was that for those students from working-class and low-income families attending the local public school, overseas travel was a pipe dream, beyond their means. Holidays to Bali were not part of the world that he inhabited while at Sandringham Secondary College, much less tours of London and Los Angeles. Most of the students had to work and save their own money just to participate, many saved for years. This was truly the Slucki Method. These trips showed the students that anything was possible, and that it was in their grasp, but they had to be open-minded, daring, collaborative, and willing to work hard.

～

Sluggo retired from teaching in 2006. Really, he was forced to retire by an elite Jewish private school that increasingly saw the performing arts as a luxury, that felt a drama teacher had no place in the school's leadership structure. Sluggo's performing arts tours of New York and Los Angeles were seen as a competitor to the school's trips to Israel, his popularity threatening to some. It was a devastating blow, one from which I don't think he fully recovered, so invested was he in his career as a teacher, so widely respected and recognized.

Schools could be ruthless when politics came to the fore, and even the most decorated drama teacher in the state was not immune. His ego was wounded, and he was lost for a few years, wandering, and not in the way that he liked. Aimlessly, without clear purpose, as he'd been used to since his midtwenties.

Ten years earlier, the school's then-principle had approached him to make an offer he couldn't refuse. He was happy enough at Sandringham, but restless, ambitious. "Don't make your living from the Jewish community," his father had warned decades earlier. They would only take advantage. But when this Jewish school approached him, offering him a senior leadership position, a bigger salary, and the opportunity to oversee the building of a state-of-the-art theatre, he could hardly say no. After decades scraping by on the salaries of two public school teachers, he now had the chance to gain some breathing space financially. Six or seven years later, things turned sour when that same principal failed to back him after a minor complaint from a parent. The next few years were full of battles, as Sluggo fought off the school's attempts to undermine the performing arts program, until they finally forced him out. That he'd been lured there with promises of institutional support made it a much crueler blow when he lost the school's backing.

The forced exit eventually led him to adapt the Slucki Method to a new life outside the classroom. He formed a company, Theatrica, through which he took school groups to New York and Los Angeles, a tried and true formula drawing on his vast experience and networks, and mainly drawing on his huge, infectious personality. He mentored individual students, helped them prepare for auditions, and resumed his work in community theatre. His passion for teaching and developing young people, giving them opportunities, never waned.

He later took that energy and method to Cambodia, where he developed a close friendship with Professor Sedtha Long, a survivor of the Khmer Rouge's genocide and a kindred spirit. Professor Long ran an orphanage in Siem Reap that Sluggo became involved with, not only helping to raise funds and awareness in Australia but also contributing his creative energy by running workshops with the children. This was the ultimate fulfillment of the Slucki Method, the application of his principles to those truly in need. He recognized some of his own family in those children: suffering from the aftermath of genocide, torn from their families and their culture by murderous fanatics, their country left in ruins, the children left to face the consequences.

∾

Just before he died, Sluggo was recognized by the peak drama teachers' organization, Drama Victoria, as one of the pioneering drama teachers in Australia, a legend of the industry. "I don't know about legend," Sluggo said, with a healthy dose of false modesty, "but it's great to be recognized." Those who worked with him—as budding actors, writers, theatre technicians—always knew this; it came as no surprise. He had built a reputation globally as an innovator in theatre education. When he died, tributes flowed in from students across the globe. Maybe one thousand people attended his funeral, many former students crowding into the *shtiebel* to pay tribute to one of the formative influences in their lives, helping to fill in the grave and close the chapter on the life of their friend. Friends and family tuned in online from the United States, Europe, Israel, and Asia to pay their respects. Professor Long held a special Buddhist mourning ceremony in Cambodia in his honor, which he broadcast through Facebook, a tribute to the wide reach and impact of the Slucki Method.

∾

Theatre provided a special bond between me and Sluggo. I grew up in his classrooms, rehearsal spaces, and theatres. I would run around backstage in the tiny dressing rooms of the Yiddish theatre, by then relocated to Melbourne's southeastern suburbs, where the Jewish community had collectively remigrated. I'd hang out with his students in the makeshift backstage of his school productions, and tag along to all manner of professional and amateur productions that he would take me to. Eventually, I started dragging him to shows that

I wanted to see. Jacob lost interest earlier than I did—he was more independent, forged his own path. But I had breathed in the sweet, musky scent of the stage, and I was hooked. Besides, it allowed us to stay connected when Sluggo was out of the house for long stretches, when he might only be able to sneak out after school to watch us at football practice, before taking us with him back to rehearsals.

Sluggo didn't just *schlep* me along, though. He involved me in the process. Sometimes he'd throw me into the chorus; at other times I'd move sets, be part of the backstage crew, help bump a show in and out. One year he had me perform an improvised stand-up act as emcee in the front-of-house café he'd built for his school production of *Guys and Dolls*. The older I got, the greater the responsibility. I must have been only eleven or twelve when he asked me to take notes during the rehearsals and run of the year twelve production, which he then insisted I deliver to the performers. At fifteen he asked me to be musical director of the school play, working with a small band to help animate the drama unfolding on stage.

I now wonder about his decision to include me. I didn't think of it at the time, but it's clearer to me now that it was something he wanted to share with me, a way for him to show belief in me, to bring me into his world. When he was a kid, because Zaida worked such long hours, Dad spent many Saturday mornings working in the knitting factory, helping out, spending some time with his parents. Bringing me to rehearsal was probably his version of that, although I came a lot more often than once a week. When I was in high school, he'd pick me up from school often and we'd drive straight back to his school for rehearsal. Sometimes I was a pest, sometimes I helped out a lot. Maybe sometimes he gave me jobs just to keep me occupied. It never felt that way, though. He used to joke that you should never work with children or animals, quoting one of his favorite comics, W. C. Fields (he was also fond of another of Fields's quips: when asked why he didn't drink water, Sluggo would respond "because fish fuck in it," always lingering just a moment before that punch line).

I also think that he was drawing on what he knew from his own childhood in the Yiddish theatre: that being part of a company and putting together a production is exhilarating, exciting, confidence building. The reality is that age was never a barrier for him; his companies in Yiddish and community-theatre settings were always multigenerational, bringing together children and adults. It made sense, then, when I was eight, nine, and ten years old, that the theatre would be my babysitter, just as it was for him. Like him, I transitioned from pest to cast member seamlessly. With his long hours of rehearsal in the evening, plus a couple of weeks' run of a show, it was a way for us still to spend some quality time together, but also to inhale that intoxicating scent of the past that lingered with each production. In this way I learned about Goldfaden, Itzik Manger, and Sholem Aleichem, and eventually about Euripides, Arthur Miller, and Cole Porter. I would run up and down the aisles of the cinema-cum-theatre at the new Kadimah, relocated to the same block as my primary school, stand on stage, pretend to perform, and play with whoever would play with me.

By the time I joined the Yiddish theatre as an eleven-year-old, despite a miniature burst of energetic creativity, it was going through a transition, a decline. Just over two years after my unremarkable debut on the Yiddish theatre stage, I rejoined the company for a production of *Fiddler on the Roof*, a hybrid production with dialogue in English and songs in Yiddish. By then, that was how we did Yiddish theatre. The market could no longer support full-length, serious theatre in Yiddish. The bilingual musical was a happy compromise that brought people through the door and could keep the tradition alive. And although it had been a productive decade, it was becoming increasingly difficult to convince people, now with their own careers and families, to commit the time required to stage a production. Rehearsals several nights a week and on weekends, with weeks-long runs of shows, were become a much harder sell than they had been to the same group of people, now more encumbered by adult life, squeezing in whatever communal involvement they could. Sluggo wasn't involved this time around; his last show was *Mazl-Tov Cobbers* in 1995, a show about early Jewish settlement in Australia.

For me, *Fiddler* was chance to carve out my own place in that tradition, that *goldene keyt*, the golden chain, out of Sluggo's shadow. I was in the chorus, a minor player in the village scenes, a ghost in Tevye's confected nightmare, a bottle dancer in the wedding scene. And this time, I was not cast simply because my dad was the director. It was a proud moment for me; more so probably for Sluggo, who still drove me to and picked me up from rehearsals.

Fiddler on the Roof, Fidler oyfn dakh, was most memorable, though, because it was where I first met Helen. After months of childish flirting, including playing hard-to-get, then easy-to-get, then hard-to-get again, we two thirteen-year-olds started dating, and we haven't been apart since. No wonder I'm so fond of Yiddish theatre.

∽

Fueled by this exposure to the stage, to the excitement, camaraderie, and—let's face it—adulation (of my parents at least), my ambition was to become an actor. In the years following, I performed in school plays and musicals, took minor roles in local companies, and studied theatre seriously at school. I went to dozens of plays and musicals, revivals and experimental new works, dragging my dad to see touring productions at the Melbourne Arts Festival and plays at the avant-garde Malthouse Theatre. Like Dad, I was interested in serious drama more than musicals, although I had a soft spot for musical theatre. Through high school, inspired by my dad's energy and charisma, I planned to study performing arts, later pursue a diploma in education. As the son of a drama teacher, I knew that actors needed a backup plan, so why not teaching? It was all mapped out.

Then, I didn't get into the creative arts degree I wanted to do, and the dream waned. I did more theatre after that, particularly when Sluggo summoned me to help out in a show. In those few years of university, I did a lot of work with Sluggo. He started to give me a lot more responsibility—he trusted me, enjoyed working with me. In the months that I produced and stage-managed his school productions of *The Wizard of Oz* and *Seussical the Musical*, we had lunch together almost every day, spent long nights in the theatre, days planning and negotiating. During rehearsals for a staged reading of *The Fist*, a play on conscientious objectors in the Israeli army in which I read for the lead character, we spent many evenings together preparing. In the best tradition of the Yiddish theatre, it was a family affair. Helen produced one show, performed in another. It was a thrill for us all to work together so closely. Sluggo gave me enormous responsibility, trusted me completely. I learned lessons beyond the theatre in how he operated. He was collaborative, democratic, endlessly creative and experimental. He wasn't afraid to fail; he knew that you learned from it. He was full of self-confidence, at the top of his game.

In a place where Yiddish culture might not have endured for as long as it has, Sluggo's dynamism and generosity of spirit helped foster an active local Yiddish theatre scene for decades. Under Sluggo's directorship, the Melbourne Yiddish Youth Theatre, later the Melbourne Yiddish Theatre, staged a whole gamut of plays and musicals. He directed classics, such as Itzik Manger's *Di megile*; translations and adaptations of well-known plays like *The Diary of Anne Frank* and *The Sunshine Boys*; and original works by local writers about immigration and early Jewish settlement in Australia. Perhaps the biggest feather in his cap as Yiddish theatre director was staging the concert, *Nign*, featuring Broadway star Theodore Bikel. But after 1995, he stepped away, his formal connection to Melbourne's Yiddish theatre severed over personality clashes, politics, and the growing sense that there were too few people willing to commit time and energy to sustaining it. Different priorities, a young family, a burgeoning career.

Sluggo planned to rekindle his work in the Yiddish theatre at the Kadimah in 2016, working with his old friend and collaborator Arnold Zable to write a new play about Sholem Aleichem to commemorate the writer's hundredth *yortsayt*, the anniversary of his death. Arnold was writing the play, and Sluggo was to direct. He had a cast in mind, a group of veterans that he had worked with for decades plus some newcomers, all spearheaded by Shane Baker, mainstay of the New York Yiddish theatre scene. They had met several times in New York to plan for the show. This was an opportunity to work with people that he knew were humble and talented, and would contribute to the success of the production. By then, he had an established formula that worked creatively and ensured a cohesive company. There was no room for egos too big, no matter the talent attached to the ego. In the best tradition of the European Yiddish stage, Sluggo prioritized putting together a group that worked effectively as a team. The success of a production depended much more on the willingness of its members to work together than it did on the star power of the most talented individuals.

It was twenty years since he had been seriously involved in Yiddish theatre. In the interim he had done his share of communal, grassroots theatre, from directing a play about women and Judaism by Melbourne novelist and playwright Yvonne Fein, to a staged reading of a new Israeli play on Israel's conscientious objectors, to an adaptation of Franz Kafka's *The Trial*, which protested Australia's cruel treatment of asylum seekers. The theatre continued to be a potent means for political expression, for him to bring his socialist sensibility to audiences, to carry on that responsibility he felt toward his father and his father's murdered family, and to do so in experimental and creative ways. He staged The *Dybbuk with* his students, gave adult education classes on the history of Yiddish theatre, and directed an adaptation of Chaim Potok's *My Name is Asher Lev* with a local Jewish company.

Sluggo was excited at the prospect of returning to the Yiddish theatre, of returning to his roots, that vehicle that launched him into the stratosphere of drama education. But it was not to be. Days after a planning meeting for this production with Shane, the curtain finally closed on Sluggo's life. He didn't make his last curtain call. But then, his productions always ended with a full company bow— there were no individual honors. He would always rather bask in the reflected glow of the actors on the stage, whom he had led, guided, and taught. They are his legacy: the thousands he mentored,

Sluggo directing his final show, *My Name is Asher Lev*.

carrying on the best of what he absorbed as a boy on the modest
stage of Melbourne's Yiddish theatre.

Theatre, in those months after Dad died, was among the jumble of
different parts of his legacy that I couldn't get out of my head. I
couldn't seem to get away from it; it was a ghost haunting me. Or
maybe I could, but didn't want to. I hadn't been involved in the theatre
for years. At some point in my midtwenties I ran away from it. My
own rebellion. I don't know why. I protested the pretentiousness of
most plays I saw, dismissed the frivolity of musicals. I missed working closely with others to create something new and exciting, the
excitement of seeing it all come together. The applause, the kudos,
the spotlight. Now I missed it all desperately.

A few weeks after I arrived back in Charleston from Dad's funeral, I accompanied Arthur on a school field trip to the theatre, a
local company doing their annual children's show for schools, *A Year
with Frog and Toad*. A cute show, catchy songs, funny punchlines.
Nicely enough done. Arthur sat on my lap to see better. He giggled
his way through. I cried. In a children's musical about two amphib-
ians in culottes. Quiet tears, little sniffles, but inside I was curled up
on the floor in the fetal position. My reaction seemed out of pro-
portion to what was unfolding in front of me. I'm glad it was dark.
Sluggo had wanted to take Arthur to see *The Lion King* in New York

the previous year, but he was a little too young. Plenty of time, we thought, you'll take him to a lot of theatre. As Arthur convulsed with giggles on my lap, the actors doing their box step only a few feet from us, all I could do was sob silently about how mistaken we had been.

Weeks later, the theatre continued to haunt me: I gave a lecture on Broadway and the Great American Songbook. I talked about the role Jews played in creating the Hollywood system, and how Jewish Tin Pan Alley composers were at the forefront of forging a new American culture. I spent that week preparing by listening to the Great American Songbook: Ella Fitzgerald and Bing Crosby singing classics of early musical theatre. Nostalgia. Musicals burned into my consciousness. *Kiss Me Kate, Anything Goes, West Side Story.* Gershwin, Berlin, Porter.

In February 2017, it all hit home. Shane Baker came to Charleston from New York City to perform a one-man show, a collection of monologues in Yiddish. After a year of planning, it was a belated tribute to Sluggo. I operated the surtitles, a minor contribution. Shane had the crowd in stitches. The audience—students, faculty, members of the Charleston Jewish community—almost to a person had never experienced the joy that Yiddish theatre brought, a secret that I had known as long as I could remember. As we set up for the performances, we sat together in the college's little black box theatre. Very low-tech, not even enough power outlets, wending our extension cords through the old rig, improvising with whatever materials we could find to make sure that the surtitles were visible from all angles. Getting the sight lines right was hugely important—something I've always known instinctively, partly because Dad often built his own theatre within the modest spaces available. It came so naturally, like I'd done it hundreds of times before.

I felt Sluggo's ghost there. I could see him sitting in the front row taking notes, encouraging the performers to experiment with their intonation, their tempo, their use of the stage. I could hear him telling his old stories about shows past, actors who had found their voice, stories that aged gracefully, that occasionally got more extravagant with each retelling, but that comforted me like an old leather jacket—reliable, familiar, providing warmth and shelter, a little tattered, but more charming as they aged. His stories always served some purpose: to inspire, to teach, to shock. I could sense him improvising solutions to the mundane problems that arise in a theatre; I could feel him encouraging us to break the rules, work out ways to jump the hurdles that we faced. Although in his last few years as a teacher he had a state-of-the-art theatre at his disposal, he was really in his element in a no-frills space where he could use all of his guile and imagination to create something. Somehow that seemed to fit with his approach: he didn't need a lot of bells and whistles, didn't rely on fancy tricks. He put his trust in the people he worked with, knew that they could get a lot out of whatever they had on hand, make the most of their talent.

I looked over to the front row and I swore I could see him sitting there, wearing a broad grin as he watched, right leg crossed over his left, ankle resting on his knee, hands clasped in his lap. Just the way he would sit and watch with satisfaction, knowing that he had done all he could to bring out the best in his people and soaking in their success. It was in these very kinds of places—basic, underdeveloped theatre spaces—that he showed me anything was possible, that he created a whole world out of nothing, that he transported me to New York in the 1950s, to Northern Ireland, to outback Australia, or to turn-of-the-century Russia.

As I sat watching Shane weave his magic, performing Sholem Aleichem stories and Yiddish monologues, as the audience reveled in the glorious flexibility and complexity of the Yiddish language, I thought, of course, about Sluggo and the legacy that I carried with me. I shed more tears. I seemed to have an endless well of tears. And that hope of Sluggo's before he died, to return to Yiddish theatre and make it viable once again in Melbourne, kept nagging at me. I had no power over that, but putting on a show in Charleston was a small way I could feel a bit of Sluggo's presence with me, as his actual presence receded further and further into the past. Yiddish theatre, it turned out, was a way for me to keep his ghost close. I wouldn't, couldn't, let it go.

8

Warsaw, My Ancestral Home

In a rear corner of the vast Warsaw Jewish cemetery, nearly impossible to find amidst the hundreds of thousands of stone memorials and overgrown trees, is a gray, mostly upright gravestone. It is in reasonably good condition, particularly compared to those that are now illegible or not even standing. Yisroel-Shmuel Slucki lies here, his eternal marker describing him as "an honest God-fearing man who walked a simple, honest path." It is a description that is in marked contrast to that on Zaida's or Sluggo's graves, in which God takes a backseat. I don't know who wrote the inscription, who was responsible for putting it up, or to what extent it reflected his life. And until I visited the grave in June 2012, my second time there, I didn't really know anything about him, and I don't really know if Sluggo knew much about his own grandfather. Perhaps the mystery meant that he wasn't particularly noteworthy or interesting. What I would come to realize was that his grave may have helped to explain more about Sluggo and his father than I could have imagined.

At the end of May 2012, I visited Warsaw to participate in a scholarly conference on the Bund. By then, my book on the post-Holocaust history of the Bund had been published, and I was part of a growing group of young scholars rediscovering the Bund as an area of academic inquiry. There was a mini-renaissance in historical interest in the Bund; my timing couldn't have been any better. The conference had originally been scheduled for Vilnius, the Bund's birthplace, but for a range of reasons, practical and political, it had to be postponed. After it was rescheduled, I didn't think I'd be able to make it. It was only months after Arthur was born. I was still wandering around tired, fueled by coffee in the mornings, soda in the afternoon, beer at night. Helen wasn't back at work yet, and we had a trip planned to New York in June. I was on autopilot, recovering from a busy semester, still trying to establish myself as a teacher and scholar. I wasn't even writing about the Bund anymore. My book had come out and been reviewed, and I was on to the next project. Or at least trying to work out what the next project would be. By then, I was probably more interested in writing about sitcoms than the Bund. Knowing that the conference was in Warsaw, though, I was determined to go. Had it been in Vilnius, once the center of a mighty Jewish civilization before World War II, I might have decided it was too hard to go. But I was drawn to Warsaw, and I was ready to go find the ghosts of my family's past, even in the sleepless haze that comes with a newborn.

I have always had a fascination with Poland, a kind of feeling of ancestral connection. When people talk about homelands, or mother countries, my mind tends toward Poland. It's difficult to explain: my mother and her parents weren't interested in the country. When I first visited in 2004, my bubba asked me: "why would you go to such a shitty country?" Although my grandparents always spoke Polish among themselves and their peers, there was no interest in Poland as a place for return or to feel affection toward. Jacob was the first in the family to visit, a year before me, with his then-girlfriend. But there was no sense of connection fostered, no feeling that Poland was anything more than a graveyard. There was no feeling that Jewish life was permanent, that Jews were anything more than a historical curiosity, that my link was a deep existential one. Still, I felt that nagging connection, always trying to pick up little Polish phrases from my grandmothers, cheering Polish Olympians, hoping one day to visit, maybe even to learn the language.

～

It was cold when I arrived in Warsaw that year, much colder than I expected. I wasn't prepared for it, having come from a Melbourne winter. I probably didn't even own a warm enough jacket for the chilly Polish spring. The trees still looked bare in the streets. The skies were mostly gray. Warsaw: gray, cold, unwelcoming, a concrete jungle, graffiti lining the shabby, communist-era apartment buildings. The clichés couldn't be layered on any thicker. It was the Warsaw that my grandparents might have remembered when they returned from Siberia: a wasteland, not the ornate, cosmopolitan central European capital of their childhood. *A sheyner shot*, a beautiful city, Zaida Izak would tell me, remembering his early years in the heart of Warsaw's Jewish neighborhood, 49 Pawia Street, now a nondescript concrete box, maybe not even standing in the same spot as it occupied when he was raised.

The conference itself was a watershed moment for me. Surrounded by this global cadre of scholars, many having a socialist outlook, mostly not Jewish, I felt at home. These were people who wrote about the Bund from a place of sympathy, even identification, with an underdog movement whose past was glorious and tragic. I learned a lot, not only because of the thoughtful papers that people presented but also by how people came to write about the Bund, and how they ended up at this workshop in Warsaw. I had always thought my pathway was obvious—I wrote about my own family, I couldn't think of why else you would choose to write about the Bund. In Warsaw, though, I discovered how deeply this movement, this past, could continue to resonate with people who were not raised or surrounded by Bundist veterans and activists. The papers at the conference were all very interesting, the discussions collegial and lively. Visiting Warsaw was a revelation for me professionally, giving me the chance to connect with like-minded young scholars from around the globe. More importantly, it gave me a week to think about the meaning of home, and of my connection to the past and to place. Walking those streets, visiting the monuments, trying to picture the ghostly Jewish landscape that could now only be conjured by a vivid imagination—this was where I tried to situate myself in the longer chain of the Slucki family.

When I visited Warsaw, I didn't really know anything about how Zaida's father, Yisroel Shmuel, lived or died. Later, I discovered that he died when Zaida was a teenager, which in part prompted Zaida to leave Warsaw. Sluggo shared his grandfather's Yiddish name, *Shmulek*, but I'm not sure he knew so much about his Zaida either. He never talked about him to me, and I don't know if his dad talked about him. I never thought too much about it. I already had one elusive grandfather, a life I could reconstruct only from the scraps of information, the small stories, quotes that Sluggo recounted. There were more pressing family matters to get to the bottom of than uncovering the layers of a great-grandfather who had died nearly a century earlier, whose name I didn't even know. But my visit to Warsaw in 2012 piqued my interest. Perhaps it was rediscovering a tangible trace of him, his tombstone, that made me feel that some connection was possible. Maybe it was that I was a new father, starting to think deeply about the role fathers play in their sons' lives, the influence they had. Perhaps I was trying also to make sense of why I wrote and taught about the Bund, about the Holocaust and its survivors, and about *di goldene keyt*, the golden chain of Jewish history and tradition of which I was a part. Although I had been reflecting on these things during my early morning walks around the sites of the old ghetto, it wasn't until the final day that I was able to really see the thing that still connected me to this place. Our visit to the Warsaw Jewish Cemetery would prove to be a revelation.

The conference organizers had set aside time for a formal tour of key historic sites: the Warsaw Ghetto Uprising monument, some important streets, the cemetery. The morning began with a short walking tour around the old Jewish neighborhood of Warsaw, the very neighborhood in which three of my four grandparents took their first steps, where they had seen joy, tragedy, poverty. Their own school of life, on the Jewish streets of Warsaw. Hard-working people, unaware that they were part of one of the most dynamic civilizations in Jewish history. It must have been hard at that time to imagine that those slums were at the center of a cultural renaissance, that the explosion of literature, theatre, newspapers, and politics around them was historic. By the time I walked those streets, they were part of a Warsaw that my grandparents wouldn't have recognized. They weren't even really the same streets, having been rebuilt after being leveled during the war. It's hard to know if my grandparents would even have been able to find the well-trodden streets on which they walked to school and played with their friends, let alone where their homes had stood. One picture of Bubba Mania and Zaida Izak from after the war shows Bubba sitting on the rubble of her old home, a look of sorrow evident on her face at the memories that must have been overflowing from her consciousness, the guilt of being the only survivor in her extended family apparent.

I tried to imagine my grandparents as children running through those streets, but my imagination couldn't make the leap. To do so, I had to not only picture my grandparents in their younger years but also imagine the streets that had vanished in the war's dusty after-math. Turns out the people weren't the only ghosts I was looking for. The buildings, parks, alleyways, and courtyards were also haunting me. I couldn't visualize how that neighborhood might have looked, it was so utterly transformed. Not like a city that gets modernized over time—a building knocked down here, a converted gas station there—but a city that was built on top of its own ruins. Each building was a steel and concrete memorial stone, a testament to what stood there before, marking the bodies and ashes buried underneath. A cemetery the size of a central European capital, without the solemnity.

We arrived at the cemetery by tram. The atmosphere among this group of scholars was upbeat. By now we had been together a few days, shared and critiqued our work, bonded over all the different kinds of Polish sausage and cheap Polish beer whose smell permeated almost every meal we ate. Those were good days for my soul, but not necessarily for my belly. As the tram rumbled through the outskirts of the old Jewish quarter, I couldn't help but think about how miserable it looked—the aftermath of communism laid bare before our eyes, a kind of concrete wasteland, punctuated by fast-food restaurants and cheap motels. Had Helen and I been to the McDonald's across from the cemetery eight years earlier? I couldn't quite remember. Something was familiar, but I couldn't pin down what. A very different Warsaw from that in which Zaida was raised, physically, culturally, politically. Jewish ghosts were palpable, Jewish life less obvious.

The visit to the cemetery that day was very somber, as any visit to a graveyard ought to be. It was windy, cold, gray. Fitting, as though someone had conspired to make my visit even more eerie. I had visited years earlier with Helen, but this time I felt much more prepared. This time I knew why I was there, which ghosts I was looking for. When I was there as a nineteen-year-old, I only knew that it was important for me to be there, that I was asserting my sense of connection to the ghosts haunting the cemetery, that I was part of the broken chain of Polish-Jewish civilization. Now, I was coming back, conscious that I was in fact a link in that chain, trying to hold it together.

The old Jewish cemetery is formidable, a vast cluster of tombstones, weeds, and overgrown trees and bushes. Thousands upon thousands of headstones in all manner of disrepair, punctuated by those that have been restored or maintained. Shiny little beacons that belie the reality of the place: not only a graveyard in the literal sense but also a symbolic graveyard for a once-thriving civilization. A veritable urban forest, very different from the cemeteries I'd been to in Melbourne, which were much more orderly, more suburban, more open, with headstones that were evenly spaced and uniform in style. Walking along the main path in Warsaw, it seemed orderly enough. The headstones were nicely polished, upright, with names occasionally familiar, the pathway wide and neatly maintained. As I walked just a little beyond the main corridor, with the security of knowing exactly where I was in relation to the exit, the cemetery took on a much more gothic feel, like something out of an Edgar Allan Poe poem. Unlike the outer suburban, sprawling cemetery of middle-class Melbourne Jewry, this graveyard seemed unplanned, assembled piecemeal by a working-class urban community trying to squeeze as many tombstones in as possible for centuries, interrupted only by the arrival of Hitler's armies. Some plots had been well preserved, such as the mausoleum built for the Yiddish writers I. L. Peretz, S. An-ski (who penned "Di shvue"), and Yankev Dinezon. Most, however, were more disheveled, covered with vines, leaning over, as though carrying the burden of history, their inhabitants unable to find peace and solace even in death.

At the symbolic grave for the Bundist martyrs fallen in the Warsaw Ghetto Uprising, we sang "Di shvue." I sang it with gusto as I looked at the names on the grave: Abrasha Blum, Mikhl Klepfisz, the Blones children, all fighters in the Warsaw Ghetto Uprising. These were the young Bundists and SKIFistn whose names we read each year at the Bund's April 19 ghetto *akademye*, whose stories were imprinted into our consciousness. These were my heroes, teens and young adults who had courageously sacrificed their lives to try to stave off the Nazi scourge a little longer, who had been murdered trying to protect their comrades and allow them to escape. I had other heroes: sporting stars, actors, singers. Those were aspirational, they represented a life I imagined for myself, starring for my football team or in a Hollywood film. Those were stars whom I wanted to emulate, the objects of my childhood dreams of fame and celebrity. The young Bundists whose remains were buried in the rubble of the ghetto were heroes of an altogether different kind. These were ghosts whose deeds inspired me, intimidated me. I knew how each of them died during the uprising, I'd known since I was seven or eight, and I knew that nothing I experienced could match their suffering, nothing I did could emulate their heroism. The best I could do was stand at their symbolic graves and sing "Di shvue."

Singing the Bund's anthem on that crisp spring afternoon, I thought of my Zaida and imagined all the old Bundists singing it at his funeral in 1978. What a sight it must have been, hundreds of true believers mourning the loss of their comrade, their elder statesmen, finally finding his long-sought peace. How did it sound to have hundreds of people sing an anthem with so much vigor, their oath of blood and tears? How did my dad feel standing by his dad's grave? I had heard so many times that they had sung "Di shvue" at his funeral, but I never knew if my dad was even able at that time to join in. A eulogy in the Bund's journal suggested Dad and his sister, Miriam, had sung with gusto, but I'm not so sure.

I imagined my dad and Zaida alongside me that day, thought how proud Zaida would have been at this gathering of young people doing their best to pay homage to his movement, his family. Singing "Di shvue" was no intellectual exercise, nor even a political statement, although perhaps it was partly those too. More than those things, singing "Di shvue" at those graves was my way of paying tribute to the ghosts that had followed me to Warsaw, and those I found on my return. The oath my Zaida and Dad must have sung hundreds of time, perhaps thousands, across continents and decades, in war and peace. It seemed a fitting tribute that I could sing it before the memorial to the fallen Bundists whose names and heroic deeds were so burned into my consciousness. Yes, this was much deeper than ideology or even a movement. This was a family matter; it was personal, visceral. This was spiritual. *Gaystik*, in Yiddish.

We followed "Di shvue" with the "Partisans' Hymn," the anthem of the underground movement in the Vilna ghetto which became the icon for Jews globally in the postwar years. This was even more a staple of my childhood than "Di shvue," with its incantation to "never say that you are walking your final path/ although blue skies may be concealed by dark clouds." Its underlying sense of hope, its urgent call to remember the past, and its plea to learn from the heroism of those who battled the Nazis routinely reminded me of my link to that tragic past. Each year on April 19, on Ghetto Day at SKIF camp, and at our school Holocaust memorial assembly, we would belt out the sacred hymn as the faces of the fallen ghetto insurgents stared down on us, their ghosts present even on the other side of the world from the rubble under which they were buried.

It was probably one of the earliest songs I knew, one of the few melodies that sends a shiver up my spine. When I was little I would secretly take pride in singing without the song sheet, standing there up on stage at *geto akademye* showing the world that I had this one down, a signal to my dad that his message was getting through, that he ought to be proud of me. Later, when I ran the Bund's Holocaust commemoration and taught SKIFistn the "Partizaner hymn," I would point to the line in the fourth stanza, "this song was written with blood and not with lead," to convey the gravity of its message to the young SKIFistn, often as young as eight years old. How could they possibly make sense of the tragedy of which they were singing without that visceral reminder that this was a song sung "between tumbling walls," "with grenades in hand"? Could they even imagine what that was like? Could I? Should we? It was unfair to expect that they would, just as it was unfair that my parents' generation and their parents expected us to make sense of it from so young an age.

The hymn always evoked tears, and at the *geto akademye* each year, people would sing it with all their heart. I certainly wasn't alone in that feeling of its solemnity. It could touch me in my bones. Sitting at a Yiddish performance at a Jewish studies conference a couple of years later, a pair of scholar/performers performed the "Partisans' Hymn" as part of a collection of Yiddish protest songs. I couldn't explain it now, but my body trembled, I felt nauseous, and I had to race out. A song that ought not be performed. It is a melody that affects my outer and inner core.

Back at the cemetery in Warsaw, we hadn't come prepared to sing the "Partisans' Hymn"; there were no song sheets, and most people didn't know it. I knew it. The melody, the words, the rhyming couplets were imprinted in my soul. So I sang it with gusto, even though I was more or less singing on my own. It seemed then like the most important thing in the world I could do, my *Kol Nidre*. April 19 is a *heylige date*. I probably wasn't even conscious of how much I had internalized Sluggo's annual refrain that April 19 was his own Yom Kippur.

～

After reflecting on the Bundists' graves and taking a formal tour down the main path, we were given the opportunity to explore on our own.

The Polish guide agreed to take me to see my great-grandfather's grave, which, luckily, was one of the still relatively few that had been catalogued. It took about ten minutes to walk to the grave. Somewhere along the way we lost Eran, my Israeli filmmaker friend who wanted to film me finding the grave, part of his documentation of his visit to Poland. I didn't mind—it seemed too personal, I wasn't sure how I'd react. The walk was perfectly peaceful, even pleasant. The deeper we got into the cemetery, the taller the trees, the more rustic the atmosphere. I was amazed at the guide's ability to find the headstone—there were no clear markers or signs that differentiated sections and rows, at least to my untrained eye. Just row after row of unkempt headstones, leaning in concert with the trees and vines providing them shade from the sun. Yet she led me straight to my destination, it seemed, without the slightest hesitation. We exchanged only a few words along the way; she was single-minded, focused on taking me to this tangible site of family memory.

Finally, we found it, further away from the entrance than I expected, toward one of the walls enclosing the vast graveyard, although I have no idea in which direction. Like most of the graves, this one was not fully upright, but it was still standing. It looked like someone had given it a little love over the past century. Vines had not yet overtaken it, and the stone inscriptions were still clear and legible. This gravestone had survived a century exposed to the elements, poverty, world wars, communism. Someone had been watching over the eternal home of this ghost, but who? The name inscribed on the tomb was Yisroel Shmuel ben Yakov—Israel Shmuel son of Jacob. That much I could decipher. I hadn't even realized before that, but my Zaida was named for his grandfather, just like Sluggo had been. A family tradition. It also meant Zaida's father died before Dad was born. I guess I knew that instinctively but hadn't thought too much about it. Jewish superstitions dictate that you don't name children after living relatives. It's considered bad luck, tempting fate. Here, I discovered another Slucki man who lost his father too young, although I don't know when or how. Turns out it's a tradition in our family.

I didn't learn any more from the text; it was in Hebrew. I did take a couple of dozen photos from all different angles. I didn't want to miss a scratch, chip, or crack in the headstone. I wanted to make sure I would later be able to decipher every letter, every bit of meaning hidden in those ancient characters. The Israelis I was with gave a basic translation, but it didn't seem right. They didn't have the religious sensibility to unpack the deeper meaning of the words. A colleague later translated it for me. It reads:

A straight [honest] God-fearing man

Who went [lived] a simple
[wholesome and moral] path

Who engaged in business faithfully
[honestly, with faith in God]

And took pleasure in the labor of his hands
[in what he earned by his labor]

Our teacher, Yisroel Shmuel

Son of reb Yaakov

Slucki

16 Nissan 5676 [19 April 1916]

We don't know a lot about Yisroel Shmuel, about his childhood, or about how he lived his life. Zaida and his brother didn't talk a lot about him to their children. Maybe they didn't remember a lot, or perhaps they didn't have many happy memories. He died while they were both young, and so neither had the influence of a father figure to guide them as they came of age.

Here's what we do know: Yisroel Shmuel was a humble shoemaker with a shop at a busy Warsaw marketplace. He was multi-talented, moonlighting as a cantor of some renown, although how renowned we don't know. Two conflicting family stories have been passed down, both highlighting his singing prowess. One story goes that in 1914, before the outbreak of the Great War, he was invited by a congregation in Berlin to lead Yom Kippur services and sing *Kol*

Grave of Yisroel-Shmuel Slucki, Warsaw.

Nidre, no doubt a great honor. The other story says that he traveled to Berlin that summer to study opera at a conservatorium. Either way, family memory insists on his talent and renown. Both stories end similarly. By the time Yisroel Shmuel was set to return to Warsaw, World War I had escalated into a continent-wide conflict, with international treaties drawing in all the major European powers. As a Russian national, an enemy subject, Shmuel was suspected of spying and was arrested by the German military. He spent months under German rule as a prisoner of war before finally being allowed to return home.

His singing voice was one of the few things that his sons talked about to their children. My aunt Miriam remembers that each year on Yom Kippur, the holiest day on the Jewish calendar, Zaida Jakub, for decades a socialist and atheist, would sing her the ritual song *Kol Nidre* with his own beautiful singing voice and would tell her this story of his father. It's a strange contrast to the story my dad always told about his father on Yom Kippur—that before the war, Zaida and his socialist friends would set up a table outside shuls and eat ham sandwiches, something Sluggo emulated in his early years. Maybe we were born with creativity flowing through our veins, or at least deep in our souls. Maybe Zaida somehow passed on his father's own creative flair to Sluggo, a link to a past that is so distant that it is almost unintelligible.

Yisroel Shmuel died in 1916, in the middle of a Europe ravaged by a senseless war, a Poland suffering under the yoke of German occupation. With hunger rampant and food in short supply, the neighboring grocery store alongside his workshop was extremely in demand, a place to pick up ever-more-scarce rations. Living under a curfew, a couple of local Jews asked Yisroel Shmuel if they could sleep on the floor of his shop so that they could line up early the following day at the shop next door. He hesitated, but the fact that it was so close to the curfew meant that he had no choice but to house them for the night. When the German soldiers saw that he was harboring people on the floor of his store, in contravention of the curfew, they beat him brutally. He died days later, a result of the bloody beating he had received at the hands of the occupying soldiers. This was not the last time Zaida would lose his loved ones at the hands of German soldiers.

In 1947, before leaving Poland forever, Zaida tried to pay one last visit to his father's grave. He knew that it would be his last opportunity before he headed to Paris and eventually to Australia, Canada, or the United States. He and Bubba were in Warsaw for a Bund conference and to say a final good-bye to comrades and friends. "My dear Eda and I walked around for a couple of hours and couldn't find our father's grave. We felt great frustration. I walked between graves that looked like they could fall at any moment." Cemeteries are remarkably resilient; they're designed to be, rows and rows of memorials built to stand the test of time, to endure far longer than the lives of those that they honor. Although Warsaw was almost razed to the ground, the cemetery survived enough to walk around. Still, Zaida couldn't find the grave. He must have been devastated: there were no graves he could visit for any of his immediate family. The final insult.

If only he'd had a guide and decades of indexing and preservation, like I did.

~

Yisroel Shmuel was pious, serious. Zaida's older sister, Chava, a well-known Yiddish writer and educator in Israel after the war, captured his earnest nature in a fictionalized retelling of her own birth. "Shmuel sat in a corner," she wrote, "with a small prayer book reciting Psalms, asking God that his wife Rivke should endure this easily." This was his only contribution to the scene, the only impression she captured of her father in her work.

His piety is the one consistency in the scraps we have. Zaida's letters give some insight, fill in some gaps. In 1950, writing from Paris, Zaida described his fear that they would struggle to make ends meet once they arrived in Australia. He recalled a childhood memory of his father, "a wholly gentle soul." When they had endured financial difficulties living at Świętojerska 18, his hard-working father struggling to bring home enough money for fish and meat for *shabbes*, the Sabbath, Zaida's mother would boil a pot of coffee to give neighbors the illusion that she was preparing a sumptuous *shabbes* feast. When it came time to observe the *shabbes* holiday, she would tightly close the doors so no one would see their shame. "With tears in his eyes," Zaida recounted to Mendel, "our father used to say, children, don't go astray, all will turn out well. Such faith he had, that even though he couldn't celebrate the holy *shabbes* with all the trappings, he could still be happy that he didn't have to accept anything from anyone. He had so many gentle character streaks that we must take and pass on to our own children and future generations."

Zaida had broken away from that path, like so many Jews in his generation. In a time when millions of Jews in Eastern Europe began to embrace modernity in politics, literature, and culture, many left the old world of religious observance and superstition behind them. In their droves, these Jews joined movements like the Bund and

Zionism; they learned the languages of their surroundings; they read the burgeoning body of secular Yiddish and Hebrew literature. They studied natural sciences and math, Karl Marx and Theodor Herzl, Simon Dubnow, Otto Bauer, Adam Mickiewicz, Leo Tolstoy. They escaped what they saw as the restrictive clutches of Judaism and joined the revolution in the Jewish world that imagined the Jews as a modern nation standing alongside the nations of the world. They saw themselves as equal to those around them, deserving of equal rights, opportunity, and safety from harm. Reading the inscription of my great-grandfather's tomb, the significance of this hit me. My Zaida was a revolutionary, not only because he was a member of a revolutionary political party but also because he was one of the millions of Jews in the early twentieth century to make a radical break with the world of their parents and imagine themselves on equal footing to their neighbors. He was revolutionary because of the enormous project in which he participated, that of transforming a traditional, premodern community into a modern civilization.

I don't know why he embraced the Bund, why he and his siblings distanced themselves from the piety of their father. Maybe he lost faith once his father died and he saw the consequences of war around him— the brutality, the famine, the way families were torn asunder. Perhaps it was a reaction to the abusive grandfather to whom his siblings were sent after Yisroel Shmuel died, who would punish Mendel harshly for lax observance and study of Jewish law. Perhaps it was simply the promise of the nascent Jewish Left, which offered young Jews a pathway to equality, which told them that they had dignity, that they were part of a Jewish nation, and that they deserved better than to remain second-class citizens in a world of expanding rights and protections.

It might be thanks to his father that he found that path. His father, the shoemaker, with unusually progressive ideas about educating his children, gave them a worldly upbringing, despite his own religious convictions. This was a rarity, Zaida would tell Mendel, for a humble shoemaker in that time and place. He had a warm, open heart, welcoming all others despite his own poor material circumstances. It was that openness, perhaps, to the modern world that

Jakub as a teenager in Warsaw. Second from the right is his sister Chava. This is the photo I most see myself in.

helped propel Zaida and his siblings into the new movements grow-ing rapidly around them.

Zaida Jakub left home as a teenager. After Yisroel-Shmuel died, his mother, Rivke, remarried. Left destitute with five children, she had little choice in order to feed her children. Her new husband promised that her five children would live with them. Once they married, though, he reneged, and her children were sent to live with Yisroel-Shmuel's father, a hard man who treated Zaida's siblings with contempt. Mendel, by then a teenager, a freethinker, and a stir-rer felt his wrath particularly. Mendel ultimately followed his broth-er's lead, leaving home as a teenager and taking their younger sister, Chasha, to the famous orphanage of Janusz Korczak, the pioneering pedagogue and children's author. Zaida and his older sister, Chava, saw the marriage as their cue to leave home. Already they objected to their mother remarrying, obviously not trusting the arrangement she had made. Very quickly, they left Warsaw, making their way to

Włocławek. It's not clear if they were simply looking for a new beginning, or if the circumstances of the Great War forced them to search for greener pastures.

Rivke also died in tragic circumstances, within a couple of years of Yisroel-Shmuel. Having fallen pregnant to her new husband, she tried herself to abort the pregnancy, unable to face the task of feeding more mouths, of delving even further into poverty and misery. She threw herself off a bed face-first to the floor. She did abort the fetus, but died shortly after from the complications of her impossible decision. Zaida and his three surviving siblings were orphaned before adulthood, forced to find their own path in a changing, unforgiving world.

World War I affected Zaida profoundly. His father was imprisoned and later murdered during its throes. He suffered hunger and the degradation of living under an occupying power. Perhaps it is no wonder he gravitated to a socialist party, with its promise of human dignity, equality, and freedom, a pathway out of the slums and degradation of Jewish working-class life and out of a world that produced the senseless violence of a world war. Socialism offered him a promise of hope where he experienced only hopelessness.

Another thing that struck me, reflecting on the translated text of the headstone, a revelation that came only years later: Yisroel Shmuel died on the 16 Nissan 5676, the second night of Passover. Or, as I discovered, April 19, 1916. April 19, the day that the young soldiers of the Jewish Fighting Organization in the Warsaw Ghetto took up arms against their own Goliath, their own Haman. April 19—the holiest day on Dad's calendar, the only day on our calendar whose ritual act of remembrance was non-negotiable. Perhaps not only because of the Warsaw Ghetto Uprising. More ghosts than we even knew.

I wish I could say that as I stood at Yisroel Shmuel's tombstone I reflected on what a remarkable and tragic life he had led; how he had been not only a witness to but a participant in some of the most explosive and extraordinary moments in the twentieth century. I would have had so many questions to ask him about World War I, about witnessing the revolution in Jewish life, about living in a world that was in total flux. The truth is, though, I didn't know any of this about him as I stood there in the cool of late spring, a gentle breeze blowing around me. Standing there, I was amazed at how peaceful it was, and the contrasts of that moment. Perhaps fifty or one hundred meters away, beyond the wall of the cemetery, the bustling city of my ancestors continued to pulse with its mix of communist gray and postmodern chic. All I could hear, though, inside those old walls and under the thick canopy of tall trees, which together soundproofed the space, was the breeze, the rustling leaves, the crunch of footsteps in the overgrown vines that covered the paths. The calm contrasted with the violence I knew not only had been part of that landscape during two world wars but must have been a daily part of my grandfather's and his family's life.

Mostly, though, I thought about the absence that this tombstone represented. I thought about the parallels between my father and me, neither of us knowing our paternal grandfathers. I hoped that the wistfulness in my father's voice when he spoke about his father was also present when Zaida told him stories about Yisroel Shmuel, if he even did talk about him.

That Yisroel Shmuel's tomb still stood there proved to me that I was connected to a longer chain of something, that I had a history that stretched much further back than World War II. I was amazed at how something so unassuming and unremarkable could have so much meaning to me. That this modest tombstone represented the most tangible link I have found to this civilization was a major revelation. Graves are funny like that; they represent permanence, a claim to the earth that the resting body inhabits. They are literally a concrete link to the dead; my family name on a century-old stone that binds me to a lost time and place. The headstone is a memorial not only to Yisroel Shmuel but to the Slucki family and to the millions of ordinary people that were part of the Polish-Jewish civilization that exists only in memory.

∽

Once again, I paused to think about the names. At the grave I learned that the names in our family were cyclical, that the name "Shmuel" went back further than I realized, that the name "Jacob" went back an extra generation. The act of naming is a meaningful but complicated one. I often think about how this simple tribute blurs the lines between absence and presence. Does the act of naming ensure a more permanent presence of the dead in our midst? Did Yisroel Shmuel see some of his father in Zaida? Did Zaida see his father in Sluggo? Was Sluggo a constant reminder to Zaida of the father that he lost at such a young age? In a way, this act of naming marks the person who assumes the name of the dead as a living memorial. They are burdened with that past, with a kind of responsibility to live up to who that person was, what he or she stood for. Was Sluggo named for his grandfather, Yisroel Shmuel, whose grave still stood in the gothic cemetery of Warsaw? Or was he named for Zaida's murdered son, Yisroel Shmuel, who had no grave? I still didn't know.

∽

On my return to my group, Eran, my new filmmaker friend, was not happy with me. "I wanted to film you visiting the grave!" "It was very emotional," declared my guide, betraying a distinct lack of emotion in her tone. She'd guided hundreds of people on these pilgrimages; I was surely just another one. These "emotional" reunions must have now become run of the mill for her. I was simply the latest in a long string of Western Jews returning to see only ghosts, ignoring what was still living in that ancestral home of mine.

The next day, my twenty-eighth birthday, I flew to New York to meet Helen and Arthur, who was now a week older than when I had seen him last. At that age, three months, a week was a long time. Would he remember me? How would he respond to seeing me after thirty hours of flying? How would all that reflecting on the role of fathers, and the absence of them, inform what kind of father I would be to Arthur? I was probably too tired and jetlagged to seriously consider those questions by the time we were reunited. Still, thinking about my great-grandfather gave me pause to think about the role fathers play in their sons' lives, and how absence and loss dictate in certain ways how we develop as parents and human beings.

When I think of Poland, and of Warsaw especially, I can't help but reflect on what home and homeland mean to me. How did my grandparents feel about Poland in the decades after they had made a new home? Did Zaida continue to feel the same sense of attachment in 1978 as he did when he left in 1948? How do immigrants relate to those places where their memories are scattered, generations buried deep in the ground? What about the descendants of those migrants? Australia is my home, but what is my homeland?

Clearly, I'm not Polish; I don't feel any sense of connection to Poland or belonging to the Polish nation, its history, or its culture. I don't speak or understand Polish, and I don't describe my grandparents as Polish ("they came from Poland," is my usual answer to questions about my surname, or "they were Polish Jews, Holocaust survivors"). I never heard them describe themselves as Polish, even though they spoke Polish with each other and with friends. What I do feel is that I'm part of a thousand-year-old continuum of Polish Jewry, of a Jewish civilization that endured many trials but that also produced one of the most intense bursts of creative and political energy in Jewish history. Warsaw, that strange tapestry of reconstructed medieval squares, Stalinist cinder blocks, and postmodern glass cubes, is my ancestral home, the city that, almost more than any other outside Melbourne, shaped my family and my life. The working-class Jewish slums in which Zaida was reared, dotted with peddlers, buskers, and courtyards, gave birth to his worldview, which eschewed material wealth and privileged the love of humanity, education, culture. The heroism of the fighters in the ghetto formed the foundational myths on which our little Bundist enclave built our universalist view of the world. That I grew up thousands of miles from there matters little. That it's essentially a different city than that

Jakub in his Polish military uniform, probably during the Polish-Soviet War. No one seems to know the date, or much about his time in the military. Dad used to tell the story that he tried to defect to the Soviet Union, enthused like many Bundists by the Russian Revolution. I'm not so sure, but it is a good story.

of my ancestors is of no consequence. My family was thrust from the land of their ancestors. Once they left, their hopes of reviving Jewish Poland, of maintaining their historic link, were snuffed out. They never went back.

It is not so much Poland or Warsaw to which I feel connected, but a mythical Jewish geographic space that exists now only in stories, history books, photographs. It is a homeland whose absence overlays that landscape in my imagination, but without walls, windows, or soil. It can only be this way because of what happened in the years 1939 to 1945. It is a space that has shaped us in ways we don't even appreciate. Its presence attests to the absence of a father figure and a grandfather, and I can't even begin to understand its centrality in shaping Zaida's journey. It was in Warsaw that I learned that Yisroel Shmuel's ghost must have hovered over Zaida, standing alongside those of his wife, Gitl, and his sons Chaim and Yisroel Shmuel. These were ghosts that he could not chase away.

9

Fathers

Zaida's second shot at fatherhood was bittersweet. He couldn't fully embrace his role, physically or emotionally. By the time Dad and Miriam came along, he was a broken, battered shell of the man he once was, none of the energy, vigor, or youthfulness that he had had in the 1930s. He did want to be a father again, to be part of the efforts to rebuild the world that had been destroyed. In late 1946, not long after returning to Poland, Bubba Eda had a miscarriage when she was around four months pregnant. Zaida described it to Mendel matter-of-factly, expressing relief that she was recovering after some time in the hospital. The episode gave him pause to consider the question of fatherhood, and whether or not he wanted to be a father again, with all the complications it would bring. "The doctors," he wrote, "consoled me that I shouldn't despair, because such a young woman will quickly be able to fall pregnant again after a miscarriage." Cold comfort for a man who only two years earlier had found out his sons had been murdered. "You [Mendel] yourself understand that one of the greatest goals now in my life is to have another generation, after my great misfortune."

Once he became a father again, though, Zaida felt a certain ambivalence about fatherhood. He wasn't ambivalent about his children, whom he loved very much and wanted to provide with a comfortable, peaceful life. But after losing his two sons at Chelmno and enduring so much, he wasn't sure he could be the father that his children needed, or how he could protect them from the burden that followed him. "I must not carry it with me into my new family life," he told

Baby Sluggo and Jakub, either in Paris or in Melbourne.

Teenage Sluggo and Jakub, Melbourne (late 1960s). Miriam is also in the photo. Dad used to keep this photo in his wallet.

Mendel. "Why should they be responsible for my pain?" He wrote to Mendel often about how torn he was watching his children grow up, and the constant painful memories of Shmulek and Chaimek.

Those memories of the first Shmulek and of Chaimek, whom Sluggo resembled, lingered constantly in the foreground, and because of his own trauma, Zaida's involvement in Dad's life wasn't as a constant presence. He didn't go to watch Dad play a single football match, didn't pick him up from school, usually wasn't around at dinnertime. He worked tirelessly in their small knitting factory, sleeping very little, unable to play a major role in the day-to-day raising of his children.

I often wondered how his father's ambivalence shaped Sluggo's own view of being a father. Did he just take the good bits and leave out the bad bits? Was it just improvisation, experimentation, learning on the fly how to be involved in your children's life when you had not witnessed it firsthand? He never said so, but I do think that to a large extent Sluggo modeled his own parenting style against that of his father. The kind of seriousness, the temper, the absence, all a part of Sluggo's childhood, were just not a part of my own. What would I take with me, and leave behind when I became a father?

~

"It's a boy . . . and he looks like Sluggo!" These were the first words Arthur heard when he entered this world. Arthur Manny Slucki was born on March 3, 2012, at 4:30 a.m., one day earlier than he was due to arrive. We were relieved he was born early—we'd seen friends whose babies came nearly two weeks late. They became the objects of people's interest, speculation. We didn't want that, people prying into our most private affairs. Arthur's early entrance, with its lack of fanfare, prevented the possibility of that. Even better, it all unfolded in the still of night, in secret, the last time he would do anything stealthily. We'd be able to control the news getting out. When everyone woke up on Saturday morning, there was a new member of the family to carry on the legacy, but until we told them, they were none the wiser.

We had lain down in bed that evening after *shabbes* dinner with Helen's family. We left Helen's parents that night, none of us expecting that the next time we saw them, they'd be Bubba and Zaida. We settled in for the night, watching television, Helen a little restless as she tried again to find a comfortable position.

And then it came, and with a big surge of pain that signaled our little tadpole was getting ready to come out, our lives changed.

We snapped into action; we were ready. We'd practiced, done our breathing exercises, gotten the hospital bag ready, made our plan. But as the old Yiddish saying goes, *a mentsh trakht un got lakht*, Man plans, and God laughs.

The surges of pain were quickly getting more acute for Helen. She tried standing, leaning over, sitting, showering. They only got worse. The nurses at the hospital told us to stay home, not to come in, that they'd ease, that we had time. We didn't want to drive in only to be sent home.

A mentsh trakht un got lakht.

We decided to head on into the hospital. The pain was too much for us to stay home and wait it out. It was close to midnight on a Friday night when we left the house; when we returned it would be a very different house—cluttered, noisy, a little dirtier, people coming and going, tired eyes the only constant. Pitch black outside as we drove, not much traffic at that time. King Street was the big worry—I had routes planned out depending on the time of day. If it was daytime, there was no way I would try to navigate King Street, one of the major business thoroughfares in central Melbourne, but at this time of night, I was confident we'd get quickly through the seedy nighttime version of King Street, dodging the drunken men spilling out of strip clubs. Helen was alarmed—the contractions were coming fast and sharp, there might still be hours of this to go. Her screams were ear piercing. I tried to be supportive, a subtle finger in my ear to dampen the decibels. Not subtle enough—it's one of Helen's most vivid memories of that night. Still, I was determined to play my part, get Helen and our tadpole there quickly and safely.

We got to the hospital, I walked Helen up to the maternity ward, and then I went to park the car. We were settling in there for the night, so I thought I'd better take it out of the tow-away zone. The nurses would take care of Helen, and I had time.

Or so I thought.

When I returned it turned out Helen was nine and a half centimeters dilated, almost ready to start pushing. We wouldn't even have time to do all the hypno-birthing techniques we learned, the breathing and visualization and sitting on the fit ball and playing the calming music that we had prepared on the iPod. It was go time.

A mentsh trakht un got lakht.

It was a quick labor, but Arthur wasn't coming out so easily, lodging his shoulder in an awkward spot. Insert Freud joke here. Two hours of pushing later, Arthur, unwilling, was yanked out by the obstetrician. Maybe he knew that he'd never again feel as safe and warm and didn't want to give that up so easily. Perhaps through some cosmic inheritance, he knew that the world was a tough place to live in and to make sense of. He didn't want to forgo the happiness and protection that only Helen could offer him.

Rabbi Simlai, a third-century Talmudic sage, taught that God gives embryos in the womb all knowledge of the Torah, and hence all knowledge of the world. When they are born, though, once they see the light of day, an angel comes down and, with a flick above the baby's mouth, takes all their knowledge away, so that life is a long process of recovering the memories that we once had. This, it is said, is how we get our fulcrum, that little recess between our nose and upper lip. Rabbi Joseph Soleveitchik, the twentieth-century American Orthodox Rabbi, took this a step further, arguing that if this was the case, then studying Torah was the process of returning to one's true self, an act of redemption. Centuries before Rabbi Simlai, Plato argued something similar: because the soul is immortal, it has seen and heard everything before. Searching and learning, therefore, are merely the process of recollection, of rediscovering what is buried deep inside one's soul. This might explain Arthur's dogged unwillingness to let Helen push him out of her womb, and his bitter struggle with the obstetrician. His first battle in life was to retain all that knowledge, to shield himself from the cruel world that saw his great-grandparents' families reduced to ashes. In the years that would follow, he rapidly began recovering those lost memories, his near-photographic memory ensuring that we had to start reckoning with how to talk to him about World War II, empires, and political violence before he was even five. Turns out, he recovered all that knowledge pretty easily.

This reminds me of a conversation I had with him when he was five. We were sitting on a park bench by the lake, having an after-school snack. It was already early in the summer, too hot to sit in the sun, but still nice enough in the shade. We had a couple of hours before the bugs came out; the perfect time for us to sit, chat, read. The kind of peaceful life I imagine Zaida yearned for. As usual, Arthur was blabbering away about some imagined football match, or something about marine life that he had been reading in a book, or recalling a Winnie the Pooh story. What pricked my ears up was something he was saying about pyramids and Pharaohs, and how different Pharaohs took on the forms of different animals. "How do you know that, bud?" I asked him. "Did you read it in a book or learn it at school?" Without skipping a beat, he said to me, "I just know it, I didn't learn it anywhere." I pressed: "But you must have learned it somehow? From school or a book?" "No," he answered, "I just knew it." Being the know-it-all I can be—*a mishpokhe feler*, a family fault—I tried one more time: "But Arthur, we don't just have knowledge from nowhere. Everything we know is because we learned it from somewhere." He wouldn't budge. Stubborn, like his father. And mother. And all his grandparents. Some traits are inherited, some knowledge must come through cosmically.

I figured he probably just couldn't remember where he'd read it, or when he'd heard it at school. I still think that, but part of me wonders if it's somehow part of that recovered memory, a glimpse into that knowledge that was whipped away as that angel slapped Arthur across the mouth, causing him to forget everything. Perhaps he knew what Plato and Rabbi Simlai taught thousands of years ago—that all knowledge is recollection, rediscovery of things that our souls have carried into this world.

～

Is this all just one big metaphor? Is this whole exercise just a way to recover these deep memories subliminally passed on from Zaida to Dad to me, and now to Arthur? Will he feel the burden of his Zaida's absence in the way I felt the absence of mine? Did Dad feel the absence of his own dead half-brothers as a weight that he had to drag behind him his whole life? Was his whole life just some way of recovering those lost memories, that lost knowledge that he didn't even know he had?

Biologists talk about epigenetics, a phenomenon in which traumatic experiences warp people's DNA, which, in turn, genetically shapes the children of the traumatized. Their own genetic makeup ends up a compendium of their parents' lived experiences. A geneticist in New York applied this idea in a 2015 study in which she claimed that children of Holocaust survivors had a higher risk of stress disorders, compared to the children of American Jews who lived through World War II in the United States. It's probably not so surprising that the trauma of the Holocaust had physiological effects on survivors. But that it then got passed down to their children genetically, and not only socially, was more unexpected. The study was controversial, criticized for its small sample size and some gaps in its methodology. Still, maybe there's something of that here, and Sluggo, Jacob, Arthur, and I are all somehow the product of the aftermath of the Holocaust, of our warped genetics. Maybe Arthur didn't come out so easily because he knew somehow what legacy he was set to inherit. Perhaps he was genetically predisposed to view the world with skepticism, fear, and suspicion.

Or maybe it is something more cosmic, something that was passed down in ways we don't even understand, but that help to mold the people we become. Perhaps there are certain kinds of knowledge we bring into the world when we exit the security of our mothers' womb.

In that moment when Arthur came into our lives, though, it was hard to feel the skepticism that came naturally to me. The sight of his head crowning and of Helen heroically pushing through the pain barrier and insisting that he join us, those first cries, cutting the umbilical cord—it was all a miracle. All I could see was the possibility that this life could offer, the innocence that could exist in the world. At that moment there was no tiredness, no anxiety, no hunger—only elation and hope. Perhaps it's too much pressure to put on Arthur, but in the very moment when I saw his little chubby legs, his face crumpled and creased like a pillow in the morning, the purple circle on his little cone head—his first yarmulke, courtesy of the suction device used to drag him out—right then I lost all my sense of the dangers of this world. All I could see in his eyes, pressed closed so

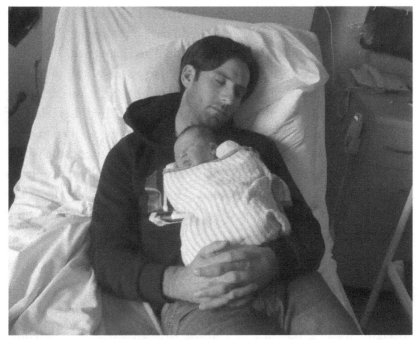

Arthur and I napping together on day one.

tightly, was possibility, redemption. Forget logic. He's just one person, and it's certainly not within his grasp to bring salvation to the world. But in that little pillowy package, I pinned the hopes of generations of the Slucki family. Unfair? Maybe. But no different, I imagine, or at least I hope, to Zaida's feelings upon his first glimpse of Dad, or Dad's the first time he held Jacob. I suspect until he died, Dad felt that same sense of elation, of hope, of possibility in me and Jacob. I hope I don't lose that feeling.

～

When Arthur was born, I was conscious of how the world had changed. He cried a lot initially, probably because of that whack across the mouth from Rabbi Simlai's angel. And then as he settled into Helen's chest, and then onto my chest, eyes closed, lips loosely pressed together, still working out how to breathe for himself, figuring out what this world was around him and who these people were, all I could do was smile and think about the kind of father I wanted to be, and the kind of boy I wanted to raise. If he could have put together the words, I'm sure he would have said: "What the hell just happened?"

When the nurses took him and Helen to go learn how to breast-feed, I walked down the street to a local coffee shop. It was drizzling a little, I was drowsy after not sleeping (not as tired as Helen, of course). The grayness and dampness of that morning seemed at odds with the massive change that had just taken place. For me, the whole world was different. For almost all of the other six billion people on the planet, it was business as usual. Mostly I just looked up at the gray sky as I wandered in my daze. All I could think was: "What the hell just happened?"

～

We called our parents at about six. They pretty much knew as soon as they got an early-morning phone call what it was about. They came at eight, wasting no time in coming to see their first grandchild, competing to hold, cradle, nurture the first of the next generation, like Sluggo had been. The pressure was on from the very beginning, consciously or not.

I remember Sluggo being tentative; it was probably decades since he'd held a newborn baby. Mostly he was aware of the distance in time between my own infanthood and Arthur's; how much had changed in terms of technology, parenting styles, and expectations; how little he remembered from his own hazy days cradling a noisy, sleepless infant. Sometimes he cited having raised us as evidence that he knew what he was talking about when it came to rearing a baby, but most of the time he deferred to us. "You'll make the right decisions," he'd tell us reassuringly as we battled sleep deprivation and frustration at a screaming baby who hadn't learned yet that it was his job to sleep, eat, and poop, and to do so on a predictable schedule.

Sometimes I wondered what Sluggo had been like as a dad when I was an infant. I always associated him with teenagers, getting the most out of his students, being able to talk to them on their level. But

I don't really remember seeing him interact with small children very often. I wondered how he'd be as a grandfather. Loving, obviously, but how would he relate to Arthur? How would he interact with him? Baby talk wasn't his shtick.

I wondered what Zaida Jakub would have been like if he'd gotten to be a Zaida. How would his personality have translated to that new relationship? Would he have played with us? Talked to us? Run around with us? Would he have looked at us, as I imagined he often did at Sluggo, and thought about the family that he could have had? About the grandchildren that might have run around the streets of Włocławek?

Parenting is hard work, relentless. We didn't believe it, no matter how often people warned us. We had been around children—Helen had worked part-time in a childcare center for years as a teenager; together we had given a hand with the middle-of-the-night feeds for our cousins' twin girls. We were ready, we thought. We'd read the books, blogs, and pamphlets, been to the classes, talked to all the people we knew with young kids. Nothing could really prepare us, though, for the enormous responsibility that comes with keeping another human being safe and healthy. The burden of just ensuring that person stays alive can itself be tough, with so many variables at play. Layer in sleepless night after sleepless night, challenges at work, boredom at home, and it can be easy to wonder why you would have children at all. Can't we go back to our uncomplicated life B.A.E (Before the Arthur Era), when we felt we had some control over the things in our life? When we were mobile? When the house was quiet? When every decision didn't feel like it carried quite as much weight as it does now? Day-to-day there seems to be more gravity in the choices we make, but the responsibility to the past seems much more urgent now, to tend to the health of the family tree, its roots decaying, maintained only by our attention and care.

Arthur is smart. He's been smart almost from the very beginning. He was alert very early on, smiling at us, recognizing us after a couple of weeks, observing the world around him and all these new and weird places: streets, houses, parks, cafés. Especially cafés. At about six or seven weeks, his pediatrician told us we were in for a tough ride: the reason he didn't sleep was because he was so smart, alert, and curious. We thought it was a little ridiculous to declare a baby smart—because he stared at his fingers? Because he cried through the night? I wonder if intelligence is something you can be born with, or if it must be learned. I've always leaned toward the nurture, rather than the nature, but since seeing Arthur develop, and seeing how much he embodies some of the best and worst personality traits in our family (kindness, stubbornness, the need to be right), I've questioned that feeling.

He hit many milestones early: talking, reading, counting. "Is he actually reading?" people would ask us as we sat together in the coffee shop reading our books. "Does he actually know how to do multiplication? He's already better at math than me!" How did he know when Hawaii became a state? When Genghis Khan conquered Asia and Europe? When Homo sapiens emerged? What hammerhead sharks eat? Arthur is a sponge, though it was hard to have imagined that Dr. Lou was right in June 2012 when she declared that this baby was such a handful because of his manifest curiosity.

Ergh, I'm *that* parent now.

No one marveled more at his intelligence and development than his grandparents. Dad thought he was the greatest child in the world, the culmination of all he had done right in raising me. "Dave, look how strong his legs have gotten. Is that normal?" he'd ask while he propped Arthur up on the coffee table. Sluggo grew into the role of Zaida. Every Monday, when Helen and I were both at work (we split the other days working from home), Dad would take Arthur for the morning. When Arthur was really small, he would work while Arthur slept. Later, they would go walking, get coffee, visit my great aunt and great uncle around the corner, play in the park. He never did the baby talk thing, but he did learn to communicate with baby

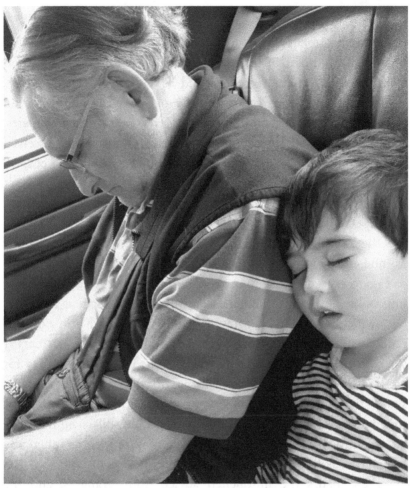

Two peas in a pod, New York City (2015).

Arthur, and then to negotiate with and spoil toddler Arthur. They played board games together, did puzzles together, drew pictures. Dad tried to teach Arthur to play chess, which he learned to do not long after Dad died. He was a loving, doting Zaida, unencumbered by the responsibilities of parenthood, by the burdens of the past. They were twins, separated by a couple of generations. Baby Arthur giggled and smiled at Zaida's antics, and reveled in his attention later. When Arthur was with Dad, he was, as Sluggo might have said, "like a pig in shit."

～

Fatherhood presents its own particular challenges. Being a father brings with it a certain set of expectations—within our family and from the world around us. Never did I feel more watched, judged, than as a father. When Arthur cried, people looked at me with pitiful stares; when I couldn't stop him crying, the stares turned to glares. When he was well behaved, I was a star, bucking some perceived trend of absent or uninterested fathers. In that way, fathers get slack that mothers don't; for many, showing up seems to be enough. I get told what a great father I am just for doing my job. For Helen, it's just expected that she'll do it all. Old attitudes die hard.

There's a flip side, though, a less generous one. People see fathers as inherently incapable of raising children, which explains why it's so easy to exceed expectation. People expect fathers to be idiots; it is impossible for many to imagine that we are equal partners in raising our own children. "You're babysitting today? Giving Mum a break?" random strangers ask as we sit quietly, minding our own business at the coffee shop on a Sunday morning. When Helen goes away for work for days at a time, or has a yoga workshop or teacher training, she is invariably asked who's looking after Arthur. "Is this the first time he's looked after him on his own?" people still asked her years later, a throwback to a time when fathers were seen as inherently lacking the skills to keep a child alive.

Then there's the unsolicited advice from strangers, and the theories, and the general sense that I must be the assistant in the child-rearing hierarchy of our house, Helen's deputy, the family shit kicker. Not to mention the almost universal cultural depictions of fathers as dopes, and mothers as primary caregivers, sharing a special bond that fathers can't understand or identify with. Bullshit.

I've also been viewed with suspicion: Can't you control your crying kid? Are you really even his dad? One day, Arthur was throwing a tantrum in the streets, and I was talking firmly but calmly to him. Who knows what the hysteria was even about? It was such a non-event: toddler wants something, doesn't get it, lets the world know.

On this day, a woman hovered, suspicious, keeping her distance but also keeping a close eye on me. Was this some test? Was she going to try to help me? Offer me some unsolicited advice? No, even worse, I think. She was making sure I wasn't kidnapping Arthur. The sight of a man with a crying child could only be interpreted in that way, apparently. A noble gesture from a stranger, maybe, but utterly humiliating for me, trying to get through a Sunday morning with a toddler behaving exactly as a toddler should, me reacting exactly as a parent should. Had Helen been in my position, this woman might very well have judged her, but would not have assumed her to be a predator, a kidnapper.

Another version of this: when Helen took Arthur to the maternal and child health nurses that the local council provided, within the first few weeks, among the standard screening questions, the nurses probed Helen on how Arthur's father was doing, how he was adjusting, coping with the stress. It became obvious quickly that what they were screening for was if her husband had been abusing her, a line of reasoning that makes perfect sense in the effort to protect women against domestic violence. The rational part of me knew that. Of course, you have to take all measures, especially when it comes to these periods of transition and stress, when a parent feels that they're losing some of the control they thought they had, when they are sleep-deprived, when they are not operating at full steam because of the major life change that has just taken place. But it still hurt: the idea that in the eyes of the state, I was a potential wife beater, vulnerable in moments of high stress to taking my frustration out on Helen and baby Arthur. It wasn't personal, but it was hard to not take it personally.

∼

Why do I even care what other people think or how they perceive me as a father? Surely it doesn't actually matter in terms of how I raise Arthur, or the values I teach him. Dad always taught me to be true to myself, to not worry about that outside noise. At his core, though, I think he cared a great deal about external perceptions, and measured his success to an extent based on how he was perceived. He wanted to be recognized for his achievements and to be judged fairly for his near misses. He reveled in former students acknowledging the outsized role he often played in their lives; brooded when they failed to reciprocate the goodwill he had shown them. He could show a streak of passive aggression when he felt aggrieved. "I gave them their first opportunity" or "I introduced them to that agent," he'd insist, before dismissing the slight. "I don't care, good luck to them," he'd say, protesting too much. He didn't want to let those things eat at him, but they did. He wouldn't like to admit it, but he also could have a delicate ego, easily stroked, easily slighted.

Some of that filtered down to me. I care far too much about what other people think, about my students' course evaluations, about book reviews. The thing I care most about, against all logic, is how I'm perceived as a father. I smart at any assumption that ours is a traditional house with antiquated gender roles, where my role in raising my son is a backseat one.

Really, what am I complaining about? I'm not a victim; I do my best as a father and husband, but given the shockingly high rates of domestic and child abuse, people *should* look at me suspiciously. In Victoria, Australia, where Arthur was born, one in four women had experienced intimate partner violence in their lives in 2016. In more than 90 percent of all domestic violence incidences, the perpetrator is a man. In South Carolina, where we live now, it's one in three women. Maybe this is evidence that we should view all fathers as potential predators, and it is just sensible in times of transition, like having a baby, that we are hypervigilant. I could never imagine raising a hand against Helen, but aren't we all susceptible to committing acts of violence, given the right circumstance? Isn't that partly what the violent twentieth century taught us, when so many ordinary citizens in so many different places participated in such gratuitous acts of evil against their fellow citizens, their neighbors, their fellow humans?

It's all very sobering to think about, particularly when raising a boy. Will he one day count among those statistics, a perpetrator? I worry almost as much about this as I do about him being that other kind of statistic. One of the challenges about modern fatherhood, and being a man today, is how to raise a young man that continues to break that mold, how to be part of a shift toward the eradication of domestic violence. More broadly, how can we, on the one hand, insulate Arthur from the fact that this exists, and at the same time instill in him the kind of fire in his soul that fights against the sexism and misogyny still so prevalent in the world around us? We show by example, certainly, by building a home in which all parties are equal, and all shoulder the burdens of raising a family equally. We talk about all people with respect and insist on their dignity and humanity. In a sense, this is the easy part. We do it every day in how we move about in the world, and just like I learned that way from my dad, Arthur will surely learn those lessons from us.

But how do we know it will work? How do we know that he will turn out as we imagine? Grow into the man we hope he will be? How do we make sure he turns out kind, compassionate, loyal? What if he turns out to be self-centered, obnoxious, and mean? It's this that is most terrifying. There is no way to know how he will internalize these legacies and the lessons that we want to pass on. He won't turn out how we want, he will be an individual, and we have only limited control over that. And if we do try to control it, we will surely only suffocate him, push him into some kind of rebellion. The only thing we can do is let go of that need to be right, the need to be in control, the need to be God.

~

This all feeds into bigger, existential questions, to which I have no answers, that keep me up at night. How do I pass on this difficult legacy that I have inherited? When do I start talking to him about what happened to his great-grandfather's wife and sons, to his great-grandmother's sister, father, aunts, uncles, and cousins? How do I strike that balance between the need to protect and the imperative to pass on the grave inheritance given to me, the kind of inheritance no one wants? I want desperately to shield Arthur from that knowledge. Who knows? He may already have it buried deep in his unconscious, waiting to rediscover it in school, in history books, on television, and at the movies. Maybe, as some of those geneticists claim, his DNA carries the scars of that past and his ability to respond to adversity is partly the result of Zaida's experiences, not to mention those of his other seven great-grandparents. But I don't want him to have that burden, the burden of simply knowing that such things are out there in the world, still today. That once upon a time, it was his own family that was the target of hatred and violence, and could be again in the future. I want to preserve his innocence for as long as I can.

But I can't. It started early, when he picked up a children's history encyclopedia and turned to the World War II page. I saw it in front of me as I pushed the pram through Hampton Park, and I looked down and staring up at me and Arthur from the page below was the man with the little moustache, his Nazi insignia splashed across the page. How would I explain that to him? I still haven't figured it out, but I knew right then that I couldn't protect him from knowing how the world worked for much longer. I couldn't keep that knowledge from him. I don't want to bullshit him, treat him like he can't handle it. The opposite: I must teach him how to handle it.

To be sure, I could easily walk away from that past, ignore it, minimize its centrality to our lives. And in a sense, it's not even the bigger story of what happened to the Jews of Europe that draws me back to this responsibility. It's the memory of Gitl, Shmulek, and Chaimek, whose names I didn't even know until I was an adult. It's those ghosts that will someday join Arthur on his journey. I don't think I can avoid that, or walk away from it.

The more I think about it all, the more muddled and complicated it seems to get. As I dig further into that past, the harder I find it to know how to filter information through to Arthur, and how to teach him in a way that is not stifling or traumatic. No one *wants* to traumatize their children. But maybe we have no choice. Maybe we just have to wing it, respond to the situations as they arise, answer the questions he asks, allow him to have his childhood without shattering his illusions about the world and other people. Either way, it's all a work in progress, and I'm not sure it can be anything else. The uncertainty is probably the only certainty.

~

So, what sort of person do I want Arthur to be? What do I want to teach him? To be a mini-me, living out all the dreams I wished for myself when I was younger, my unfulfilled ambitions, to be an astronomer, an actor, a footballer? No, none of those things. He'll carve out his own path and I'll support him, like Sluggo supported me. I want him to be true to himself, whatever that means. I want him to question everything, to eschew orthodoxies. I want him to recognize how the past shapes the present, his present, and to make his decisions with that as the jumping-off point. I want for him to be ambitious, but for his ambitions to stretch far beyond his own career and material success. I hope that he'll value his family as we do, in all its messiness and beauty, and embrace as family even those whose blood we don't share. I want him to be flexible, to be able to make a home in any place he finds himself. I want him to go through the world with a sense of adventure, of awe, and of fearlessness despite what he will invariably learn about the world. I want him to see the beauty in the world and in the people with whom he interacts every day. I want him to feel empowered and to empower others. I want him to value the leg up that he has gotten in this life, generations in the making, with freedoms and privileges his great-grandparents could only dream of. I want him also to recognize that his security and prosperity are built on the back of the dispossession of other peoples and the exploitations of their bodies and their labor. This legacy that has consumed me also does not excuse us from that. I want him to stay curious, to seek out the complexity in all situations, to feel empathy with others, and to act on that empathy. I want him to want to change the world for the better, even if I believe it is only possible for an individual to do so much.

I guess that in the end these are all things I prize in the aftermath of Zaida and Sluggo's lives, all traits of their personalities, all things they inherited or picked up along the way that I want for my life and for Arthur's. What I've come to learn is that there is no point trying to replicate the parenting of the generation before; circumstances have changed, expectations are different, and the world is a very different place. All I can do is bring myself to the role, carrying a messy potpourri of knowledge, experiences, and beliefs that I've picked up along the way, and hope that, like I did and like Sluggo did, he takes the good stuff and learns from the bad.

10

Ghosts

"Make sure you sing this at my funeral," my father said to me after belting it out for what would be the last time in his life, on December 26, 2015. We had just finished singing "Di shvue."

We didn't know then that three days later he'd be dead, and eight days after that we would indeed be singing it by his graveside, just as he had by his father's graveside thirty-eight years earlier.

At that moment in New York City, though, together with his son at an event celebrating the Bund, Sluggo had a spring in his step. Reconnecting with friends whom he hadn't seen for forty-five years, he worked the room as if it were one of his own events, planning future projects, catching up on half a lifetime apart. We had just spent six weeks together in Charleston and New York City. On this night, two days before he was due to depart for Australia, we celebrated the living legacy of the movement that had been central to our family for more than one hundred years. After all he knew about the violent twentieth century, Dad still maintained a kind of sunny optimism, a sense that he was still a revolutionary, that he could still change the world.

≈

Sluggo died on December 29, 2015. It was sudden, unexpected. The shock was unimaginable. An hour earlier we had spoken on the phone. He had called from Los Angeles to say goodnight to Arthur. We spoke about the everyday, banal things: who he had caught up with that day, updates on family. Nothing out of the ordinary. Arthur

Last family photo, New York City (December 28, 2015).

tried to show him his new pajamas and socks over the phone, still trying to work out this old technology, the telephone. It was about 7:20 or 7:25 at night, past Arthur's bedtime. I rushed him off the phone. We'll talk to you to tomorrow, I said. We didn't. Arthur went to bed, I did some work. Helen got home around ten o'clock from yoga. I went to bed, down in the basement of the townhouse we had been renting with my parents in Harlem. When Helen rushed down the stairs screaming, I thought she was laughing.

Then she told me to sit down.

I knew.

I don't know why, but there was that look in her eyes.

I knew.

The call had come from Los Angeles, where my parents were stopping over to visit family and friends on their way home from their six weeks with us. Dad had been out walking; he collapsed in the street, suffered a heart attack, and was dead before he arrived at the hospital.

Just like that.

First thing the next morning, Helen told Arthur. I wanted to, but I wouldn't even have been able to get the words out if I'd tried. My reconstructed version of what she said: "I have something very sad to tell you. Last night, Zaida Sluggo got very sick. His heart stopped working and he died." I remember Arthur's reaction. I was sitting on the stairs sobbing, but I don't think I'll easily forget his response: "Can you please say that again?" He was shocked; he understood the gravity of what Helen was telling him perfectly well. That afternoon he told Helen: "Mummy, I want to die before you." Helen told him that would be a tragedy, that parents should pass before their children. Arthur responded that he didn't want to be lonely, by himself. Hopefully, Helen said, you'll have someone that you love when we pass away. "But now Bubba Mich is lonely by herself," he answered. Forced to face his own mortality at three; conscious of how Zaida's death affected us all.

It was fitting that Dad would die in the most melodramatic way possible. Ever the dramatist, he had a flair for the spectacular. I knew he was never going to be someone who got old and sick and faded away. He would die with panache, with gusto, just as he had lived. He wasn't going to go gently into that good night. No matter the inconvenience, his passing would make a splash all over the world. Within hours, tributes flowed in from Australia, the United States, Mexico, France, Israel, and Cambodia. Students, friends, and family sent their fondest memories, expressed their own grief and their solidarity with us. His funeral featured on the local news bulletin, an obituary appeared in the New York Yiddish *Forverts* (Forward) newspaper. Local Jewish community organizations and drama education bodies eulogized Sluggo. The Cambodian orphanage he supported held a traditional Buddhist mourning ceremony. He would have found it all fitting. Just right. The recognition he deserved. No one would have reveled in it more than he. The irony.

~

The next weeks were hectic. I met Mich in Los Angeles. We flew home to Melbourne, landing early Saturday morning. That journey home was surreal. We were well looked after by Qantas, Australia's national carrier. Business-class seats, first-class lounge at LAX, shepherded through security, customs, immigration. It was the most luxurious trip I've taken, probably the most luxurious trip I'll ever take.

Mich and I sat in a private room in the Qantas lounge at the airport, messaging Jacob, worried that he was alone; messaging Helen, hoping that Arthur was coping with the news, processing it as best as a three-year-old could. We could choose anything off the menu. Neither of us had eaten for days. We still weren't hungry, but we ordered some food, thought it would be best to eat something. The server came in and out, not sure whether to give us space or to keep an eye on us. She sat with Mich for half an hour; they wept together. Death brings perfect strangers together, friends by necessity. I ordered calamari and fries—the oily batter filling my stomach, making me feel a little more human with every bite, washed down with swigs of diluted whiskey, the ice in the glass melting as quickly as the tears pouring from my red eyes. I needed something to help me sleep on the flight. It was New Year's Eve, somewhere between 11:00 p.m. and midnight. I only remember that because I can still see the NBC New Year's Eve celebrations from Times Square, where Mich and Sluggo had celebrated New Year's Eve the previous year with Arthur, on the TV in the background. One of the early reminders that everything would bring the trauma back home to us in a visceral way. I asked our server to change the channel. This was no time for celebration. Happy fucking new year.

There was a lot of weeping on the long, restless flight, red-eyed on the red-eye. After being shepherded through immigration control in Melbourne, we found Jacob waiting for us. The look in his eyes betrayed his emotions. This was unusual for Jacob, so reserved, so stoic. He doesn't usually give a lot away. When our grandparents died, he wore his sunglasses throughout the funerals, inside and out, no matter how bright or gloomy it was. He didn't want to reveal his vulnerability. That's always been his way. Our grandmother, Bubba Mania, used to tease him: "You're such a *tsinik* [cynic]," she'd say, in her charming linguistic cocktail of Polish, Yiddish, and English. That Saturday morning in Melbourne, there was no hiding what lay beneath. His eyes showed a mix of utter bewilderment, sorrow, and pity that usually wouldn't penetrate his gruff exterior. He didn't cry out loud like me, but that look said it all.

It was a look we'd see repeatedly over the next week from hundreds of people, as we saw family and friends for the first time since my dad collapsed. They'd come to Mich's house (Mum's house now, not Mum and Dad's), knock on the door, put down the cake or bagels they brought with them, and cry into our shoulders. I hadn't expected to come back to Melbourne for at least another eighteen months. We had visited only months earlier. It was surreal to be back, among family, friends, strangers. Everyone seemed a little like a stranger. The world had changed irreversibly (although what change is reversible)—no one was the same person we knew before. Everyone was navigating a world without Sluggo. The same things repeated over and over, as people tried to work through their shock:

"How could this happen?"

"Was he unwell? He seemed so vibrant."

"He just messaged me on Facebook last week!"

"We were going to meet for coffee when he got back."

"I was looking forward to working with him our new project."

We weren't the only ones seeking words of comfort, an explanation; not the only ones refusing to accept that Sluggo was gone. People sat around the table, in the living room, or by Dad's study stunned, trying to find the right words, usually failing. We were in a daze, everyone navigating through the fog with half-finished cups of tea, stale biscuits, and two-day-old bagels.

The line between mourner and comforter blurred as we all tried to come to grips with this new, post-Sluggo world. Everyone felt like they'd lost a friend, a guide, a father figure. Sluggo had a way of giving all of himself to people. Everyone felt that their relationship with him was special, unique. How could there be a world without Sluggo? What would the world look like without his boundless energy and positivity? So many people whose lives were shaped by his wisdom and his generosity now bereft. He was, as so many people reminded me, "larger than life." How small life seemed now without him.

～

Those few days we waited, waited, waited for my dad's body to be flown back. Funeral, minyan, shiva. A whirlwind. Hundreds of hugs, maybe thousands. Stories we hadn't heard, stories we'd heard many times before. People coming and going. Food. So much food being brought. Even in the luxurious kitchen pantry my parents had built, and in the enormous fridge, we couldn't find space for all the cakes, bagels, cookies, and frozen meals. Jews sure do know how to do death. The Jewish custom is that mourners bury the body within twenty-four hours, something about moving quickly into the mourning phase. They say that in that period, the focus is directed toward the deceased, but after the burial, it shifts to the mourners. Jewish mourning rituals are tightly structured, millennia-old traditions that help those grieving get back to their lives. By burying the body quickly, you don't have to worry long about the logistics of funerals, burials, keeping watch over the body. You can get on with the brutal business of grieving, self-pity, and readjustment. We didn't have such luxury. With Dad stuck in Los Angeles with the coroner, we didn't even know exactly when the funeral would be scheduled, something usually very predictable. We couldn't tell family and friends until after he had been delivered to the hands of the Melbourne Chevra Kedisha, the local Jewish burial society. That wasn't until Tuesday morning. On top of all that we were processing, we also had to deal with the coroner and Chevra Kedisha in Los Angeles, and the airline that was flying him home for the final time. This trans-Pacific flight, which he'd made so many times since his first visit to Los Angeles in 1959, was his last. Those days he spent thirty thousand feet above the Pacific Ocean were some of his most restful, the only time he really could sit back quietly, uninterrupted, captive in the air for those fifteen hours. That last flight would be the most peaceful one yet.

For some, death comes as a relief, after a period of suffering. For others, it marks the endpoint of a difficult relationship, an opportunity to start afresh. Yet others are sparked into a kind of soul-searching, a period of coming to terms with what their relationship meant, what the legacy would be. I had no such confusion; I knew exactly the impact my father had had on me and so many others. I was lucky—my father was a mentor, a comrade, a friend. He showered me with unending, unconditional love throughout my life. All he wanted was for me to succeed. As someone wrote to me the day after his death: "You really lucked out with your dad." The loss cut deep; the scars would be enormous. It was hard to see myself as lucky, though. How would I come to terms with my father dying? What would I do, losing the person who was my biggest influence, my biggest cheer squad? The person I wanted to ask about this, the person who had been through this journey I was now forced into, was Sluggo. The irony was not lost on me.

Thirty-one is an unnerving age to lose someone. I had friends who had lost parents at a much younger age. I felt lucky that I had been able to develop such a close bond to my dad in different phases of my life. But I was too young to lose him, to imagine the rest of my life without that guiding light, like I was being sent out on my own really for the first time. He was in a strange, in-between phase where he had lived such a full life, but had so much left in him, where *we* had so much left. He was ready for this chapter, a born elder statesman, there to guide his followers through all stages of their own lives. And Mich was now staring into the void, a lonely life ahead. She had just retired, had been looking forward to the reward of a life of leisure and travel and being a bubba that she had earned after decades of life as a working mother. My mother, robbed of her just rewards, married since she was twenty, now destined to fend for herself.

On the morning of my dad's funeral, I walked down the street to a local coffee shop near my parents'—no, my mum's—home. It was a walk I'd done hundreds, maybe thousands, of times throughout my childhood, to the milk bar—something like a small grocery store—to the pharmacy, to the fish-and-chip shop, to the news agent, to the pizzeria, or to the train and bus stations. The sun was out. It was summer, although when I arrived in Melbourne a few days earlier it had been overcast. Now, with the sun shining down, I felt a particular kind of warmth and a shiver down my spine. I looked up. Like Dad, I don't believe in heaven or afterlives, but that was the first time I was aware that my dad's ghost was somehow alongside me. The warmth of the sun was like an embrace from my dad. He would be alongside me that day as I would do the hardest thing in my life—bury him.

Burying a loved one is a surreal experience. I'd seen it from a distance previously, having lost three grandparents, all in their eighties, all succumbing to periods of illness. The mechanics of a funeral, the financial burden, the need to be detail-oriented—these are all at odds with the raw emotional state that typifies grief. It's the worst possible time to make important decisions. Which burial plot would Dad have liked? Should we put a death notice in the local Jewish newspaper? What should we do with his car? What should we do with all the bagels that our loved ones kept bringing? How were we going to observe shiva?

At times, I envied those whose loved ones died with some advance warning; at least they could plan for death, get their affairs in order, so to speak. Can you ever plan for death? We watched both my grandmothers take their final breaths after months in hospitals and hospices. I'm lucky I never saw my dad sick. I don't have to live with memories of his decaying body and mind. The sickest I ever saw him was probably with a cold. I don't have to remember feeding him when he couldn't feed himself, like I helped do with Zaida Izak. Nor do I have the image of his lifeless body in the hospital room like I do with Bubba Eda, that sense of relief that her suffering had ended mixed in with the raw grief. Only grief, now, and pain, and thoughts of what might have been.

In any case, in those days and the months following, we were all in shock. The suddenness of his death pierced our souls, crushed our spirits. We felt a little of everything: sadness, anger, fear, nostalgia. We tried to understand how it could happen. People gave us their theories: he was overweight; too unhealthy; too much Diet Coke; too much junk. Fuck you all and your theories. I just want my dad back.

No, we were in no frame of mind to be making decisions.

I am the family eulogist. Not through any official decision. I simply inherited my father's knack for public speaking, and perhaps just a little of his eloquence, his ability to weave a compelling story. Whenever there was any kind of minyan or memorial, he would always insist on saying a few words, sharing a few stories and recollections. At one particularly awkward minyan, when the eulogies didn't avoid discussing the checkered past of the deceased, Sluggo managed to cut through the tension and paint a picture of a warm and funny friend. He had a way of seeing the best in people. He was a natural storyteller. Not above embellishing details for dramatic effect. "Don't ruin a good story with the truth," he used to joke. He didn't give the eulogy at his father's funeral, much too hard at the time. But I don't remember him ever missing an opportunity to tell a story about someone or share some memories. He reveled in the spotlight, his natural habitat.

Mostly, I wrote Dad's eulogy sitting at his favorite café—his "office" for the past few years, now my office in the days leading up to the funeral. He would meet us there for a coffee or a Diet Coke in between meetings with students, budding actors, or people going to Cambodia or New York who needed a contact. He wasn't even a coffee drinker; he just loved the buzz of the place, and they loved him there. He became a fixture. The staff there were devastated. His infectious personality, his generosity of spirit, his massive heart had left their impression, as they always did.

I didn't pay for a coffee in those few days. The little things. A sure sign that the love you put out into the world gets returned in kind.

One thing that people said and wrote to me over and over in those weeks was that my dad had a massive heart. Always open, always embracing. Ironic that he died of a heart attack, or maybe very appropriate. Maybe his heart just couldn't handle being so open to everyone. Perhaps it overflowed. A friend of mine who had been a student of Sluggo's told me a story of when she was in his drama class. On the first day of class, Dad told the students that he kept a stash of coins and some bills in the top drawer of his desk. His office was always open for students to hang out or work in, even if he wasn't there. If they needed some cash for lunch or anything, they could take what they needed, as long as they replaced it. A small but simple act of kindness and trust, but one that typified how he related to the world around him. If you put your trust in people, if you treated them with respect (*derkherets* in Yiddish—he would always use the Yiddish word with me, as though it had some deeper meaning than the pedestrian English translation), then they would ultimately respond in kind. He was never about punishing students, or me and Jacob. He favored empowerment, giving his charges the feeling that they mattered, that they had worth.

On the day of the funeral we drove the roughly forty-five-minute drive to the newer Jewish cemetery on the outskirts of Melbourne. We weren't the first there, but we arrived well ahead of time. We knew there'd be a lot of people and wanted to make sure we could easily get a parking spot. Even in times of grief, we managed to plan for those small things. It was difficult to get into the *shtiebel*, the chapel at the cemetery. There were already dozens of people there. I was overwhelmed. The first person I saw at the doorway was Fletcher, a student of Sluggo's from the early 1990s who went on to forge a career as an actor. Of course, Sluggo was very proud of Fletch's career in the industry, and they also shared a bond through their mutual love of cricket. I don't know why, but seeing Fletch, probably for the first time in twenty years, I broke down. Then I saw Michael, for whom Sluggo (Charlie, to him) had been a formative influence and a father figure. I broke down again in his arms. His beard was much longer than I'd ever seen it, a wispy, scruffy long beard, like a Chassidic Jew, or one of the lead singers from ZZ Top. His bristly whiskers pressed into me, or I pressed into them, as we both wept for the father and father figure that we'd lost. I remember the distinct feeling of crying into his beard as it absorbed my tears, a comforting, scratchy bed of straw.

One after another, people came up to me, people I hadn't seen in a couple of years since moving to the United States; people I hadn't seen in decades, since my dad put them on their path into adulthood as their drama teacher. I had a cried a lot already. The wrinkles around my eyes stung constantly from the salty tears. "You don't remember me," they'd introduce themselves. I remembered more of them than they realized. I spent long nights and days with his students growing up. They babysat me, played with me, entertained me when I was becoming an awkward teenager. They always treated me with respect, always as a human being, just as my dad treated them and expected people in his charge to behave. I had two working parents—they often didn't have a choice but for me to spend time in rehearsals, backstage, and, occasionally, in classes with him. The dozens of those former students that hugged me that day brought a flood of memories that had been hidden in the background. "Your dad was a great man," they said to me. "He was so proud of you." Grief overlapped with nostalgia for a simpler time, when my bushy-bearded, energetic dad, darting around in his salmon-colored shorts, pencil in his sock, Diet Coke bottle in his right hand, would take me to rehearsal, trusting that I would behave myself and that his students would help keep an eye on me. I pined—I still pine—for those days, when he would find me small jobs backstage or minor roles in the shows. He brought me into his world, blurring the boundaries between family and work. His death a rude shock. I can't shake my nostalgia for those early years.

When I saw the casket, I virtually collapsed. It was too much. It was the first time I'd "seen" my father since our teary good-bye in Harlem two weeks earlier. I couldn't have known then how teary a good-bye could be. I went outside for some fresh air and quiet, out the back of the *shtiebel*. My brother-in-law, Zak, kept people away. He formed an invisible boundary that no one could cross, although everyone just wanted to comfort me, grieve with me. Zak, my own personal bodyguard, my hero for five minutes. That week I had a succession of heroes, people who looked after me just like Zak as my life unfolded in slow motion, in a haze.

Rabbi Ralph, who worked with Sluggo at his last school, was late. We didn't have a rabbi to whom we were attached; we weren't

members of a congregation. My parents had never taken me to synagogue except for life cycle events. Shul was like a foreign country
to me, I didn't even know the basics. Still, we wanted the rabbi who
buried Sluggo to be someone who knew him, who could talk to the
mourners of his generosity of spirit. Someone who could offer us
some real comfort, not in a cookie-cutter, generic way. Sluggo and
Rabbi Ralph had a relationship built on mutual respect. Despite
their very different backgrounds and understandings of Judaism,
they shared certain values, worldviews. They had common ground
through which they fulfilled their shared mission of sending young
people out into the world to make it a more caring place. Sluggo had
a knack for getting along with people no matter their religious or political background, something he had inherited from his own father.
If he could find common ground, he could find a kindred spirit.

Rabbi Ralph called from the car—he had never seen so much
traffic into the cemetery. The line of cars was at least a kilometer long,
backing up onto the highway. The *shtiebel* filled up, an estimated one
thousand people crammed in, although who knows—when I looked
up it was a sea of faces. Standing room only: friends, family, acquaintances spilling outside, watching on the monitors set up outside the
shtiebel. There's something altogether macabre about the intermin-
gling of technology and mourning rituals, but on that day I was
grateful that the funeral could be broadcast to the people outside the
shtiebel, be they outside the door or across the Pacific Ocean. It allowed me to feel that Helen and Arthur were there alongside me, in
spirit at least. The journey was too difficult for us all to do, so Helen
stayed in New York with Arthur and her parents. Knowing that they
were watching helped give me some extra strength, when my reserves
of strength had long since been sapped. The proceedings began with
the traditional Jewish customs: mourners rending our shirts, an out-
ward sign of grief. I had imagined that moment. I decided I should
wear a shirt that I liked; maybe it would be more meaningful to ruin
something to which I was attached, rather than a disposable shirt I
wouldn't wear anyway. The little decisions we had to make in those
moments, as though everything hinged on whether I wore a red or a

purple shirt. I thought it would be visceral; I imagined a loud tearing sound. It was anticlimactic in the end: no audible rip, no catharsis. Just the pain of losing my dad, and a ruined shirt. After rending the shirts, we heard psalms and a few words from Rabbi Ralph. I don't even remember what he said. I couldn't listen. I was caught up in my own muddled thoughts, my overactive brain in overdrive. Before I knew it, I was up.

Strangely, I had imagined this moment. When I moved to the United States, I thought about the possibility even more. What would I do if someone got sick, or worse, died? My parents weren't getting younger. How could I leave them now? I didn't think it would come so soon, but I had thought it possible. My dad had talked about death enough. Whenever he'd buy us something or take us for dinner, he'd tell us: "This is your *yerishe* [inheritance]. I'd rather see you enjoy it while I'm alive." When we'd tell him he needed to sleep more, when he was obviously weary after another night on the phone to New York or London, he'd tell us: "I'll have plenty of time to sleep when I'm dead." When we went to a funeral or to a Bund function, he'd insist: "Make sure you sing "Di shvue" at my funeral." Most of all, in his insistence that we make the most of the short time we've got on this world, he'd remind us: "You never know when you're going to get hit by a bus." Strange to think that I had visualized giving a eulogy at his funeral at some time in the distant future. Still, nothing prepares you for the reality.

There I was, standing at the lectern, shaking, my father's casket displayed in a glass box, a religious sleight of hand allowing the participation of *Cohanim*, descendants of the priestly caste of Jews ritually prohibited from sharing a room with the dead. Jews don't do open caskets, thank goodness. I wouldn't have coped. Giving the eulogy was strange, surreal. Basically, I was looking out on all the different parts not only of his life, but of my own. The family and friends with whom we had always been so close; the colleagues and students that he had collected in thirty years of teaching. I'll never again see such a broad cross section of the different parts of my life, figures from my childhood and adulthood, family, friends, and community.

I tried to keep it short. At least, short for a Slucki speech. Brevity is not our strong point. I could have talked for hours about Dad, telling stories about the minor and important moments in our lives together, about the absolute force of his personality, about his unqualified commitment to me and Jacob and Helen and Arthur, about his total and utter devotion to my mum. But I tried to keep it short. He taught me that audiences get restless. Keep it short, leave them wanting more.

I painted a picture of Sluggo as father and family man, and also of what I had observed of him as a teacher and community activist. I kept it together, mostly. Occasionally I turned toward the casket and talked to him directly, told him what a major hole this created in all our lives. The only time I got choked up was when I lamented that he wouldn't get to see Arthur grow up, and be the inspiration to him that he was to so many young people over five decades. Mostly, though, I was performing, just as he would have wanted. I put on a brave face, told jokes, told stories, made sure to mention the names of the most important people in his life.

He would have liked my eulogy. He would have liked the jokes and the anecdotes. He would have liked my sense of theatricality, the way that his personality and his flair for storytelling shone through me. He would have liked my ability to improvise and riff on certain points without reading a script. He prided himself on his ability to talk off the cuff, no notes, no script. Most of all, though, he would have basked in the public way in which I talked about how important he was to us. The last few years he had struggled to adapt to his new role in our lives—a father of adult sons, out in the world, independent. A grandfather to a baby boy. He never really worked out quite what a father's role was, if not to be the guiding light, the mentor, the taxi, the bank, the innkeeper. He was a natural at these, but he found it harder to take the backseat. He would have loved how I described his ongoing presence in our lives, and how he shaped us as individuals and the way we see the world. He would have bragged later about how much we appreciated him as a father and a friend. He would have liked to have heard that all he did for us did not go unnoticed. Sometimes he needed to hear it, but we didn't tell him enough. I wish we'd all told him more.

Too little, too late.

When the official proceedings were over, the hard part began. Hundreds of people—friends, family, former students—marched closely behind us as we walked the couple of hundred meters to Sluggo's final resting place. The longest walk of my life. We weren't ready to say good-bye, not ready for the permanence of putting him into the ground. I can barely remember it, except the feeling of my mum leaning in toward me, barely able to keep herself standing. Despite the presence of so many, there was a deathly silence outside. The cemetery was still relatively new, relatively empty. Very peaceful, picturesque, dotted with what seemed like only a handful of graves, surrounded by enormous tracts of farmland. As always, my dad was a pioneer, willing to go where no one had gone before. We chose a plot by a tree, not because he was particularly fond of nature but because it would be easier to visit and more peaceful for us.

In the Jewish tradition, the mourners pour the first shovelfuls of dirt onto the casket after it is lowered. I won't easily forget those first few thuds, when the clumps of earth landed on top of the casket, when the reality struck that my father was now returned to the earth and would be with me only as a ghost. It was real, final.

I was no novice at funerals. One of the quirks of growing up in shtetl Melbourne, or maybe just in our Bundist circle, is that you end up going to a lot of funerals. For all the relatives, close and distant, for all the parents and grandparents of friends, for all the old Bundists who had been fixtures of your childhood, at your grandparents' table, shouting at Bund meetings. The first funeral I can recall attending was for my mum's uncle, Shyje. It was early 1996, and I was eleven. I might well have been to others before that, but I don't remember them. This one left an impression. I can still see the throng of people crowding around the labyrinth of graves in their uniform dark marble with gold lettering. The sky was cloudy, the only way it should be when visiting a cemetery. I can still hear his widow, Asia, wailing, that god-awful screeching sound. I don't know if I was old enough to understand or feel empathy. I felt a little scared at that noise, though, wafting over the hushed murmuring of those squeezed into the narrow pathway that separated row after row of private memorial.

That's the first time I can remember my mum crying, my dad the stoic, philosophical, calming presence. We've got to support her, he told me. *Vayter furt di ban,* the train continues on its journey, his grandmother used to say. This was maybe the first time I heard him say it, although I'm not sure now. He probably said it. I was confused at my mum crying. I didn't even remember her uncle; what was she crying about? They weren't close. It was the first time I saw, though, the way you ought to behave in that setting, a kind of training for the future.

Between 2005 and 2011, I would lose my three grandparents, watching each of them deteriorate over months or years. Their funerals were all well attended. I gave a eulogy at each of them, and standing before the large crowd gave me a feeling of satisfaction. The full *shtiebel* gave me *naches* for my grandparents. They mattered. We matter. All those people coming out to honor them proved it, all the nice things people said about them proved it. I contrasted this with funerals I went to at which there were very few attendees. I always felt bad for the families. I found myself measuring people's lives based on the attendance at their funerals. Maybe that's what happens when you go to a lot of them.

As dozens of close family and friends helped to fill in the grave of my father and belted out "Di shvue," there was a numbness. Probably we were all still in a state of shock, unable yet to make sense of the fact that our lives were now turned upside down. For me, the words of my father rang in my ears: "Make sure you sing this at my funeral," although now with so much more urgency. He said it pretty much every time we sang it at a Bund event. But I still hear those words exactly as he said them that night, standing in that outdated hall by Battery Park. Or maybe I don't. Maybe I've reconstructed them, remembering only the fact that he said them and clinging to the memory, anything that reminds me of a time when he was still standing alongside me. In any case, they ring in my ears, like a final warning or a message.

In hindsight, it was strange to be singing "Di shvue" at that time and place. A quaint, archaic oath to a movement that barely still exists, it calls for its members to swear their loyalty without boundaries. It was "an oath of blood, and an oath of tears," that would be witnessed by the heavens and the earth. Did we still believe that? Did he still believe it? The song is not a manifesto, it doesn't lay out the movement's ideas or its commitment to socialism and Yiddish culture. It's much more visceral than that. Perhaps the answer lies in the lyrics themselves. "Heaven and earth will hear us/The bright stars will bear witness/An oath of blood, an oath of tears/We swear, we swear, we swear!" His father, who loomed so large in his life, had sworn that oath his whole life. Sluggo had sworn it since he was a child. It was their oath to a movement, a community, a civilization cut down so tragically.

~

A few days later, I flew home to Charleston, a flight very different to my flight home to Melbourne. I have two homes; I'm not really sure which to call home, where I live, or where my memories reside. On the return trip I wasn't looked after in quite the same way as on the way out. No business class, no first-class lounge, not even a working TV this time, usually my saving grace on the long haul. A full flight, chaos at the airport, and a thirty-plus-hour journey all on my own. In some ways, this is when reality began to set in; this was now life without my father. I'm not sure why. I hadn't traveled with Sluggo in years, and I had taken the long-haul flight on my own many times. But now I felt alone, disconnected, between two worlds. Hours waiting for the delayed flight on my own, trying to work to keep my mind busy. Then in limbo over the Pacific Ocean, cut off from everyone, alone with my grief and hundreds of strangers uncomfortably crammed into the aircraft—the world felt so vast and unknowable, yet so small and insignificant.

I didn't have my usual flying anxiety; that was the last thing on my mind. On that long-haul flight, I often feel overwhelmed by the sense of disconnection, dislocation. Unable to connect with Helen, my family, or my friends, I am often overcome with feelings of isolation. This might be part of that Holocaust legacy: the Sluckis like to keep tabs on each other. What if something happens while I'm up there? What if someone dies? Morbid thoughts, but hard to escape. In fact, when I landed in Los Angeles, I switched on my cell phone to a message from Jacob that David Bowie had died. Even though it felt as though the world should stand still while I was in flight, it didn't. Bowie was trying to upstage Dad, Jacob wrote. I laughed out loud, felt grounded again.

Mostly, though, I knew I had to just get through the flight, get home. I took a sleeping pill, dozed on and off. No TV, but the aisle seat a small saving grace. After a stressful few hours' delay in Melbourne, I knew already I'd miss my connecting flight in Los Angeles and I'd have to spend the day there. Lucky for me, I could spend it with family. Henry picked me up. I wasn't alone, at least. I spent the afternoon at Henry and Carole's, some time with cousin Danny, dinner with cousin Dennis, and then back to LAX for the last two legs, the red-eye to Charlotte and then the short flight home. I'd get home half a day later than I planned. It felt like a week.

The day I arrived back to Charleston was quiet. Helen picked me up from the airport, and Arthur was already at school. The house was empty, the whole world felt empty. I was at a loss. What should I do now? I didn't want to work, and probably couldn't have even if I had wanted to. I still had about twenty-four hours left of shiva. I had never really considered how I would do shiva when the time came along. I was surprised at how seriously I took it. I didn't cover the mirrors, as is the custom, but I did shave before the funeral, knowing I wouldn't do so again at least for the month of mourning that was to come. Even on that last day, I sat on a low chair, just as I had for the whole week since the funeral. I didn't switch on the TV, didn't put on music. Just sat, talked to whoever was around, walked. Tried to get some fresh air. It was surprisingly warm in Charleston for early January. It had been a warm winter. Even in New York, where we'd spent the previous month, we went around without coats, unseasonably warm. I can barely recall arriving back, actually. I do remember the relief when I saw Helen through the new glass wall that had recently been unveiled at the exit of Charleston's airport. A wave of warmth and comfort came over me as we reunited. We were apart for only a week and a half, but we experienced a lifetime worth of sorrow. I don't know that I cried so many tears on reunion. Just felt that wave of relief, then back to the numbness. Even though we hadn't talked a lot while I was in Melbourne, there wasn't really a lot to say. We were both in shock. For her, stuck in the United States and unable to join the family to grieve, that week was excruciating. Sluggo was like a father to her, too, and she and Arthur had to mourn from a vast distance, separated in time and space.

That night, Shari and Eric, close friends of ours in Charleston, organized a shiva minyan, something like a last-minute memorial service. About twenty-five to thirty people came, I think, but I'm not sure. Our apartment felt full, everyone milling around, waiting for the proceedings to begin. I was overwhelmed by the support. We had lived only a couple of years in Charleston, but we had somehow managed to surround ourselves with wonderful, caring people. Colleagues, friends, both Jewish and non-Jewish, rallied around us. At the same time, I wanted them all to leave. Everyone standing, me slumped in the low beach chair, the best we could rustle up. I couldn't have felt any smaller. I just wanted to shrink into nothing. I don't remember who led the service, maybe Eric or Josh. I stumbled through kaddish, the mourner's prayer, slowly, mumbling some of the words, racing through others. I don't know why I recited it, or why it had an impact on me. It was probably the fourth or fifth time I had said it that week and it didn't get easier. Strangely emotional to recite the kaddish; by the end, it felt like I'd just got back from a long run, light-headed, my knees weak, my breath shallow. My father-in-law, Sam, visiting us in the United States as my parents were leaving, gave a mini-eulogy, reflecting on his friendship with Sluggo and painting a picture of Dad for those in the room, most of whom had met him but didn't really know him. I barely remember it—mostly I remember sitting down low, head in my hands, sobbing. Partly I was embarrassed to be in such a state in front of people; mostly I had no choice, no control. Another day, another set of tributes, dozens more sets of eyes looking at me with pity, not sure what to say, hoping to not say something dumb. I didn't know what to say in return.

The next morning I stood up from shiva and went for a walk around the block, as is the custom—a symbolic reentry into the world. The worst of it out of the way, perhaps. I learned quickly, though, that this was just the beginning of the dense fog that had surrounded us so suddenly. We had no idea how far we would have to go to get through that cloud—certainly the path isn't linear, and probably we'll never be fully through the mist. It is the ghost that always surrounds us, Sluggo's spirit always present, always teasing us, reminding us of what we are missing. A few days after I stood up from shiva, I had a dream about Sluggo. I'm not sure if it was the first one, but to that point it was the most vivid, the most frightening, where that ghost teased me with his presence. I dreamed he hadn't really died—it was all just a mistake. He had returned to us, we were back in New York, in the Bronx, I think, where he had lived for a period in the early 1970s. As we planned to unveil his return to all those present, friends and family from Melbourne and New York, me walking down the stairs ahead of Dad, I felt his body crumple over my back, the weight of his collapsing body weighing me down, crushing my spirit. He really was dead, his ghost haunting my dreams.

This wasn't the last time I'd dream that we had been fooled in that way, and the nightmares got more intense. I would wake up sweating, or sometimes I was woken up by Helen, alarmed that I was crying, wailing in my sleep. Usually I didn't go back to sleep those nights. Turns out, I believed in ghosts too. And I was afraid of them.

Epilogue

Just Like Him

"You sound just like him," Alicia said to me as she broke down crying at the other end of the line when I called to ask her to sing at Dad's minyan. "You sound just like him," Rock said to me when I returned his call in the year following Dad's death. "You sound just like him." This was something I heard hundreds of times throughout my life, answering the phone at home or being introduced to people who had known Sluggo for decades. Dad's coworker Alan used to just call me "Dolly," after the Scottish sheep who was the first mammal to be successfully cloned. I was Dad's clone, his "mini-me."

For years we were inseparable. For four years, I worked as an integration aide at his school, helping students with learning disabilities. Dad and I often had lunch together, carrying around our bottles of Diet Coke, watching assemblies and performances from the back of the hall, arms folded, taking notes in our heads for our debrief in the car later. I'd shadow him when he put on shows, eventually helping him run them, a father-son theatre team. We'd drive into work together, even when I lived in the opposite direction from school to him. When I was a graduate student, we'd regularly meet for lunch. Once I started working full time, we'd meet for coffee. We were together a lot. Mich used to say she was jealous of how much time we got to spend together.

I sounded like him, I looked like him. We shared interests, passions, ambitions. We had the same dorky, dad sense of humor. We had a similar worldview. I shared his enthusiasm for theatre and the arts, I was a student of history, I was an extrovert like him. Two peas in a pod. If I looked and sounded like Sluggo, in what other ways was I like him? Did I want to be like him?

He was a towering figure in the lives of so many young people who had seen difficult times and who had forged successful careers. He commanded the respect of so many. Within the performing arts community in Melbourne, in the education world, and among Melbourne Jews, Dad's name carried with it a sense of recognition and esteem. He had a reputation as bold, daring, warm, lighthearted, and totally committed to improving the lives of those around him. Sluggo went far beyond being a teacher: he was a mentor, a life coach, a career counselor, a family counselor, a sounding board. He thrived helping guide people through their careers and lives.

He reveled in the idea that I was "just like him." Although he wanted to me to forge my own path, follow my own interests and passions, he took a great deal of satisfaction in having this clone following him around with the bottle of Diet Coke, the nasal twang. His own shadow, thirty-six years younger, but such a strong match.

"Are you Charles's son? He changed my life." To his students, I was "Charles's son." "Oh, are you Sluggo's son? I grew up with him in Carlton." To the seemingly endless cavalcade of Melbourne Jews he knew, I was Sluggo's son. Wherever we went, Dad knew someone, and they always sang his praises to me. Someone he had taught twenty-five years ago, someone with whom he had gone to SKIF in Carlton, someone whose kids went to his school. Someone to whom he had shown generosity, goodwill, or offered time, advice, contacts.

Usually I was proud to be "Charles's son." I basked vicariously in the respect that association commanded. I was proud of my dad, and I thought it reflected well on me. I didn't realize then that it didn't actually reflect on me at all. It was merely an accident of history that I was Sluggo's son, a happy accident, but nothing for which I could claim credit.

Sometimes it bothered me, especially the older I got, the more I tried to forge my own path. Occasionally it was just irritating. I

When Helen and I moved into our new house in 2010, we had a costume party. The theme was what I want to be when I grow up. I dressed up as Dad.

know, Sluggo's amazing, but I'm just trying to do my grocery shopping, or catch the train to the footy, or finish my workout at the gym. I don't need to constantly hear it.

It brought expectations, unspoken, but hovering. To what extent did I embody his achievements, his abilities, the force of his personality? How much did I carry on the hopes placed upon him by his father, and now upon me, to lead a moral life, to carry on the legacy of a family whose branches had been severed? It sounded simple enough, but sometimes it felt as though it was impossible to be selfless and giving all the time. These obligations could be draining and often led to guilt. Was I really living up to the example he set? Was I generous, caring? He never put pressure on me to follow in his footsteps. He just insisted I treat others with respect, *derkherets*. That was the most important thing. But it often felt as though so much was at stake, that because the path we were following was littered with the corpses of family senselessly murdered, the injunction to respect others mattered so much more.

There was also a kind of pressure, maybe that I brought on myself, that I should grow up to be as accomplished, prolific, recognized, well loved as Sluggo. After Dad died, many people commented that they hoped someday people would speak so lovingly of them, that they would be as well respected. It is not always easy to be in the shadow of a giant.

We struggled to transition to our new roles as father and son once I grew older and relied less on him, once he began aging and I had to worry about him more than he had to worry about me. When he no longer loomed quite so large in my life, when I earned a living, raised my own family, he wasn't sure what it meant to be the father of adult children. After all, he hadn't had a father through most of his adult life to model it to him. It didn't sit comfortably with him. He was used to, I think, playing an outsized role in my development and in the decisions I made. He was used to being a sounding board, my own Sherpa guiding me through the mountainous terrain of life. As

I grew up, he felt that he lost his usefulness to me, that he had less and less to offer. This led to our biggest fight, one that saw us not talk for a whole weekend. Maybe not so long for most people. For me and Sluggo, it felt like a lifetime.

One Friday night, in the midst of a chilly Melbourne winter, Sluggo and I went to the football, as we usually did together each weekend through the winter. This was something we'd done together since I was five, me running up and down the gently raking aisles of the Melbourne Cricket Ground, Australia's answer to the Coliseum, a sporting stadium where we'd lived some of our happiest moments and some of our most enduring heartbreak. Football bound us together. On this night, though, just months before Helen, Arthur, and I were due to leave Melbourne for who knew how long, our usual trip home on the train and in the car was solemn and tense. Sluggo had, as he did most weeks, bumped into some old friend on the train platform coming back from the game, and had gone and spoken to him for some time. I was annoyed, possessive, jealous. My reaction was infantile: we came together to the footy, I wanted to spend the time with him, debrief, or even stand on the train silently together while he listened to the after-game commentary on his trusty transistor radio, loudly relaying his outrage at the broadcasters' analysis. When he came back to tell me who the old friend was, I didn't hide my agitation, responding insolently that I didn't care, that I never really cared who they were. I tried to couch it in a sarcastic, smart-alecky tone, but my petulance came through loud and clear.

"Do you have to be such a cunt?" he snapped back. I was stunned into silence. He was embarrassed into silence. This was not a word he ever used, and certainly not against his own son. That heavy silence weighed on us for the rest of the train ride. We barely exchanged another word that weekend. Probably the longest we hadn't talked while both living in Melbourne. Ever.

He was right to be angry at me, even if his reaction was off target and his words hurtful. I had regressed into a surly teenager, and our relationship had long since progressed past the point where I could be jealously possessive or behave bitterly when I didn't get my way. I was being a brat. It wasn't a one-off, either. I'd probably made a habit of being a smart-arse, dismissive, impatient with his generosity. Maybe I was jealous at his endless popularity, his smiling, easygoing good nature.

Mich tried to mediate. She called me on Sunday afternoon, which was itself unusual. It was typically Sluggo who called. "Have you seen his e-mail?" she asked. He had sent me an e-mail explaining himself, but it had gone straight to my spam folder. Mich forwarded it to me. He had sent it at 2:43 a.m., Sunday morning. He must have been up all night mulling over the incident. It was written hastily on his phone, with shoddy punctuation, a little rambling, but with pathos struck through each word. I imagine he had been writing it in his head for twenty-four hours.

```
David
I love you. I am sorry that I upset you Friday. I just
feel that after a lifetime (yours) I have completely
lost your respect and that I have nothing more to
contribute to you and your family. I want family.
It is so important to me and I hoped to bring up my
children to feel the same. I only want good things
for you and yours and if I am holding that back then
I know what I should do. Just remember that all my
actions including questions are because I care. I love
you no matter Your father
```

I ran to the car and drove straight over there; at the time, we were only living about a mile apart, a pleasant walk, but I drove anyway. He had, as he usually did, taken the first step toward reconciliation. He never wanted to waste time fighting, or holding grudges, at least not with those he cared about most. So I didn't want to waste time either. We sat in his cramped, improvised study, a makeshift office while they built their dream home. It was dark, lit only by the upright lamp, he at his desk, me on the sofa, both crying, both trying to explain ourselves. He just wasn't sure anymore of what his role was, especially as I prepared to leave Melbourne, taking my family with me. His usual professional advice was less relevant to me as I forged my own career; he wasn't confident offering parenting advice, being so far removed from raising a toddler. He felt we were growing apart, and I pushed him over the edge with my own insensitivity. He felt like he was losing his son.

I hadn't seen him cry many times in my life. When his mother died, and his in-laws. Twice, maybe three times. After his bar mitzvah in 1961, when Mendel and Ruchel left Melbourne to return to Los Angeles, Zaida wrote that Dad kept his tears in when everyone else around was crying. Like a man, he wrote. Dad also wrote a letter to Mendel and Ruchel in which he said something similar about Zaida. Taking it like a man. For someone who wore his heart so much on his sleeve, he didn't cry a lot. He was usually just philosophical, pragmatic when things went wrong, always trying to put things into perspective. I guess when you grow up with the knowledge he had, nothing seems so bad.

It was the worst fight we had. Not the only one, and certainly mild compared to the turbulent relationships many have with their parents. He was my father and I was his son, after all, and conflict is part of the complicated, unique relationship between children and their parents. That standoff was part of a broader transition we were both going through, the culmination of several years of shadowboxing, working out who was responsible for what and when and how. Who was looking after whom now? We were both losing our identities, mourning that thing that defined us. I was still "Sluggo's son," but what did that mean when I was going out into the world, going to be living ten thousand miles away, where a daily phone call was difficult, where there would be no pop-ins, where we'd be fending for ourselves without Sluggo's seemingly endless supply of wisdom?

And what about him? Facing his mortality, losing his identity when there might not be much more time to forge a new one, or to make sense of that being thrust on him. That unflappable exterior had begun to show cracks as I grew older. I didn't respect my father any less, but I also saw more and more that he wasn't perfect. I better understood his strengths and weaknesses, and how his identity was interwoven with his professional success and the accolades that accompanied it.

But he wasn't my teacher. I couldn't see him, or worship him, like his students did. I was too close to him for that. I saw the chinks in his usually impenetrable armor. And the older he got, the more chinks appeared. I worried for him; he seemed to slow down, and we were all blindly feeling our way through the transition into a new kind of relationship. Whether I liked it or not, I had a lot invested in my identity as Sluggo's son, he as the father of two young men. It was not easy simply to accept that those things meant something different now that I had my own son, my own career, my own story in which he was a less central character.

This was surely a situation Dad had faced from the other side, when the dynamic between him and his father began to flip. In a sense, he had played that role from a young age; his first visit to Los Angeles, after all, was as an interpreter for Zaida. He was the son of a father who was so damaged, who needed caring, understanding, patience. Zaida always worried about Dad and what kind of person he would turn out to be. He cared for him, provided for him, tried to be a role model. But his ability to be involved, as he knew well, was limited. The ghosts were never far away. When did Dad become aware of Zaida's ghosts? When did he know to start worrying about his father? When did he start to understand his father and the sorrow that laced every breath he took? When did he realize that the dybbuks of his past inhabited his body?

And what of the pressure on Sluggo, the replacement son for a father who never stopped mourning his two sons. Bearing the name of his dead half-brother—what was it like to be his father's son? What was it like to carry that pressure, that burden?

Zaida died of a heart attack on November 22, 1978, thirty-nine years to the day since he said good-bye to his beloved Gitl, Shmulek, and Chaim in Włocławek and took the journey into his new life. It was less than two weeks after aunt Miriam married Joe. There were visitors from across the world for Miriam's wedding. Mendel and Ruchel were in Melbourne. So, too, were Zaida's cousins from Paris, Avram and Reyzl. They would stay up late into the night catching up, telling stories of their childhood, the three cousins reunited, in the same room perhaps for the first time ever. Certainly, the first time in over fifty years. Probably it was the largest gathering of family Zaida had seen since the war. Zaida seemed to be waiting for the right moment, when he could say good-bye to as many of his family as possible. Although he was by then quite frail, and retired, no one saw it coming. As with Dad, his heart gave way unexpectedly. But I wonder if Zaida knew. Did he hold on just long enough to be together with his brother and cousin? To see his youngest child walk the aisle? Were the loose ends tied up?

Helen and I worried a lot about Sluggo in his last few years. He aged in subtle but unmistakable ways. He never lost his flair for storytelling, his zest for meeting new people. Physically, he only seemed to get stronger, healthier, as he improved his diet and looked after himself. And for those not around him often, they probably didn't see how he was slowing down; how it took him longer and longer to overcome his jetlag when traveling; how his joints were a bit stiffer when he knelt to play with Arthur. Just that little bit more forgetful, that little bit slower to react. He was more detached, introspective, philosophical. He could seem more distant. It took him that extra few moments to work out which platform to take on the subway in New York City, which he'd been catching for forty-five years.

There was also a different kind of restlessness, a lack of focus. That wasn't new. He could often find it hard to keep focus. He always had so many things going on at any one time, his brain darted in so many directions, every little task more urgent than the previous one, every phone call had to be answered now. But now there was a kind of reflectiveness, and he worried about his own mortality, his legacy. He seemed to be constantly assessing what he had accomplished in his life.

He often told me he wasn't scared of death, but I think underneath his flippant attitude toward his mortality, he really was. He talked about it often enough, which I think was a way to mask his anxiety about what lay before him. Each time someone in his cohort died or got sick, or when he once had a minor cancer scare a few months before he died, that angst came to the surface, betraying his usual devil-may-care demeanor.

When Dad died, we didn't see it coming, just as he hadn't seen it coming with his own father in 1978. I was raised by a fatherless father, like Sluggo was, and like Arthur will be. This new ghost has been added to the family of ghosts that have always been there in the background, whether we knew it or not. I don't know if we'll ever truly recover from the shock. And I know that the accumulation of shock and grief over the past century will continue to make its mark on our family. The ghosts of Zaida, of Gitl, Shmulek, and Chaim, of Chasha, of Zaida's own father have always lingered, I think, never far below the surface. I don't know how it will affect Arthur, to have lost his Zaida so young, to grow up with this specter, hearing all about him, but unable to truly know him. And I don't know how to free him of the burden of our history, or even if I should. I think one way that past affected me was that I have often been afraid: afraid of catastrophe, afraid something will happen to my loved ones, a nervous parent, husband, son. And that balance of how to draw lessons from the ghosts and raise a child who is confident, fearless, yet circumspect is one of my greatest challenges as a father.

Like my own parents did, and like their parents before them, we'll just have to keep improvising. Work out how to be comfortable with those ghosts, comfortable with that knowledge and with the gaps in what we know. Even if we don't chase those ghosts, they find their way to us.

Acknowledgments

This is the fun part, where I finally get to publicly acknowledge all the wonderful and generous people that helped me make this book a reality. One thing I've learned since Dad died is to make sure to tell people that you're grateful for them, so here goes.

The seeds of this book were planted in August 2016 in Los Angeles when I was visiting faculty for Yiddishkayt LA's Helix Program. I am so grateful to Clare Fester and Robbie Peckerar for their invitation to talk about the Bund, and their flexibility with me going on tangents about Dad and Zaida. I'm also thankful to all the participants, including fellow faculty Nick Underwood and Mindl Cohen, for their openness and their willingness to allow me to experiment with this work.

Numerous sets of eyes looked over various versions of this manuscript. I'm especially thankful to Victoria Aarons, David Shneer, and Jordy Silverstein, whose feedback on the entire thing helped shape it into something more cohesive and focused.

Thanks to Krystyna Duszniak, who translated the Polish letters and postcards that Gitl wrote to Zaida from the Włocławek ghetto.

A very special mention to Henry and Carole Slucki, who let me rummage through their garage to find Zaida's letters, and who are always hospitable when I visit Los Angeles.

I am lucky to be surrounded by talented and supportive colleagues at the College of Charleston. It's a long list, but to highlight just a few: Shari Rabin and Joshua Shanes have created a truly collegial atmosphere in the Yaschik/Arnold Jewish Studies Program. I have learned a great deal from their scholarship and the discussions we have in formal and informal settings. Thanks also to Dale Rosengarten and Brandon Reid in the Special Collections at the library, who digitized an album of family photos, some of which appear here. Jewish Studies is well supported by dedicated staff, particularly Enid Idelsohn and Mark Swick, who have been constants in my time at CofC. There are many, many more faculty to whom I owe a debt of gratitude.

Various colleagues helped encourage me to write this book. I thank Nick Underwood and Joel Berkowitz, who pushed me to write a blog post on Dad's involvement in the Yiddish theatre that became the nucleus of a chapter. I also thank Moshe Rosenfeld (Rock), Irena Klepfisz, and Shane Baker for inviting me to New York to speak twice, giving me the opportunity to present parts of the manuscript and develop my voice. I'm grateful to Debra Caplan for sharing her interview notes with me from an interview she did with Dad. I'm also very lucky to have a lot of mentors who encouraged me at different stages of writing, who gave me the confidence to write something that fell outside the conventions of my discipline. My thanks to Jack Jacobs, Jeremy Dauber, Tony Michels, Hasia Diner, Laura Levitt, Avi Patt, Gabriel Finder, Adam Mendelsohn, Adam Ferziger, Noah Shenker, and Daniella Doron. Again, this is only a partial list.

Judy Heath helped me get through the first year of grieving after Dad died and showed me that there would be some light at the end of the long tunnel. She was very supportive of this project, and I'm grateful for her wisdom and support.

I have a long list of friends who were just there when I needed them after Dad died. In Melbourne, I thank Hanna, Alon, Shai, Josh and Cara, Raph and Libby, Tim and Linda, Pete and Marta, Zak and Amy, Eve and Josh, Naomi and Adam, Daniel, Mark, Danny and Becky and the boys, and Troy and Kelly. In Charleston, my friends who created a strong sense of community that helped me to feel a little less alone: Shari, Eric, Josh, Jessica, Becca, Hannah and Casey, Dan, Amanda, Mark, Noah and Jill, Arlene and Peter, Alan and Neda, and Mickey and Patti. Also thanks to Ross, Jaymie, and all of the crew at Black Tap/Second State, where I wrote most of this book. Elsewhere around the world: Sam, Adi and Sheryl, Avi and Shiri, David, Sofija and Michael, Jason and Steph, and Chonkers.

To my agent, Cherry Weiner: this is not just another book for you. The story it tells is parallel to yours, and your own upbringing was deeply embedded in the neighborhoods I describe. I appreciate your counsel, your close reading of my work, and your willingness to take in me, Helen, Arthur, and Harry when hurricanes were pointed right at the Lowcountry.

I have been blessed to work with the ultimate professionals at Wayne State University Press. I am extremely thankful to Kathy Wildfong for championing this manuscript from the seedling of an idea I brought to her at the Association for Jewish Studies conference in 2016. I'm grateful also to Annie Martin, Rachel Ross, Kristin Harpster, Emily Nowak, Kristina Stonehill, and Jamie Jones for their work in bringing the book to fruition. And to Sandra Judd for her extremely careful reading and editing of the manuscript. It's encouraging when your editors really get the project.

This would have been a very different book without the generosity of family and friends who shared their memories with me. For this, I am especially grateful to Hania and Gooter Goldberg, Moshe Goldberg, Bronia Witorz, Arnold Zable, and Henry Slucki. Henry Nusbaum also shared photos with me, some of which appear here. A very special mention must go to my aunt Miriam Gelbart, whose own life story is tied up in this book and who very generously answered any questions I had and told me stories of her father, even though it was at times very difficult for her.

My biggest cheerleaders are probably my parents-in-law, Sam and Fay Eichenbaum, who were extremely close with Dad. I thank them for their unwavering support and interest in my work.

My brother, Jacob, read the manuscript and was characteristically understated in his response, pointing out some areas in which he disagreed with my interpretation, or where his memories were different. I'm grateful for his close reading and for his willingness to talk about the book and the things that it brought up for both of us. Lily came into our lives in the last months of Dad's life, and Mich and I met her the week after Dad died. She was like a guardian angel for our family and we were all so overjoyed when she and Jacob were married, even though we weren't invited!

To Mich, for whom the loss of Dad has cut most deeply: don't forget that you are loved and cherished. You have always thought I was capable of greatness. I don't know that this book takes me there, but your belief in me has helped me get a step closer. I am truly grateful for your love, support, and guidance.

While writing this book, Helen and I celebrated our twentieth anniversary together. We've seen some of everything along the way, and our bond grows stronger each day. You believed in me, encouraged me, talked me through my hesitations. You had the grave responsibility of delivering me the bad news about Dad. This book was possible because of you, and the life we lead is only possible because of your love, warmth, and unwavering belief. Arthur and I are both so lucky.

Finally, to Arthur. This book is for you. I wrote it so that you'll feel connected to a past and a story that is so much bigger than our own. We sat together for many hours in our writers' retreats, and your very presence helped give this project life. Your presence gives me life.

About the Author

DAVID SLUCKI grew up in Melbourne, Australia, and now lives in Charleston, South Carolina. He is an author and historian who has written widely on the aftermath of the Holocaust. His first book, *The International Jewish Labor Bund after 1945: Toward a Global History*, was published in 2012. He has also coedited two volumes: *In the Shadows of Memory: The Holocaust and the Third Generation*, with Jordana Silverstein and Esther Jilovsky, and *Laughter After: Humor and the Holocaust*, with Gabriel Finder and Avinoam Patt. His scholarship has appeared in journals and publications in the United States, Europe, and Australia. He is an assistant professor in Jewish studies at the College of Charleston, where he teaches about the Holocaust and other genocides, and about modern Jewish history, politics, and culture. You can usually find him drinking coffee and playing chess with his son at Second State Coffee.

CPSIA information can be obtained
at www.ICGtesting.com
Printed in the USA
FFHW012305090519
52386992-57777FF